O9-AIE-339

Taste of Home's
CONTEST WINNING
ANNUAL RECIPES 2006

Taste of Home Books

Taste of Home's
CONTEST WINNING
ANNUAL RECIPES 2006

Editor: Heidi Reuter Lloyd
Art Director: Lori Arndt
Associate Editors: Beth Wittlinger, Jean Steiner
Senior Editor/Books: Julie Schnittka
Proofreader: Julie Blume Benedict
Editorial Assistant: Barb Czysz

Food Editor: Janaan Cunningham
Associate Food Editors: Coleen Martin, Diane Werner
Assistant Food Editor: Karen Scales
Senior Recipe Editor: Sue A. Jurack
Recipe Editors: Janet Briggs; Mary King
Food Photographers: Rob Hagen, Dan Roberts, Jim Wieland
Associate Photographer: Lori Foy
Food Stylists: Joylyn Trickel, Sarah Thompson
Set Stylists: Sue Myers, Jennifer Bradley Vent, Stephanie Marchese

Creative Director: Ardyth Cope
Senior Vice President, Editor in Chief: Catherine Cassidy
President: Barbara Newton
Founder: Roy Reiman

Taste of Home Books
© 2006 Reiman Media Group, Inc.
5400 S. 60th St. Greendale WI 53129
International Standard Book Number: 0-89821-499-8
International Standard Serial Number: 1548-4157
All rights reserved.
Printed in U.S.A.

PICTURED ON FRONT COVER:
Strawberry Lover's Pie (p. 205)

PICTURED ON BACK COVER:
Rich 'n' Cheesy Macaroni (p. 136), Chocolate Chip Cheesecake Bars (p. 179)
and Cheddar-Chili Bread Twists (p. 152).

To order additional copies of this book, write to *Taste of Home* Books, P.O. Box 908, Greendale, WI 53129.
To order with a credit card, call toll-free 1-800/344-2560 or visit our Web site at ***www.reimanpub.com***.

Table of Contents

Old-Fashioned Strawberry Soda, p. 14

Creamy White Chili, p. 51

Scalloped Potatoes and Veggies, p. 133

Cookie Dough Brownies, p. 168

Double Chocolate Fudge, p. 210

359 Winners from our National Recipe Contests—All in One Must-Have Cookbook

WELCOME to the third edition of *Taste of Home's Contest Winning Annual Recipes*—a book that readers suggested we make a few years back. We liked the idea, too, and now we'd like to say thank you for supporting our past two volumes.

This 2006 edition is our best yet! It's packed full of 359 recipes—each of which is a prize winner in a national recipe contest sponsored by *Taste of Home* or one of its sister magazines.

We think of this cookbook as the "cream of the crop" because it contains only contest-winning recipes. But the real winner is you because you get an entire year's worth of winning entries from five of our publications, all under one cover. That's *Taste of Home*—the No. 1 cooking magazine in North America—plus *Quick Cooking, Light & Tasty, Country Woman* and *Country* magazines.

So how exactly does a recipe become a prize winner? It starts when home cooks from across the country read our call for contest entries and send in their tried-and-true family favorites—the recipes that friends and family ask for again and again.

Our professional home economists then sort through the stacks of mail we receive and test the most promising entries. Then they prepare the top contenders for our taste-test panel, which consists of experienced food editors, fellow home economists and magazine editors with a knack for picking winners. After much sampling (a tough job, but somebody has to do it!), a grand prize winner and runners-up are announced.

Winners from Dozens of Contests

The contests featured in this cookbook offer an appealing assortment of recipes—snacks and beverages; salads and dressings; soups and sandwiches; entrees; side dishes and condiments; breads and rolls; brownies, bars and cookies; cakes and pies; and special desserts! This year we added a chapter of prize-winning breakfast & brunch recipes, too!

For a complete list of chapters, please see the Table of Contents on page 3. Here a quick summary of the year's worth of contests and the top prize winner of each category:

- **Cheers for Cheese:** Think outside the box—of macaroni and cheese, that is! This homemade version of the traditional favorite will have you putting those unused cardboard boxes in the recycling bin. Fresh and creamy is oh-so-good! You'll find Rich 'n' Cheesy Macaroni on page 136.

- **Favorite Cookie Collection:** Imagine a cookie that combines the best of malted milk balls and toffee candy bars. Actually, you don't have to imagine it at all. Just turn to the recipe for Toffee Malted Cookies on page 175 and start making 'em!

- **Oodles of Noodles:** Italian Manicotti gets a south-of-the-border spin in warm and comforting Mexican Chicken Manicotti on page 110.

- **Fantastic Fruit Pies:** Your family will be berry, berry happy when you bake the grand prize winner, Raspberry Meringue Pie, on page 195. Truth is, you can't go wrong with the other winners, either. Peaches 'n' Cream, Apple Blackberry and Glazed Pineapple pies were among those that earned honors!

Mexican Chicken Manicotti, p. 110

Orange-Glazed Cornish Hens, p. 95

- **Colorful Carrots:** Scalloped Carrots and Oven-Roasted Carrots make great side dishes, but what if you're sweet tooth is acting up? Grand Prize Winner Harvest Snack Cake, on page 200, is a delicious solution.

- **Regal Roasts:** Whether it's for a special occasion or a Sunday dinner, the winners from our roast contest are simply divine. You'll find No. 1, Glazed Holiday Pork Roast, on page 123.

- **Great Grilled Fare:** Zesty Mustard Chicken on p. 115 took the Grand Prize in this sizzling contest.

- **Healthy Harvest of Grains:** The variety will impress you and your taste buds. The top two finishers make a great lunch—try Whole Wheat Pumpkin Nut Bread (p. 153) with Cream of Wild Rice Soup (p. 65).

- **Freezer Fare:** Delicious dinner choices come out of the cold and into your warm kitchen. Try Taco-Filled Pasta Shells (p. 96) or Italian Chicken Roll-Ups (p. 92).

- **30-Minute Side Dishes:** Want great sides with a minimum of fuss? Creole Green Beans (p. 140) and Southwestern Spuds (p. 131) are sure to please.

- **Swift 'n' Thrifty Recipes:** Short on time and money? These inexpensive choices taste rich! Moist Chocolate Cake (p. 190) and Cheeseburger Meat Loaf (p. 120) will stretch your grocery budget.

- **5-Ingredient Dishes:** They're simple and delicious: No-Bake Cheesecake Pie (p. 197) is a satisfying ending to a hearty dinner of Pork Chops with Apples and Stuffing (p. 117).

- **Bake Sale Bonanza:** Need a recipe that will stand out at your next church bake sale? Caramel Apple Cupcakes (p. 203) is guaranteed to do the trick!

- **Delicious Company Dishes:** Impress guests with a menu of winners, such as Orange-Glazed Cornish Hens (p. 95), Hearty Twice-Baked Potatoes and Maple-Mocha Brownie Torte (p. 206).

- **Classic Cakes:** Having your cake and eating it too is possible if you make the top two vote getters! Toffee-Mocha Cream Torte (p. 196) and Lemon Meringue Cake (p. 194) will win over everybody!

- **Chili Cook-Off:** When it's cold outside, warm up your insides with Pepperoni Pizza Chili (p. 60) or Bold Bean and Pork Chili (p. 53).

- **Come for Brunch:** Liven up the table with Croissant French Toast (p. 87) or Ham 'n' Cheese Omelet Roll (p. 89).

- **Chock-full of Chips:** Who would have thought those little morsels could have such big impact? Try Three-Chip English Toffee (p. 214) and Cappuccino Cake Brownies (p. 170).

- **Tempting Tomatoes:** Summer's bounty never tasted so good! Tomato-Onion Phyllo Pizza (p. 93) and Four-Tomato Salsa (p. 8) are extraordinary!

- **Hearty Meat Pies:** Feeling the need for comfort food? Pick an entree from this dynamic duo: Creamed Chicken in a Basket (p. 79) and Beef Stew Pie (p. 107).

Now you know you'll come out a winner with this *Taste of Home's Contest Winning Annual Recipes 2006* cookbook! You be the judge of which fabulous recipe to try first!

Toffee Mocha Cream Torte, p. 196

Tangy Fruit Punch, p. 8

Garden Focaccia, p. 13

Almond Cheddar Appetizers, p. 11

Snacks & Beverages

Whatever the occasion—a family dinner or a gathering of friends—this chapter offers a wide variety of appetizers and beverages to satisfy your guests.

Old-Fashioned Strawberry Soda, p. 14

Creamy Caramel Dip, p. 17

⚜ ⚜ ⚜
Tangy Fruit Punch

(Pictured on page 6)

Ann Cousin, New Braunfels, Texas

The fruity flavors mingle in this rosy, refreshing punch. It's a popular beverage for a brunch, since its versatile, sweet-tart taste goes wonderfully with all kinds of foods.

- 1 can (46 ounces) pineapple juice
- 1 can (12 ounces) frozen orange juice concentrate, thawed
- 3/4 cup lemonade concentrate
- 1 cup water, *divided*
- 1/2 cup sugar
- 2 large ripe bananas
- 1 package (20 ounces) frozen unsweetened whole strawberries, thawed
- 2 liters ginger ale, chilled

1. In a punch bowl or large container, combine pineapple juice, orange juice concentrate, lemonade concentrate, 1/2 cup water and sugar.

2. Place bananas, strawberries and remaining water in a blender; cover and process until smooth. Stir into the juice mixture. Cover and refrigerate. Just before serving, stir in ginger ale. **Yield:** 25-30 servings (about 5 quarts).

⚜ ⚜ ⚜
Four-Tomato Salsa

Connie Siese, Wayne, Michigan

A variety of tomatoes, onions and peppers makes this chunky salsa so good. Whenever I try to take a batch to a get-together, it's hard to keep my family from finishing it off first! It's a super snack with tortilla chips or as a relish with meat.

✓ Uses less fat, sugar or salt. Includes Nutritional Analysis and Diabetic Exchanges.

- 7 plum tomatoes, chopped
- 7 medium tomatoes, chopped
- 3 medium yellow tomatoes, chopped
- 3 medium orange tomatoes, chopped
- 1 teaspoon salt
- 2 tablespoons lime juice
- 2 tablespoons olive oil
- 1 medium white onion, chopped
- 2/3 cup chopped red onion
- 2 green onions, chopped
- 1/2 cup *each* chopped sweet red, orange, yellow and green pepper
- 3 pepperoncinis, chopped
- 3 pickled sweet banana wax peppers, chopped
- 1/2 cup minced fresh parsley
- 2 tablespoons minced fresh cilantro
- 1 tablespoon dried chervil

Tortilla chips

1. In a colander, combine the tomatoes and salt. Let drain for 10 minutes. Transfer to a large bowl.

2. Stir in the lime juice, oil, onions, peppers, parsley, cilantro and chervil. Serve with tortilla chips. Refrigerate or freeze leftovers. **Yield:** 14 cups.

Nutritional Analysis: One serving (1/4 cup salsa) equals 16 calories, 1 g fat (0 saturated fat), 0 cholesterol, 63 mg sodium, 3 g carbohydrate, 1 g fiber, 1 g protein. **Diabetic Exchange:** Free food.

Editor's Note: Look for pepperoncinis (pickled peppers) and pickled banana peppers in the pickle and olive aisle of your grocery store.

Horseradish Crab Dip

Kathleen Snead, Lynchburg, Virginia

I depend on this mildly seasoned crab dip when hosting parties. It's a terrific time-saver when accompanied by celery sticks or your favorite raw veggies. It's so simple to prepare that it gives me time to get other appetizers ready or mingle with my guests.

✓ Uses less fat, sugar or salt. Includes Nutritional Analysis and Diabetic Exchanges.

- 1 package (8 ounces) cream cheese, softened
- 2 to 3 tablespoons picante sauce
- 1 to 2 tablespoons prepared horseradish
- 1 can (6 ounces) crabmeat, drained, flaked and cartilage removed

Celery sticks

In a mixing bowl, beat cream cheese, picante sauce and horseradish; mix well. Stir in the crab. Serve with celery. **Yield:** about 1-1/2 cups.

Nutritional Analysis: One 1/4-cup serving of the dip (prepared with reduced-fat cream cheese and 2 tablespoons picante sauce) equals 119 calories, 7 g fat (4 g saturated fat), 46 mg cholesterol, 257 mg sodium, 4 g carbohydrate, trace fiber, 10 g protein. **Diabetic Exchanges:** 1-1/2 fat, 1 lean meat.

Ranch Snack Mix

Linda Murphy, Pulaski, Wisconsin

This is a wonderful, fast-to-fix munchie. The recipe makes a generous 24 cups and doesn't involve any cooking. It's a cinch to package in individual snack bags, keeps its crunch and is a savory alternative to the cakes and pies usually offered at bake sales.

- 1 package (12 ounces) miniature pretzels
- 2 packages (6 ounces *each*) Bugles
- 1 can (10 ounces) salted cashews
- 1 package (6 ounces) bite-size cheddar cheese fish crackers
- 1 envelope ranch salad dressing mix
- 3/4 cup vegetable oil

In two large bowls, combine the pretzels, Bugles, cashews and crackers. Sprinkle with dressing mix; toss gently to combine. Drizzle with oil; toss until well coated. Store in airtight containers. **Yield:** 6 quarts.

✿ ✿ ✿
Sausage Wonton Stars

Mary Thomas, North Lewisburg, Ohio

These fancy-looking appetizers are ideal when entertaining large groups. The cute, crunchy cups are stuffed with a cheesy pork sausage filling that kids of all ages enjoy. We keep a few in the freezer so we can easily reheat them for late-night snacking.

- 1 package (12 ounces) wonton wrappers
- 1 pound bulk pork sausage
- 2 cups (8 ounces) shredded Colby cheese
- 1/2 medium green pepper, chopped
- 1/2 medium sweet red pepper, chopped
- 2 bunches green onions, sliced
- 1/2 cup ranch salad dressing

1. Lightly press wonton wrappers onto the bottom and up the sides of greased miniature muffin cups. Bake at 350° for 5 minutes or until edges are browned.

2. In a large skillet, cook sausage over medium heat until no longer pink; drain. Stir in the cheese, peppers, onions and salad dressing. Spoon a rounded table-spoonful into each wonton cup. Bake for 6-7 minutes or until heated through. **Yield:** about 4 dozen.

✿ ✿ ✿
Feta Bruschetta

Stacey Rinehart, Eugene, Oregon

You won't believe the compliments you'll receive when you greet guests with these warm appetizers. Each crispy bite offers the savory tastes of feta cheese, tomato, basil and garlic. They're terrific for holiday parties or most any gathering.

- 1/4 cup butter, melted
- 1/4 cup olive oil
- 10 slices French bread (1 inch thick)
- 1 package (4 ounces) crumbled feta cheese
- 2 to 3 garlic cloves, minced
- 1 tablespoon minced fresh basil *or* 1 teaspoon dried basil
- 1 large tomato, seeded and chopped

1. In a bowl, combine butter and oil; brush onto both sides of bread. Place on a baking sheet. Bake at 350° for 8-10 minutes or until lightly browned on top.

2. Combine the feta cheese, garlic and basil; sprinkle over toast. Top with tomato. Bake 8-10 minutes longer or until heated through. Serve warm. **Yield:** 10 appetizers.

🎀🎀🎀
Almond Cheddar Appetizers

(Pictured on page 6)

Linda Thompson, Southampton, Ontario

I always try to have a supply of these on hand in the freezer. If guests drop in, I just pull some out and reheat them. You can serve them as a snack, for brunch or along with a lighter lunch.

    1 cup mayonnaise
    2 teaspoons Worcestershire sauce
    1 cup (4 ounces) shredded sharp cheddar cheese
    1 medium onion, chopped
  3/4 cup slivered almonds, chopped

    6 bacon strips, cooked and crumbled
    1 loaf (1 pound) French bread

1. In a bowl, combine the mayonnaise and Worcestershire sauce; stir in cheese, onion, almonds and bacon.

2. Cut bread into 1/2-in. slices; spread with cheese mixture. Cut slices in half; place on a greased baking sheet. Bake at 400° for 8-10 minutes or until bubbly. **Yield:** about 4 dozen.

Editor's Note: Unbaked appetizers may be frozen. Place in a single layer on a baking sheet; freeze for 1 hour. Remove from the baking sheet and store in an airtight container for up to 2 months. When ready to use, place unthawed appetizers on a greased baking sheet. Bake at 400° for 10 minutes or until bubbly.

🎀🎀🎀
Cheesy Asparagus Bites

Lois McAtee, Oceanside, California

When I managed a cafeteria, I would cook up different snacks for the staff. These tiny squares with a big asparagus flavor never lasted long and prompted lots of recipe requests.

  1/2 cup diced onion
    1 garlic clove, minced
    2 tablespoons vegetable oil
    2 cups (8 ounces) shredded sharp cheddar cheese
  1/4 cup dry bread crumbs
    2 tablespoons minced fresh parsley
  1/4 teaspoon salt
  1/4 teaspoon pepper
  1/8 to 1/4 teaspoon dried oregano
  1/8 teaspoon hot pepper sauce
    4 eggs, beaten
    1 pound fresh asparagus, trimmed and cut into 1/2-inch pieces

1. In a skillet, saute onion and garlic in oil until tender. Combine cheese, bread crumbs, parsley, salt, pepper, oregano and hot pepper sauce. Stir in the onion mixture and eggs.

2. Cook asparagus in a small amount of water until crisp-tender, about 3-4 minutes; drain well. Stir into cheese mixture.

3. Pour into a greased 9-in. square baking pan. Bake at 350° for 30 minutes or until a knife inserted near the center comes out clean. Let stand for 15 minutes. Cut into small squares; serve warm. **Yield:** 5 dozen.

🎗🎗🎗 Cheddar-Bacon Dip

Carol Werkman, Neerlandia, Alberta

Both children and adults enjoy this dip. I like it, too—it's so quick to prepare. I make it for special occasions…birthdays, Christmastime parties, etc.

      1 package (8 ounces) cream cheese, softened
      1 cup (8 ounces) sour cream
      5 green onions, thinly sliced
      4 medium tomatoes, chopped
      1 large green pepper, chopped
      1 jar (16 ounces) taco sauce
      2 cups (8 ounces) shredded cheddar cheese
      1 pound sliced bacon, cooked and crumbled
Tortilla *or* taco chips

1. In a mixing bowl, beat cream cheese and sour cream. Spread in an ungreased 13-in. x 9-in. x 2-in. dish or on a 12-in. plate. Combine onions, tomatoes and green pepper; sprinkle over the cream cheese layer.

2. Pour taco sauce over the vegetables. Sprinkle with cheddar cheese. Refrigerate. Just before serving, sprinkle with bacon. Serve with tortilla or taco chips. **Yield:** 10-12 servings.

🎗🎗🎗 Jalapeno Pepper Appetizers

Peggy Roberts, Lockney, Texas

These appetizers are so easy to make and they taste so good. I have to warn you that eating them is habit-forming!

      10 medium fresh jalapeno peppers
       4 ounces cream cheese, softened
      10 bacon strips, halved

1. Cut peppers in half lengthwise; remove seeds, stems and center membrane. Stuff each half with about 2 teaspoons of cream cheese. Wrap with bacon and secure with a toothpick.

2. Place on a broiler rack that has been coated with nonstick cooking spray. Bake at 350° for 20-25 minutes or until bacon is crisp. Remove toothpicks. Serve immediately. **Yield:** 20 appetizers.

   Editor's Note: When cutting or seeding hot peppers, use rubber or plastic gloves to protect your hands. Avoid touching your face.

🎗🎗🎗
Corny Snack Mix

Sandy Wehring, Fremont, Ohio

It's hard to stop munching this yummy snack mix! Melted vanilla chips make a delightful coating for the crisp corn chips, cereal and popcorn. This snack mix is simple to toss together. I like to keep it on hand for when our grandchildren visit.

- **3 quarts popped popcorn**
- **1 package (15 ounces) Corn Pops**
- **1 package (15 ounces) corn chips**
- **2 packages (10 to 12 ounces *each*) vanilla *or* white chips**

1. In several large bowls, combine the popcorn, Corn Pops and corn chips. In a saucepan over medium-low heat, melt chips; stir until smooth. Pour over popcorn mixture and toss to coat.

2. Spread in two 15-in. x 10-in. x 1-in. pans. Cool. Store in airtight containers. **Yield:** 7-1/2 quarts.

🎗🎗🎗
Garden Focaccia

(Pictured on page 6)

Mary Ann Ludwig, Edwardsville, Illinois

Frozen bread dough is the convenient base for this herb-flavored flat Italian bread. These savory slices are a super appetizer at a summer gathering. It's a fun and delicious way to use up abundant garden tomatoes and fresh zucchini.

☑ Uses less fat, sugar or salt. Includes Nutritional Analysis and Diabetic Exchanges.

- **1 loaf (1 pound) frozen bread dough, thawed**
- **1 tablespoon olive oil**
- **1 tablespoon minced fresh rosemary *or* 1 teaspoon dried rosemary, crushed**
- **1 tablespoon minced fresh thyme *or* 1 teaspoon dried thyme**
- **1 package (8 ounces) cream cheese, softened**
- **1/4 cup finely chopped onion**
- **1 garlic clove, minced**
- **4 large fresh mushrooms, sliced**
- **3 medium tomatoes, sliced**
- **1 small zucchini, thinly sliced**
- **1/4 cup grated Parmesan cheese**

1. On a lightly floured surface, roll dough into a 15-in. x 10-in. rectangle. Place in a greased 15-in. x 10-in. x 1-in. baking pan. Cover and let rise for 30 minutes.

2. Using your fingertips, press indentations into the dough. Brush with oil; sprinkle with rosemary and thyme. Bake at 400° for 12-15 minutes or until golden brown. Cool slightly.

3. In a mixing bowl, combine cream cheese, onion and garlic. Spread over crust. Top with mushrooms, tomatoes and zucchini; sprinkle with Parmesan cheese. Bake for 12-15 minutes or until lightly browned. Cool for 5 minutes before cutting. **Yield:** 20 slices.

Nutritional Analysis: One slice (prepared with reduced-fat cream cheese) equals 109 calories, 4 g fat (2 g saturated fat), 7 mg cholesterol, 185 mg sodium, 14 g carbohydrate, 1 g fiber, 5 g protein. **Diabetic Exchanges:** 1 vegetable, 1 fat, 1/2 starch.

🎗 🎗 🎗
Avocado Salsa

Susan Vandermeer, Ogden, Utah

When I found this recipe, I was planning a party and thought it might be a fun, different salsa to set out with chips. It was an absolute success. People love the garlic, corn and avocado combination.

  1 package (16 ounces) frozen corn, thawed
  2 cans (2-1/4 ounces *each*) sliced ripe olives, drained
  1 medium sweet red pepper, chopped
  1 small onion, chopped
  5 garlic cloves, minced
1/3 cup olive oil
1/4 cup lemon juice
  3 tablespoons cider vinegar
  1 teaspoon dried oregano
1/2 teaspoon salt
1/2 teaspoon pepper
  4 medium ripe avocados
Tortilla chips

1. In a large bowl, combine corn, olives, red pepper and onion. In a small bowl, combine garlic, oil, lemon juice, vinegar, oregano, salt and pepper; mix well. Pour over corn mixture and toss to coat. Cover and refrigerate overnight.

2. Just before serving, chop avocados and stir into salsa. Serve with tortilla chips. **Yield:** about 7 cups.

🎗 🎗 🎗
Old-Fashioned Strawberry Soda

(Pictured on page 7)

Ginger Hubbard, Anderson, Missouri

With just a quick pulse of the blender, you will have what I call a "refreshing sipper"—and you'll be asked for more!

  1 cup milk
1/2 cup fresh *or* frozen strawberries
1/2 cup vanilla ice cream, softened
  2 tablespoons sugar
  2 to 3 drops red food coloring, optional
  1 cup ginger ale, chilled

In a blender container, combine the first five ingredients; cover and process until smooth. Pour into two tall glasses. Add ginger ale and serve immediately. **Yield:** 2 servings.

★ ★ ★
Peanut Butter Popcorn Bars

Kathy Oswald, Wauzeka, Wisconsin

If you're looking for a fun snack for kids, try these chewy popcorn treats that have a mild peanut butter taste. They're easy to stir up and can be pressed into a pan to form bars or shaped into balls.

> 10 **cups popped popcorn**
> 1/2 **cup sugar**
> 1/2 **cup light corn syrup**
> 1/2 **cup creamy peanut butter**
> 1/2 **teaspoon vanilla extract**

1. Place popcorn in a large bowl; set aside. In a saucepan over medium heat, bring sugar and corn syrup to a boil, stirring constantly. Boil for 1 minute. Remove from the heat.

2. Stir in peanut butter and vanilla; mix well. Pour over popcorn and mix until well coated. Press into a buttered 13-in. x 9-in. x 2-in. pan. Cool slightly before cutting. **Yield:** 2 dozen.

★ ★ ★
Spiced Nut Mix

Patti Holland, Parker, Colorado

When we were newlyweds, our first Christmas was pretty lean. I usually made presents, but that year I had no idea what I could afford to put together. A good friend gave me a special gift—this recipe and a sack of ingredients. I think of her every time I stir up this mix.

> 3 **egg whites**
> 2 **teaspoons water**
> 2 **cans (12 ounces** each**) salted peanuts**
> 1 **cup whole blanched almonds**
> 1 **cup walnut halves**
> 1-3/4 **cups sugar**
> 3 **tablespoons pumpkin pie spice**
> 3/4 **teaspoon salt**
> 1 **cup raisins**

1. In a mixing bowl, beat egg whites and water until frothy. Add nuts; stir gently to coat. Combine sugar, pie spice and salt; add to nut mixture and stir gently to coat. Fold in raisins. Spread into two greased 15-in. x 10-in. x 1-in. baking pans.

2. Bake, uncovered, at 300° for 20-25 minutes or until lightly browned, stirring every 10 minutes. Cool. Store in an airtight container. **Yield:** about 10 cups.

🎗🎗🎗 Two-Fruit Frosty

Angie Hansen, Gildford, Montana

This is a refreshing and colorful drink to serve for brunch. The cinnamon and nutmeg give it just the right amount of zing.

1-1/2 cups fresh *or* frozen blueberries *or* huckleberries
    1 cup frozen unsweetened sliced peaches, thawed
    1 cup milk
    1 cup (8 ounces) vanilla yogurt
  1/4 to 1/3 cup honey
  1/2 teaspoon ground cinnamon
  1/2 teaspoon ground nutmeg
Cinnamon sticks, optional

1. Combine blueberries, peaches and milk in a blender; cover and process on high. Add yogurt, honey, cinnamon and nutmeg; blend well.

2. Pour into glasses. Garnish with cinnamon sticks if desired. Serve immediately. **Yield:** 4 (1-cup) servings.

🎗🎗🎗 Garlic-Mushroom Appetizer

Rosanna Houlton, Fort Collins, Colorado

My grandfather, who was a hotel chef for many years, created this recipe. He prepared these mushrooms for big family gatherings, and they always were gone quickly.

    1 cup chopped onion
  1/2 cup olive oil
    3 tablespoons butter
    2 pounds fresh mushrooms, sliced
    1 can (28 ounces) crushed tomatoes in puree, undrained
    1 teaspoon salt
  1/4 teaspoon pepper
  1/2 cup red wine vinegar
    1 bunch fresh parsley, finely chopped (about 1-1/2 cups)
    3 garlic cloves, minced
Sliced French bread

1. In a saucepan, saute onion in oil and butter until transparent. Add the mushrooms; cook for 2 minutes. Add tomatoes, salt and pepper; cover and simmer for 20-30 minutes. Add vinegar, parsley and garlic; mix well.

2. Cover and simmer for 10 minutes. Chill several hours or overnight. To serve, spoon onto slices of French bread. **Yield:** 12-16 servings.

♚♚♚
Creamy Caramel Dip
(Pictured on page 7)

Karen Laubman, Spruce Grove, Alberta

Because I feed three hungry "men" (my husband, a member of the Royal Canadian Mounted Police, and our two boys), I love satisfying snacks that are easy to make like this dip. I modified a friend's recipe. We sure appreciate this cool, light treat in the summertime.

 1 package (8 ounces) cream cheese, softened
 3/4 cup packed brown sugar
 1 cup (8 ounces) sour cream
 2 teaspoons vanilla extract
 2 teaspoons lemon juice
 1 cup cold milk
 1 package (3.4 ounces) instant vanilla pudding
   mix
Assorted fresh fruit

1. In a mixing bowl, beat cream cheese and brown sugar until smooth. Add the sour cream, vanilla, lemon juice, milk and pudding mix, beating well after each addition.

2. Cover and chill for at least 1 hour. Serve as a dip for a variety of fruit. **Yield:** 3-1/2 cups.

♚♚♚
Salmon Cheese Spread

Raymonde Bernier, St. Hyacinthe, Quebec

Here's a delightful hors d'oeuvre that's excellent for any occasion. The combination of salmon, cream cheese and curry powder gives it terrific flavor.

 2 packages (3 ounces *each*) cream cheese,
   softened
 3 tablespoons mayonnaise
 1 tablespoon lemon juice
 1/2 teaspoon salt
 1/2 teaspoon curry powder
 1/4 teaspoon dried basil
 1/8 teaspoon pepper
 1 can (7-1/2 ounces) salmon, drained, bones
   and skin removed
 2 green onions, thinly sliced
Crackers

In a mixing bowl, combine the cream cheese, mayonnaise and lemon juice. Add the salt, curry powder, basil and pepper; mix well. Gently stir in salmon and onions. Cover and refrigerate for at least 1 hour. Serve with crackers. **Yield:** 1-1/2 cups.

🎗 🎗 🎗
Cheesy Sausage Nachos

Jane Sodergren, Red Wing, Minnesota

This dish is very versatile. It can be served as an appetizer or as a filling main dish. It gets rave reviews either way.

- **3/4 pound bulk pork sausage**
- **1/4 cup chopped onion**
- **3 cups diced fresh tomatoes**, *divided*
- **3/4 cup picante sauce**
- **4 cups tortilla chips**
- **3 cups (12 ounces) shredded Monterey Jack cheese**, *divided*
- **1 medium ripe avocado, diced**

1. In a skillet, cook sausage and onion over medium heat until meat is no longer pink; drain well. Add 2 cups tomatoes and picante sauce. Bring to a boil. Reduce heat; simmer, uncovered, for 20 minutes or until most of the liquid has evaporated.

2. Sprinkle tortilla chips over a 12-in. pizza pan. Top with 2 cups cheese and the sausage mixture; sprinkle with remaining cheese. Bake at 350° for 8-10 minutes or until cheese is melted. Sprinkle with avocado and remaining tomatoes. **Yield:** 8-10 servings.

Maple-Glazed Chicken Wings

Janice Henck, Clarkston, Georgia

Some wonderful maple syrup I brought back from a trip to Vermont inspired my recipe. These wings have been a hit with family and friends. They can be used for snacks, hors d'oeuvres for parties or showers, or appetizers...or double or triple the recipe and make the wings a main dish you can serve with a salad or corn on the cob on the side.

> 2 to 3 pounds whole chicken wings
> 1 cup maple syrup
> 2/3 cup chili sauce
> 1/2 cup finely chopped onion
> 2 tablespoons Dijon mustard
> 2 teaspoons Worcestershire sauce
> 1/4 to 1/2 teaspoon crushed red pepper flakes

1. Cut chicken wings into three sections; discard wing tip section. In a large resealable plastic bag or shallow glass container, combine remaining ingredients. Reserve 1 cup for basting and refrigerate.

2. Add chicken to remaining marinade and turn to coat. Seal bag or cover container; refrigerate for 4 hours, turning occasionally. Drain and discard marinade.

3. Grill chicken, covered, over medium heat for 12-16 minutes, turning occasionally. Brush with reserved marinade. Grill, uncovered, for 8-10 minutes or until juices run clear, basting and turning several times. **Yield:** 6-8 servings.

Editor's Note: The wings may be baked in a 375° oven for 30-40 minutes or until juices run clear.

Fiesta Cheese Ball

Virginia Horst, Mesa, Washington

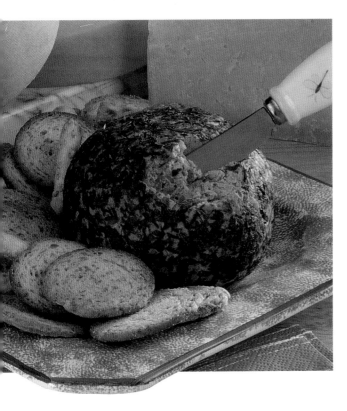

Whenever I bring this zippy cheese ball to church functions, showers or parties, folks ask for the recipe. A deliciously different appetizer, it makes even a plain plate of crackers seem festive.

> 1 package (8 ounces) cream cheese, softened
> 1/4 cup shredded Colby-Monterey Jack cheese
> 3 to 4 tablespoons minced fresh cilantro
> 2 to 3 tablespoons grated onion
> 1 tablespoon chili powder
> 1 teaspoon dried minced garlic
> 1/2 teaspoon garlic salt
> 1/4 teaspoon dried oregano
> 1/4 teaspoon crushed red pepper flakes
> 1/8 teaspoon ground cumin
> 1/8 to 1/4 teaspoon hot pepper sauce
> 1/4 cup minced fresh parsley

Assorted crackers

1. In a mixing bowl, beat cream cheese. Add the next 10 ingredients and mix well. Cover and refrigerate for at least 1 hour.

2. Shape into a ball. Roll in parsley. Cover and refrigerate for 8 hours or overnight. Serve with crackers. **Yield:** 1 cheese ball.

★ ★ ★
Appetizer Roll-Ups

Marcella Funk, Salem, Oregon

Cream cheese and a variety of herbs and vegetables make even deli cold cuts a fancy and filling appetizer. Bite-size pieces look so pretty set on a platter in a circle. But the arrangement never stays complete for long once this snack is served.

ROAST BEEF:
    4 ounces cream cheese, softened
  1/4 cup minced fresh cilantro
    2 to 3 tablespoons minced banana peppers
    1 garlic clove, minced
  1/2 pound thinly sliced cooked roast beef

HAM AND TURKEY:
  12 ounces cream cheese, softened
 1/2 cup shredded carrot
 1/2 cup shredded zucchini
   4 teaspoons dill weed
 1/2 pound thinly sliced fully cooked ham
 1/2 pound thinly sliced cooked turkey

1. In a bowl, combine the cream cheese, cilantro, peppers and garlic. Spread about 2 tablespoons on each slice of beef. Roll up tightly and wrap in plastic wrap.

2. In another bowl, combine cream cheese, carrot, zucchini and dill. Spread about 2 tablespoons on each slice of ham and turkey. Roll up tightly; wrap in plastic wrap. Refrigerate overnight. Slice into 1-1/2-in. pieces. **Yield:** 6-7 dozen.

🎖🎖🎖
Cucumber Party Sandwiches

Rebecca Rose, Mount Washington, Kentucky

This is one of my favorite appetizers. We have lots of pig roasts here in Kentucky, and these small sandwiches are perfect to serve while the pig is roasting.

> 1 package (8 ounces) cream cheese, softened
> 1/2 envelope (2 teaspoons) Italian salad dressing mix
> 2 tablespoons mayonnaise
> 30 slices snack rye bread
> 30 thin slices cucumber

Fresh dill sprigs

In a bowl, combine the cream cheese, dressing mix and mayonnaise. Allow to stand at least 30 minutes. Spread on rye bread. Top with a slice of cucumber and a sprig of dill. Cover and refrigerate until serving time. **Yield:** 30 appetizers.

🎖🎖🎖
Spicy Cranberry Warmer

Marlene Cartwright, Sierra City, California

This drink tastes great in winter when sitting in front of the fireplace. It warms you up, plus the kitchen smells so good!

> 3 whole cloves
> 2 cinnamon sticks
> 2 whole allspice
> 4 cups apple cider
> 1/3 cup packed brown sugar
> 4 cups cranberry juice

Additional cinnamon sticks, optional

1. Place first three ingredients in a double thickness of cheesecloth. Bring up corners of cloth and tie with a string. Place with cider in a large saucepan. (Or, if desired, place loose spices in saucepan and strain before serving.)

2. Simmer, covered, for 5 minutes. Stir in sugar and simmer for 5 minutes. Add cranberry juice and heat to simmering temperature. Serve hot in mugs. Garnish with cinnamon sticks if desired. **Yield:** 8-10 servings.

★ ★ ★
Rye Party Puffs

Kelly Thornberry, La Porte, Indiana

I can't go anywhere without taking along my puffs. They're pretty enough for a wedding reception yet hearty enough to snack on while watching football on television. A platterful of these will disappear even with a small group.

　　1　cup water
　1/2　cup butter
　1/2　cup all-purpose flour
　1/2　cup rye flour
　　2　teaspoons dried parsley flakes
　1/2　teaspoon garlic powder
　1/4　teaspoon salt
　　4　eggs
Caraway seeds
CORNED BEEF FILLING:
　　2　packages (8 ounces *each*) cream cheese, softened
　　2　packages (2-1/2 ounces *each*) thinly sliced cooked corned beef, chopped
　1/2　cup mayonnaise
　1/4　cup sour cream
　　2　tablespoons minced chives
　　2　tablespoons diced onion
　　1　teaspoon spicy brown *or* horseradish mustard
　1/8　teaspoon garlic powder
　10　small stuffed olives, chopped

1. In a saucepan over medium heat, bring water and butter to a boil. Add flours, parsley, garlic powder and salt all at once; stir until a smooth ball forms. Remove from the heat; let stand for 5 minutes. Beat in eggs, one at a time. Beat until smooth.

2. Drop batter by rounded teaspoonfuls 2 in. apart onto greased baking sheets. Sprinkle with caraway. Bake at 400° for 18-20 minutes or until golden. Remove to wire racks. Immediately cut a slit in each puff to allow steam to escape; cool.

3. In a mixing bowl, combine the first eight filling ingredients; mix well. Stir in olives. Split puffs; add filling. Refrigerate. **Yield:** 4-1/2 dozen.

★ ★ ★
Picnic Stuffed Eggs

Rebecca Register, Tallahassee, Florida

My dad loves these stuffed eggs, which are a Southern favorite. I've been cooking since I became a teenager, and this is one of my original recipes.

　12　hard-cooked eggs
　1/2　cup mayonnaise
　1/4　cup sweet pickle relish, drained
　　1　tablespoon honey mustard
　　1　teaspoon garlic salt
　1/2　teaspoon Worcestershire sauce
　1/4　teaspoon pepper
Fresh parsley sprigs, optional

1. Slice eggs in half lengthwise; remove yolks and set whites aside. In a small bowl, mash yolks with a fork. Add the mayonnaise, pickle relish, mustard, garlic salt, Worcestershire sauce and pepper; mix well.

2. Stuff or pipe into the egg whites. Refrigerate until serving. Garnish with parsley if desired. **Yield:** 2 dozen.

🎖 🎖 🎖
Orange Lemonade
Wendy Masters, Grand Valley, Ontario

This juice is a favorite at our place. I'll often double the batch and send a jar next door to my mother-in-law! I was looking for a way to sweeten lemonade without using more sugar when I came up with the recipe. I make it more often in summer, but we enjoy it year-round. It's good for special occasions also—I've served it at bridal showers and dinners.

1-3/4 cups sugar
2-1/2 cups water
1-1/2 cups fresh lemon juice (about 8 lemons)
1-1/2 cups fresh orange juice (about 5 oranges)
2 tablespoons grated lemon peel
2 tablespoons grated orange peel
Water

1. In a medium saucepan, combine sugar and water. Cook over medium heat, stirring occasionally, until sugar dissolves. Cool.

2. Add juices and peel to cooled sugar syrup. Cover and let stand at room temperature 1 hour. Strain syrup; cover and refrigerate.

3. To serve, fill glasses or pitcher with equal amounts of fruit syrup and water. Add ice and serve. **Yield:** 12 servings.

✿ ✿ ✿
Smoked Salmon Cherry Tomatoes

Pat Cronin, APO, Paris, France

These festive bites are a showstopping finger food during the holiday season, at Easter and for the Fourth of July. With the smoked salmon filling, these appetizers look elegant…and they're convenient because you can prepare them ahead of time.

> **30 cherry tomatoes**
> **3 ounces smoked salmon, finely chopped**
> **1/3 cup finely chopped onion**
> **1/3 cup finely chopped green pepper**

Salt and pepper to taste
> **1 package (3 ounces) cream cheese, softened**
> **1 teaspoon milk**

Fresh dill sprigs

1. Cut a thin slice off each tomato top; scoop out and discard pulp. Invert tomatoes on paper towels to drain. In a bowl, combine the salmon, onion, green pepper, salt and pepper; mix well. Spoon into tomatoes.

2. In a small mixing bowl, beat the cream cheese and milk until smooth. Insert a star tip into a pastry or plastic bag. Pipe a small amount of cream cheese mixture onto tomatoes. Garnish with dill. **Yield:** 2-1/2 dozen.

🎖🎖🎖
Mock Eggnog
Susannah Wayman, South Jordan, Utah

I found a mock eggnog recipe in a newspaper and made a few changes, which resulted in this delicious mixture. Our family loves it during the holidays.

> 2 quarts cold milk
> 1 package (3.4 ounces) instant French vanilla *or* vanilla pudding mix
> 1/4 cup sugar
> 1 teaspoon ground nutmeg
> 1 teaspoon vanilla extract
> 1/8 teaspoon salt, optional
> 1 cup heavy whipping cream

Additional nutmeg, optional

1. In a mixing bowl, beat milk and pudding mix on low speed for 2 minutes. Beat in the sugar, nutmeg, vanilla and salt if desired.

2. In another mixing bowl, beat cream until thickened, about 3 minutes. Stir into pudding mixture. Refrigerate until serving. Sprinkle with additional nutmeg if desired. **Yield:** about 2-1/2 quarts.

🎖🎖🎖
Zucchini Herb Pate
Melissa Sullivan, Iuka, Kansas

A friend gave me the recipe for this pate after she'd served it at a formal wedding reception. But I make it most often to spread on crackers at picnics, potlucks and other casual get-togethers.

> 4 medium zucchini (about 1 pound)
> 2 teaspoons tarragon vinegar
> 2 teaspoons sugar
> 2 teaspoons salt, *divided*
> 1/2 cup packed fresh parsley sprigs
> 1/2 cup snipped fresh chives *or* 1/4 cup dried chives
> 1 package (8 ounces) cream cheese, softened
> 1/2 teaspoon pepper

Crackers, bread slices or fresh veggies

1. Line a mixing bowl with a double thickness of cheesecloth. Coarsely shred zucchini into prepared bowl. Sprinkle with vinegar, sugar and 1 teaspoon salt. Toss gently; cover with a towel and set aside for 1 hour.

2. Meanwhile, in a blender or food processor with the chopping blade, mince parsley and chives. Gather ends of cheesecloth, squeezing out as much liquid as possible.

3. Add drained zucchini to food processor and process until pureed. Add cream cheese, pepper and remaining salt; process until smooth. Press pate into a small bowl. Cover and refrigerate overnight. Serve with crackers, bread or veggies. **Yield:** 1-1/2 cups.

Italian Pasta Salad, p. 34

Cranberry Orange Vinaigrette, p. 30

Layered Ham and Spinach Salad, p. 29

Salads & Dressings

Versatility makes salad a perfect choice for any season. In summer, chilled salads make a refreshing main course. Other times of the year, salads are a great starter or side dish.

Molded Egg Salad, p. 32

German Cucumber Salad, p. 36

🎗🎗🎗
Barley Corn Salad

Mary Ann Kieffer, Lawrence, Kansas

A great alternative to pasta salads, this colorful side dish adds refreshing herb flavor to corn, barley and red and green peppers. Bring it to your next get-together, and you'll see how fast it disappears!

☑ Uses less fat, sugar or salt. Includes Nutritional Analysis and Diabetic Exchanges.

　2　cups cooked medium pearl barley
　2　cups frozen corn, thawed
1/2　cup chopped sweet red pepper
1/2　cup chopped green pepper
　3　green onions, chopped
　1　tablespoon minced fresh cilantro
　2　tablespoons lemon juice
　2　tablespoons canola oil
1/2　teaspoon salt
1/2　teaspoon dried thyme
1/8　teaspoon pepper

In a large bowl, combine the first six ingredients. In a jar with a tight-fitting lid, combine the lemon juice, oil, salt, thyme and pepper; shake well. Pour over salad and toss to coat. Cover and refrigerate for at least 2 hours before serving. **Yield:** 6 servings.

Nutritional Analysis: One serving (2/3 cup) equals 163 calories, 5 g fat (trace saturated fat), 0 cholesterol, 201 mg sodium, 29 g carbohydrate, 4 g fiber, 3 g protein. **Diabetic Exchanges:** 1-1/2 starch, 1 vegetable, 1 fat.

🎗🎗🎗
Southwestern Pork Salad

Sue Cunningham, Prospect, Ohio

As pork producers, we're proud to cook and serve the delicious product we raise. This tempting salad is refreshing and colorful.

It's a succulent showcase for pork. I know your family will enjoy it as much as we do.

　2　cups cooked pork strips
　1　can (16 ounces) kidney beans, rinsed and drained
1/2　cup sliced ripe olives
　1　medium onion, chopped
　1　large green pepper, chopped
　1　large tomato, chopped
　2　tablespoons sugar
1/4　cup cider vinegar
1/4　cup vegetable oil
　1　teaspoon ground mustard
　1　teaspoon ground cumin
　1　teaspoon dried oregano
1/2　teaspoon salt
　2　tablespoons minced fresh parsley

1. In a large bowl, toss pork, beans, olives, onion, green pepper and tomato. Combine remaining ingredients in a jar with tight-fitting lid; shake well.

2. Pour over pork mixture; toss gently. Cover and refrigerate for 4-6 hours, stirring occasionally. **Yield:** 4 servings.

Layered Ham and Spinach Salad

(Pictured on page 26)

Beverly Sprague, Baltimore, Maryland

Here's a delicious salad that's sure to be a favorite with your family and friends. It's very easy to make.

- 16 cups torn fresh spinach
- 1 teaspoon sugar
- 1 teaspoon pepper
- 1/4 teaspoon salt
- 6 hard-cooked eggs, chopped
- 1-1/2 cups cubed fully cooked ham
- 1 medium red onion, sliced
- 1 envelope ranch salad dressing mix
- 1-1/2 cups mayonnaise
- 1 cup (8 ounces) sour cream
- 2 cups (8 ounces) shredded Swiss cheese
- 1/2 pound sliced bacon, cooked and crumbled

1. Place two-thirds of the spinach in a 4-qt. salad bowl. Sprinkle with half of the sugar, pepper and salt. Top with eggs, ham and remaining spinach. Sprinkle with remaining sugar, pepper and salt. Arrange onion slices on top.

2. In a bowl, combine the dressing mix, mayonnaise and sour cream. Spread over onions. Sprinkle with cheese and bacon. Refrigerate until serving. **Yield:** 8-10 servings.

Kielbasa Summer Salad

Sara Primarolo, Sauquoit, New York

The unexpected combination of flavors and textures in this cool salad sparks taste buds. It can be a main course for a luncheon or a side dish at a dinner or a barbecue. I received many compliments when I shared it as a potluck dish.

☑ Uses less fat, sugar or salt. Includes Nutritional Analysis and Diabetic Exchanges.

- 1 pound fully cooked smoked kielbasa *or* Polish sausage
- 1 can (15-1/2 ounces) black-eyed peas, rinsed and drained
- 2 medium tart apples, cut into 1/2-inch chunks
- 1 medium green pepper, chopped
- 4 large green onions, thinly sliced

DRESSING:

- 1/3 cup vegetable oil
- 3 tablespoons cider vinegar
- 1 tablespoon Dijon mustard
- 2 teaspoons sugar
- 1/2 to 1 teaspoon pepper

1. Halve sausage lengthwise and cut into 1/4-in. slices. In a nonstick skillet, brown sausage. Drain on paper towels.

2. In a bowl, combine peas, apples, green pepper, onions and sausage. Combine the dressing ingredients in a small bowl; mix well. Pour over sausage mixture and toss to coat. Cover and refrigerate for 4 hours or overnight. **Yield:** 10 servings.

Nutritional Analysis: One 1-cup serving (prepared with reduced-fat smoked turkey sausage) equals 192 calories, 561 mg sodium, 28 mg cholesterol, 14 g carbohydrate, 9 g protein, 12 g fat. **Diabetic Exchanges:** 1 starch, 1 meat, 1 fat.

🎗🎗🎗
Crab Pasta Salad

Kathryn Anderson, Wallkill, New York

This salad has a very good blend of flavors. It's easy to make and especially delicious on a hot day.

> 2 cups uncooked medium shell pasta
> 1-1/2 cups imitation crabmeat, chopped
> 1 cup broccoli florets
> 1/2 cup diced green pepper
> 1/2 cup quartered cherry tomatoes
> 1/4 cup chopped green onions
> **DRESSING:**
> 1/2 cup mayonnaise
> 1/4 cup creamy Italian salad dressing
> 1/4 cup grated Parmesan cheese

1. Cook pasta according to package directions; drain and rinse in cold water. Place in a large bowl. Stir in the crab, broccoli, green pepper, tomatoes and onions.

2. Combine dressing ingredients; pour over salad and toss gently to coat. Cover and refrigerate for 2-4 hours before serving. **Yield:** 4-6 servings.

🎗🎗🎗
Cranberry Orange Vinaigrette

(Pictured on page 26)

Toni Serpe, Dania, Florida

I eat a lot of salad and this is one of my favorite dressings. Living in Florida, I like using orange products produced in our state.

> 1/4 cup cranberry juice concentrate
> 1/4 cup orange juice concentrate
> 1/4 cup red wine vinegar
> 1/4 cup olive oil
> 1 teaspoon Dijon mustard
> 1/2 teaspoon salt
> 1/2 teaspoon pepper
> **Torn salad greens**
> **Sliced radishes and sweet yellow and orange peppers or vegetables of your choice**

In a jar with a tight-fitting lid, combine the first seven ingredients; shake well. Serve over greens and vegetables. Store in the refrigerator. **Yield:** 1 cup.

🎗🎗🎗 Spiced Peach Salad

Karen Hamilton, Ludington, Michigan

This refreshing salad is my most requested recipe. A touch of cinnamon makes it taste like fresh peach pie. My father-in-law is an especially big fan of this fruity salad, and I know you'll love it, too.

- 1/2 cup sugar
- 3 tablespoons vinegar
- 2 cups water
- 1 tablespoon whole cloves
- 4 cinnamon sticks
- 1 package (6 ounces) peach-flavored gelatin
- 1 can (29 ounces) peach halves

1. In a medium saucepan, combine sugar, vinegar and water. Tie cloves and cinnamon in a cheesecloth bag; place in the saucepan. Bring to a boil. Reduce heat; simmer, uncovered, for 10 minutes.

2. Remove from the heat and discard spice bag. Add gelatin; stir until dissolved. Drain peaches, reserving syrup; set peaches aside. Add water to syrup to equal 2 cups. Add to gelatin mixture; stir well.

3. Chill until slightly thickened. Thinly slice peaches; add to gelatin. Pour into a 2-qt. glass bowl; chill until firm. **Yield:** 8-10 servings.

Editor's Note: If desired, 1/2 teaspoon ground cinnamon and 1/4 teaspoon ground cloves may be substituted for the whole spices; combine with the gelatin before adding to sugar mixture.

🎗🎗🎗 Creamy Cauliflower Salad

Pat Payne, Harrison, Tennessee

Friends always ask for this recipe whenever I make this dish for a special occasion. It's so good and goes a long way.

- 1 medium head cauliflower, broken into florets
- 1 cup thinly sliced radishes
- 3/4 cup thinly sliced green pepper
- 1 cup (8 ounces) sour cream
- 2 tablespoons grated onion
- 4 to 5 teaspoons lemon juice
- 1 tablespoon Caesar salad dressing mix
- 1 teaspoon vegetable oil
- 1/4 teaspoon seasoned salt
- 1/4 teaspoon pepper

1. In a large bowl, combine the cauliflower, radishes and green pepper. In a small bowl, combine the remaining ingredients; mix well.

2. Pour over cauliflower mixture and toss to coat. Cover and refrigerate for at least 2 hours before serving. **Yield:** 8-10 servings.

🎀🎀🎀
Molded Egg Salad

(Pictured on page 27)

Lois Chapman, Ridgefield, Washington

When I have company I like to be able to just pop the food on the table, so this recipe's a real favorite of mine. I got it from a friend who made it for our church get-togethers.

> 3 envelopes unflavored gelatin
> 1 cup water
> 2 cups mayonnaise
> 12 hard-cooked eggs, chopped
> 1/2 cup sweet pickle relish
> 1/2 cup chopped celery
> 1/2 cup chopped sweet red pepper
> 1/2 cup sliced green onions
> 1 teaspoon salt
> 1/4 teaspoon pepper
> **Thinly sliced fully cooked ham, optional**

1. In a medium saucepan, soften gelatin in water for 5 minutes. Stir over low heat until gelatin dissolves. Remove from the heat. Whisk in mayonnaise. Stir in eggs. Add relish, celery, red pepper, onions, salt and pepper; mix well.

2. Pour into an 8-cup mold coated with nonstick cooking spray. Chill overnight. Unmold onto a serving platter. If desired, use ham as a garnish around the sides of the mold, or place several pieces in the center if using a ring mold. **Yield:** 8-10 servings.

🎀🎀🎀
Pickled Carrots

Cecilia Grondin, Grand Falls, New Brunswick

The trick to pickled carrots is cooking them just long enough to retain a harvest-fresh "snap." These tangy treats are terrific for perking up a buffet table or relish tray or serving alongside a hearty sandwich.

> 1 pound carrots, cut into 3-inch julienne strips
> 3/4 cup water
> 2/3 cup white vinegar
> 3/4 cup sugar
> 1 cinnamon stick (3 inches), broken
> 3 whole cloves
> 1 tablespoon mustard seed

1. Place 1 in. of water in a saucepan; add carrots. Bring to a boil. Reduce heat; cover and simmer for 3-4 minutes or until carrots are crisp-tender. Drain and rinse in cold water. Place in a bowl and set aside.

2. In a saucepan, combine water, vinegar, sugar, cinnamon, whole cloves and mustard seed. Bring to a boil. Reduce heat; simmer, uncovered, for 10 minutes. Cool; pour over the carrots.

3. Cover and refrigerate for 8 hours or overnight. Discard cloves and cinnamon. Serve carrots with a slotted spoon. **Yield:** 6-8 servings.

★ ★ ★
Broccoli Slaw

Konny Thomas, Citrus Heights, California

Here's a new twist on traditional coleslaw. It's easy to make and so delicious.

- 4 cups broccoli florets
- 1 medium carrot, shredded
- 2 cups shredded red cabbage
- 1/2 cup raisins
- 1 small sweet onion, chopped
- 1 bottle (16 ounces) coleslaw dressing

In a serving bowl, combine all ingredients. Cover and refrigerate for at least 2 hours. Stir before serving. **Yield:** 6 servings.

★ ★ ★
Mandarin-Cashew Tossed Salad

Sheri Shaffer, Northfield, Ohio

Mandarin oranges and chopped red onion add a touch of color to mixed greens and sweet roasted cashews in this refreshing salad. You're sure to be handing out the recipe once friends and family get a taste of the tangy honey dressing.

- 5 cups torn red leaf lettuce
- 5 cups torn iceberg lettuce
- 3 cups torn Boston lettuce
- 2 cans (11 ounces *each*) mandarin oranges, well drained
- 3/4 cup chopped green pepper
- 1 celery rib, thinly sliced
- 1/4 cup chopped red onion

HONEY LIME DRESSING:
- 1/4 cup vegetable oil
- 1/4 cup honey
- 1/2 teaspoon ground mustard
- 1/2 teaspoon grated lime peel
- 1/4 teaspoon paprika
- 1/8 teaspoon salt

Dash white pepper
- 1 cup honey roasted cashews

1. In a large salad bowl, combine the lettuces, oranges, green pepper, celery and onion.

2. In a small bowl, combine oil, honey, mustard, lime peel, paprika, salt and pepper; mix well. Drizzle over salad. Add cashews; toss to coat. Serve immediately. **Yield:** 10-12 servings.

Here's a salad with some zip to it. I've also served the spicy dressing with mixed vegetables, fruit and tossed salads.

- 4 cups torn fresh spinach
- 1 cup minced fresh parsley
- 1 cup sliced fresh mushrooms
- 2 medium tomatoes, cut into wedges
- 2 celery ribs, chopped
- 1 cup canned bean sprouts, rinsed and drained
- 1-1/2 cups (6 ounces) shredded cheddar cheese
- 1 cup salted sunflower kernels
- 1/4 teaspoon *each* salt, garlic salt and pepper

DRESSING:
- 1/2 cup vegetable oil
- 1/4 cup honey
- 1/4 cup cider vinegar
- 1/4 cup chopped onion
- 3 tablespoons chili sauce
- 1-1/2 teaspoons Worcestershire sauce
- 1/4 teaspoon salt

1. In a large salad bowl, combine the spinach, parsley, mushrooms, tomatoes, celery, bean sprouts, cheese, sunflower kernels and seasonings.

2. In a jar with a tight-fitting lid, combine the dressing ingredients; shake well. Drizzle desired amount over salad and toss to coat. Serve immediately. Refrigerate any leftover dressing. **Yield:** 12 servings.

🎀 🎀 🎀

Spinach Salad with Spicy Honey Dressing

Barbara Martineau, Hudson, Wisconsin

🎀 🎀 🎀

Italian Pasta Salad

(Pictured on page 26)

Tina Dierking, Canaan, Maine

This zesty recipe combines vegetables and pasta in a creamy dressing. Refreshing and filling, this change-of-pace salad is perfect as a side dish. It's always popular at a potluck.

- 3/4 cup uncooked spiral pasta
- 1-1/2 cups halved cherry tomatoes
- 1 cup sliced fresh mushrooms
- 1/4 cup chopped sweet red pepper
- 1/4 cup chopped green pepper
- 3 tablespoons thinly sliced green onions
- 1-1/2 cups zesty Italian salad dressing
- 3/4 cup mayonnaise
- 1/2 cup grated Parmesan cheese
- 1/3 cup cubed provolone cheese
- 1 can (2-1/4 ounces) sliced ripe olives, drained

Leaf lettuce, optional

1. Cook pasta according to package directions; rinse with cold water and drain. Place in a bowl; add the tomatoes, mushrooms, peppers, onions and salad dressing. Cover and refrigerate for at least 4 hours or overnight; drain.

2. In a bowl, combine the mayonnaise and Parmesan cheese; stir in the provolone cheese and olives. Gently fold into the pasta mixture. Serve in a lettuce-lined bowl if desired. **Yield:** 6 servings.

Green Salad with Onion Dressing

Cara Bonnema, Painesville, Ohio

This is such an elegant salad. It will dress up any table. The caramelized onion in the dressing tastes fantastic. It's never failed to be a hit whenever I've served it.

> 1 large onion, peeled and cut into eighths
> 8 tablespoons olive oil, *divided*
> 1-1/2 teaspoons sugar
> 1/4 cup chicken broth
> 2 tablespoons cider vinegar
> 1/4 teaspoon salt
> 14 cups torn salad greens
> 1 cup chopped walnuts, toasted
> 1/2 cup thinly sliced red onion

1. Place onion in a baking dish. Drizzle with 1 tablespoon oil; sprinkle with sugar. Bake, uncovered, at 400° for 30 minutes. Turn and bake 25-30 minutes longer, stirring several times, until the onion is tender and lightly browned. Cool for 30 minutes.

2. Place onion in a blender or food processor; add broth, vinegar, salt and remaining oil. Cover and process

until smooth (mixture will be thick). Chill.

3. Just before serving, toss greens, walnuts, red onion and dressing in a large salad bowl. **Yield:** 12 servings.

Creamy Fruit Salad

Brittany Tyrrell, Manchester, Iowa

Cream cheese and yogurt are combined in the light dressing that coats this fast fruit medley. The salad is a snap to assemble because it takes advantage of canned peaches, pineapple chunks and mandarin oranges, which you likely keep in your pantry. Miniature marshmallows add a touch of sweetness.

> 1 can (11 ounces) mandarin oranges, drained
> 1 can (8-1/4 ounces) sliced peaches, drained
> 1 can (8 ounces) pineapple chunks, drained
> 1 cup miniature marshmallows
> 4 ounces cream cheese, softened
> 1/2 cup plain yogurt
> 1/4 cup sugar

In a bowl, combine the oranges, peaches, pineapple and marshmallows. In a small mixing bowl, beat the cream cheese, yogurt and sugar until smooth; pour over fruit and toss to coat. Refrigerate for 15 minutes. **Yield:** 4 servings.

✿ ✿ ✿
German Cucumber Salad

(Pictured on page 27)

Julie Koren, Kennesaw, Georgia

This recipe came from a friend who ran his own inn in Germany. It's a very cool, light salad with an exhilarating taste that's delicious any time of the year—especially when made with fresh-from-the-garden cucumbers and tomatoes.

    2 medium cucumbers, thinly sliced
    4 green onions, thinly sliced
    3 small tomatoes, sliced
    2 tablespoons snipped fresh parsley
DRESSING:
    1/4 cup sour cream
    1/4 teaspoon prepared mustard
    2 tablespoons minced fresh dill
    1 tablespoon vinegar

    1 tablespoon milk
    1/2 teaspoon salt
    1/8 teaspoon pepper

In a bowl, combine cucumbers, onions, tomatoes and parsley. Combine dressing ingredients; pour over cucumber mixture and toss gently. Cover and chill for at least 1 hour. **Yield:** 4-6 servings.

✿ ✿ ✿
Blue Cheese Dressing

Barbara Nowakowski, N. Tonawanda, New York

I tasted this tangy dressing for the first time at a friend's house. She gave me the recipe, and now I make it every week. I always keep some in my refrigerator. It tastes much better than bottled blue cheese dressing and is a snap to make.

1-1/2 cups mayonnaise
    1/2 cup sour cream
    1/4 cup cider vinegar
    4 teaspoons sugar
    1/2 teaspoon ground mustard
    1/2 teaspoon garlic powder
    1/2 teaspoon onion powder
    1 package (4 ounces) blue cheese, crumbled

In a bowl, combine the first seven ingredients. Stir in the blue cheese. Cover and chill at least 2 hours. Store in the refrigerator. **Yield:** 2 cups.

Tuna Salad Pepper Cups

Ellen Boucher, Denver, Colorado

I came up with this recipe on a summer day when I didn't feel like cooking. I frequently make it when friends come for lunch, and they all love it. Stuffed into a pretty pepper half, the fresh-tasting tuna mixture gets crunch from cucumber and green onions.

> 2 large green peppers
> 2 cans (6 ounces *each*) tuna, drained
> 1 medium cucumber, chopped
> 2 green onions, chopped
> 1/2 cup mayonnaise
> 1/4 cup dill pickle relish

Cut green peppers in half lengthwise; remove seeds and membranes. In a bowl, combine the tuna, cucumber, onions, mayonnaise and relish. Spoon into pepper cups. Serve immediately. **Yield:** 4 servings.

Dilly Veggie Pasta Salad

Anna Emory-Royal, Murfreesboro, Tennessee

My sister shared the recipe for this fresh, crunchy salad seasoned with dill. It's handy because you can assemble and eat it right away…or cover and refrigerate it to take to a picnic or potluck the next day. The longer it chills, the more tangy it is.

2-3/4 cups uncooked medium shell pasta
> 1 cup halved cherry tomatoes
> 1 cup sliced green pepper
> 1 cup (4 ounces) shredded cheddar cheese
> 1/2 cup chopped green onions
> 1/2 cup sliced ripe olives

DRESSING:
> 1/4 cup olive oil
> 2 tablespoons lemon juice
> 2 tablespoons white wine vinegar
> 1 teaspoon dill weed
> 1 teaspoon dried oregano
> 1 teaspoon salt
> 1/8 teaspoon pepper

1. Cook pasta according to package directions; drain and rinse in cold water. Place in a large bowl. Add tomatoes, green pepper, cheese, onions and olives.

2. In a small bowl, whisk together the dressing ingredients. Pour over salad and toss to coat. Cover and refrigerate until serving. **Yield:** 8 servings.

🎗🎗🎗
Creamy Celery Seed Dressing

Patricia Dougherty, Dunkirk, New York

This recipe originated with my Aunt Mazie, a superb cook from West Virginia. I like this dressing because of its versatility. It's wonderful with potatoes, macaroni, hot or cold sliced meat or vegetables. I've shared it with many friends and have had it published in several fund-raising cookbooks.

      1/2 cup butter
        1 cup vinegar
        3 eggs, lightly beaten
  1-1/2 teaspoons celery seed
        1 teaspoon salt
      1/4 teaspoon white pepper
        2 cups mayonnaise
      3/4 cup prepared Italian salad dressing
      1/2 cup sugar

1. In a saucepan, melt butter. Meanwhile, combine vinegar, eggs, celery seed, salt and pepper. Gradually add to butter, stirring constantly. Cook and stir over medium heat until slightly thickened, about 5 minutes.

2. Remove from the heat and allow to cool. Mix in mayonnaise, Italian dressing and sugar. Cover and chill for at least 1 hour. Serve over coleslaw, vegetables or pasta. **Yield:** 4-1/2 cups.

🎗🎗🎗
Brown Rice Salad With Grilled Chicken

Glenda Harper, Cable, Ohio

This delightful dish is nutritious and simple to fix. It brightens up a buffet table, and I think it's a terrific way to use up leftover chicken.

☑ Uses less fat, sugar or salt. Includes Nutritional Analysis and Diabetic Exchanges.

        3 cups cooked brown rice
        2 cups cubed grilled chicken breast
        2 medium tart apples, diced
        1 medium sweet red pepper, diced
        2 celery ribs, finely chopped
      2/3 cup chopped green onions
      1/2 cup chopped pecans
        3 tablespoons minced fresh parsley
      1/4 cup cider vinegar
        3 tablespoons canola oil
        1 tablespoon lemon juice
        1 teaspoon salt
      1/4 teaspoon pepper
  Lettuce leaves, optional

1. In a large bowl, combine the first eight ingredients. In a jar with a tight-fitting lid, combine the vinegar, oil, lemon juice, salt and pepper; shake well.

2. Pour over the rice mixture and toss to coat. Serve immediately or refrigerate. Serve in a lettuce-lined bowl if desired. **Yield:** 9 servings.

Nutritional Analysis: One serving (1 cup) equals 236 calories, 11 g fat (1 g saturated fat), 26 mg cholesterol, 295 mg sodium, 23 g carbohydrate, 3 g fiber, 12 g protein. **Diabetic Exchanges:** 1-1/2 fat, 1 starch, 1 lean meat, 1/2 fruit.

Tropical Turkey Salad

Rosalind Canada, White Bluff, Tennessee

Forever on the lookout for simple dishes to prepare, I tried this delicious salad while on a trip. It's lovely and satisfying with a mixture of turkey, fruits and vegetables. The tangy raspberry dressing is irresistible.

5 cups torn fresh spinach
3 cups torn lettuce
2 cups cooked cubed turkey
2 slices red onion, separated into rings
1/2 cup chopped green pepper
1/2 cup mandarin oranges
1/2 cup sliced celery
1/2 cup pineapple chunks
1/3 cup vegetable oil
1/4 cup raspberry syrup
2 tablespoons red wine vinegar
1-1/2 teaspoons honey
1/2 teaspoon celery seed
1/2 cup sliced almonds, toasted
1/4 cup flaked coconut, toasted

1. Line a large salad bowl with spinach and lettuce. Combine the next six ingredients; spoon into bowl.

2. In a jar with tight-fitting lid, combine oil, raspberry syrup, vinegar, honey and celery seed; shake well. Pour over the salad. Top with almonds and coconut. Serve immediately. **Yield:** 6 servings.

🎀🎀🎀

Spicy Beef Salad

Peggy Allen, Pasadena, California

This recipe was inspired by my love of spicy flavors and light, nutritious entrees. The pretty salad has an appealing variety of textures. I make it year-round because it's fast and easy to prepare after a long day at work.

☑ Uses less fat, sugar or salt. Includes Nutritional Analysis and Diabetic Exchanges.

- 1/2 **pound boneless sirloin steak**
- 1/3 **cup fresh lime juice**
- 1 **tablespoon brown sugar**
- 1 **tablespoon soy sauce**
- 1 **tablespoon minced fresh basil** *or* 1 **teaspoon dried basil**
- 2 **teaspoons minced fresh mint** *or* 3/4 **teaspoon dried mint**
- 1 **jalapeno pepper, minced**
- 1 **teaspoon grated fresh gingerroot**
- 2 to 3 **garlic cloves, minced**
- 1 **large sweet red pepper, julienned**
- 1/2 **medium cucumber, chopped**
- 6 **cups torn mixed salad greens**

1. Partially freeze beef. Slice across the grain into thin strips; set aside. For dressing, combine lime juice, sugar, soy sauce, basil and mint; set aside.

2. In a medium nonstick skillet that has been coated with nonstick cooking spray, saute jalapeno, ginger and garlic for 30 seconds. Add beef; stir-fry until cooked as desired. Remove beef from pan; gently toss with red pepper and cucumber.

3. Place greens in a large bowl or divide among individual bowls or plates; top with beef mixture. Add dressing to pan and bring to a boil; remove from the heat and drizzle over salad. Serve immediately. **Yield:** 4 servings.

Editor's Note: When cutting or seeding hot peppers, use rubber or plastic gloves to protect your hands. Avoid touching your face.

Nutritional Analysis: One serving (prepared with reduced-sodium soy sauce) equals 152 calories, 171 mg sodium, 45 mg cholesterol, 11 g carbohydrate, 17 g protein, 5 g fat. **Diabetic Exchanges:** 2 very lean meat, 2 vegetable.

✿✿✿ Water Chestnut Pea Salad

Maree Waggener, Cheney, Washington

A local restaurant serves a pea salad that everyone raves over, so I came up with a similar version my family likes even better. My husband requests the well-dressed crunchy combination often during the summer.

- 2 medium carrots, chopped
- 1 package (16 ounces) frozen peas, thawed
- 1 can (8 ounces) sliced water chestnuts, drained
- 2 green onions, thinly sliced
- 1/2 cup shredded mozzarella cheese
- 1/2 cup prepared ranch salad dressing
- 5 bacon strips, cooked and crumbled
- 1/4 teaspoon pepper

1. Cook carrots in a small amount of water until crisp-tender; drain and rinse in cold water. Place in a serving bowl; add the peas, water chestnuts, onions and cheese.

2. In a small bowl, combine the salad dressing, bacon and pepper; mix well. Pour over salad and toss to coat. Chill until serving. **Yield:** 6 servings.

✿✿✿ Sunflower Strawberry Salad

Betty Malone, Humboldt, Tennessee

We have an annual Strawberry Festival in our town, so recipes with strawberries are popular here. I've served this salad at luncheons and have always received compliments.

✓ Uses less fat, sugar or salt. Includes Nutritional Analysis and Diabetic Exchanges.

- 2 cups sliced fresh strawberries
- 1 medium apple, diced
- 1 cup seedless green grapes, halved
- 1/2 cup thinly sliced celery
- 1/4 cup raisins
- 1/2 cup strawberry yogurt
- 2 tablespoons sunflower seeds

Lettuce leaves, optional

In a large bowl, combine strawberries, apple, grapes, celery and raisins. Stir in the yogurt. Cover and refrigerate for at least 1 hour. Add sunflower seeds and toss; serve on lettuce leaves if desired. **Yield:** 6 servings.

Nutritional Analysis: One 1-cup serving (prepared with sugar-free yogurt and unsalted sunflower seeds) equals 98 calories, 23 mg sodium, 0 cholesterol, 18 g carbohydrate, 2 g protein, 3 g fat. **Diabetic Exchanges:** 1 fruit, 1 fat.

❦ ❦ ❦
Banana Poppy Seed Dressing

Gloria Kirchman, Eden Prairie, Minnesota

Here's a lightly sweet, refreshing dressing that lets the flavor of banana come through. A homemaker with four grown children, I have an extensive recipe collection. This dressing is so good over crisp greens or fresh fruit. Give it a try!

- 1 ripe banana
- 1 cup (8 ounces) sour cream
- 1/4 cup sugar
- 1 tablespoon poppy seeds
- 1 tablespoon lemon juice
- 1 teaspoon ground mustard
- 3/4 teaspoon salt

Salad greens
Orange and grapefruit sections

1. In a small bowl, finely mash banana. Add sour cream, sugar, poppy seeds, lemon juice, mustard and salt.

2. Chill for at least 30 minutes. Arrange salad greens and fruit on a platter or individual salad plates. Serve with dressing. **Yield:** 1-3/4 cups.

❦ ❦ ❦
Festive Tossed Salad

Isabell Burrows, Livermore, California

This is a delightful salad that has a wonderful blend of flavors. It has a crunchy texture and looks good, too, with its variety of colors.

- 1 cup coarsely chopped walnuts
- 3 tablespoons butter
- 1/4 cup sugar
- 1 teaspoon coarsely ground pepper
- 1/4 teaspoon salt
- 12 cups torn mixed salad greens
- 3/4 cup dried cranberries
- 4 ounces crumbled feta cheese

DRESSING:
- 1/4 cup red wine vinegar
- 1/4 cup vegetable oil
- 1/2 cup loosely packed fresh parsley sprigs
- 1/4 cup chopped red onion
- 2 garlic cloves, peeled
- 1 tablespoon sugar
- 1/2 teaspoon dried oregano
- 1/8 teaspoon salt
- 1/8 teaspoon pepper

1. In a skillet, cook and stir walnuts in butter until toasted, about 5 minutes. Remove from the heat; stir in the sugar, pepper and salt.

2. In a salad bowl, toss the greens, cranberries, cheese and walnuts. Place the dressing ingredients in a blender or food processor; cover and process until smooth.

3. Drizzle desired amount over salad; toss to coat. Serve immediately. Refrigerate leftover dressing. **Yield:** 12 servings.

🏅 🏅 🏅
Mexican Garden Salad

Dianne Esposite, New Middletown, Ohio

I'm always watching for new recipes to try. When I found this salad, I knew it would taste as good as it looks. Although similar to a traditional taco salad, this recipe adds tasty extras like broccoli and shredded carrot. It's stunning on the table.

- 1 pound ground beef
- 1 jar (16 ounces) thick and chunky salsa, *divided*
- 1/4 cup water
- 1 envelope taco seasoning mix
- 1-1/2 heads iceberg lettuce, torn
- 3 cups broccoli florets (about 1/2 pound)
- 1 small red onion, thinly sliced into rings
- 1 medium carrot, shredded
- 1 large tomato, chopped
- 1 can (4 ounces) chopped green chilies, drained
- 1/2 to 1 cup shredded cheddar cheese
- 1 cup (8 ounces) sour cream

Tortilla chips, optional

1. In a skillet, cook ground beef over medium heat until no longer pink; drain. Add 1 cup salsa, water and taco seasoning; bring to a boil. Reduce heat and simmer for 20 minutes; cool.

2. In a 3- or 4-qt. glass bowl, layer vegetables in order given. Top with chilies, beef mixture and cheese. Combine sour cream and remaining salsa; serve with salad and tortilla chips if desired. **Yield:** 6-8 servings.

🎗 🎗 🎗
Swiss Tossed Salad

Sherian Peterson, High Ridge, Missouri

This simple, green salad requires just a few ingredients, yet its blend of flavors and combination of textures make it seem special. You can toss all the ingredients with the basic dressing or dollop it over individual servings.

> **12** bacon strips, diced
> **1** bunch red leaf lettuce, torn (about 10 cups)
> **1** small red onion, julienned
> **1** block (8 ounces) Swiss cheese, cubed
> **1/4** cup sliced ripe olives
> **1/3** cup mayonnaise
> **1/3** cup sour cream

1. In a skillet over medium heat, cook bacon until crisp. Remove to paper towels to drain.

2. In a large bowl, combine lettuce, onion, cheese, olives and bacon. In a small bowl, combine mayonnaise and sour cream. Serve with the salad. **Yield:** 8-10 servings.

6 large red potatoes (about 3 pounds), cubed
1/3 cup vegetable oil
1/4 cup cider vinegar
1 tablespoon sugar
2-1/2 teaspoons chili powder
1-1/2 teaspoons hot pepper sauce
1 teaspoon salt
1/4 teaspoon onion powder
1/4 teaspoon ground cumin
1 can (15-1/4 ounces) whole kernel corn, drained
1 can (2-1/4 ounces) sliced ripe olives, drained
1/2 cup minced fresh cilantro
2 tablespoons chopped seeded jalapeno peppers

1. Place potatoes in a large saucepan and cover with water; cover and bring to a boil. Reduce heat; cook for 20-30 minutes or until tender. Drain; place in a large bowl.

2. In a jar with a tight-fitting lid, combine the oil, vinegar, sugar, chili powder, hot pepper sauce, salt, onion powder and cumin; shake well. Pour over potatoes and toss to coat.

3. Cover and refrigerate for at least 1 hour. Just before serving, stir in the corn, olives, cilantro and peppers. **Yield:** 8-10 servings.

Editor's Note: When cutting or seeding hot peppers, use rubber or plastic gloves to protect your hands. Avoid touching your face.

🎗 🎗 🎗
Spicy Potato Salad

Donna Lefurgey, Prescott, Arizona

This is a great potluck or picnic dish. It's always gobbled up quickly. One of the best things is that it's a snap to fix.

🎗 🎗 🎗
Broccoli Waldorf Salad

Vicki Roehrick, Chubbuck, Idaho

This salad is as easy to prepare as it is to eat! A colorful combination of apples, raisins and pecans jazzes up broccoli florets in this summery side dish. Its tangy-sweet flavor makes it a standout at company picnics.

✓ Uses less fat, sugar or salt. Includes Nutritional Analysis and Diabetic Exchanges.

6 cups broccoli florets
1 large red apple, chopped
1/2 cup raisins
1/4 cup chopped pecans
1/2 cup prepared coleslaw dressing

In a large serving bowl, combine the first four ingredients. Drizzle with dressing; toss to coat. Refrigerate leftovers. **Yield:** 10 servings.

Nutritional Analysis: One 3/4-cup serving (prepared with reduced-fat coleslaw dressing) equals 87 calories, 4 g fat (trace saturated fat), 3 mg cholesterol, 133 mg sodium, 14 g carbohydrate, 2 g fiber, 2 g protein. **Diabetic Exchanges:** 1 vegetable, 1 fruit.

Roast Beef Sandwich Roll, p. 52

Vegetarian Chili, p. 56

Southwestern Tomato Soup, p. 49

Shrimp Patty Sandwiches, p. 55

Soups & Sandwiches

If ever there was a perfect pairing, it would have to be soups and sandwiches. They comfort and warm us; they cheer and nourish us. With their homemade goodness, they bring smiles to our faces in every season.

Creamy White Chili, p. 51

Salmon Salad Sandwiches, p. 58

My husband and I savor every spoonful of this hearty soup. It makes a real stick-to-your-ribs meal when served with crusty, oven-fresh bread.

1-1/2 **cups dried great northern beans**
  3/4 **pound Italian sausage links, casings removed**
    1 **large onion, chopped**
    1 **large carrot, chopped**
    3 **garlic cloves, minced**
    6 **cups chicken broth**
    3 **cups water**
    2 **tablespoons dried currants**
    1 **teaspoon dried basil**
    1 **can (14-1/2 ounces) diced tomatoes, undrained**
    1 **cup uncooked small shell pasta**
Grated Parmesan cheese

1. Place beans in a Dutch oven or soup kettle; add water to cover by 2 in. Bring to a boil; boil for 2 minutes. Remove from the heat; cover and let stand for 1 hour. Drain and rinse beans, discarding liquid.

2. In the same pan, cook the sausage, onion, carrot and garlic over medium heat until the meat is no longer pink; drain. Add the broth, water, currants, basil and beans. Bring to a boil. Reduce heat; cover and simmer for 1-1/2 to 2 hours or until the beans are tender, stirring occasionally.

3. Add the tomatoes and pasta; bring to a boil. Reduce heat; cover and simmer for 15 minutes or until pasta is tender. Serve with Parmesan cheese. **Yield:** 12 servings (3 quarts).

🎗 🎗 🎗
White Bean and Pasta Soup

Michelle Harbour, Lebanon, Tennessee

🎗 🎗 🎗
Baked Bean Chili

Nancy Wall, Bakersfield, California

Who says a good chili has to simmer all day? This zippy chili—with a touch of sweetness from the baked beans—can be made on the spur of the moment. It's an excellent standby when unexpected guests drop in. Served with bread and a salad, it's a hearty dinner everyone raves about.

    2 **pounds ground beef**
    3 **cans (28 ounces *each*) baked beans**
    1 **can (46 ounces) tomato juice**
    1 **can (11-1/2 ounces) V8 juice**
    1 **envelope chili seasoning**

In a Dutch oven, cook beef over medium heat until no longer pink; drain. Stir in the remaining ingredients. Bring to a boil. Reduce heat; simmer, uncovered, for 10 minutes. **Yield:** 24 servings.

Sourdough Cheeseburgers

Michelle Dommel, Quakertown, Pennsylvania

Here's a mouth-watering cheeseburger that's easy and quick. I came up with it one night when I realized I'd run out of hamburger buns. My husband loved the tang and toasty crunch of the sourdough bread.

      3 tablespoons mayonnaise
      1 tablespoon ketchup
      1 tablespoon sweet pickle relish
  1/2 pound ground beef
Salt and pepper to taste
      1 small onion, sliced and separated into rings
      4 tablespoons butter, *divided*
      4 slices sourdough bread
      4 slices Swiss cheese

1. In a small bowl, combine the mayonnaise, ketchup and relish; cover and refrigerate. Shape beef into two oval patties.

2. In a large skillet, fry burgers over medium heat for 4-5 minutes on each side or until a meat thermometer reads 160°. Season with salt and pepper; remove and keep warm. In the same skillet, saute onion in 1 tablespoon butter until tender. Remove and keep warm.

3. Using 2 tablespoons of butter, butter one side of each slice of bread. Melt remaining butter in the skillet. Place bread, buttered side up, in skillet; cook for 2-3 minutes or until golden brown. Turn; top two pieces of bread with two slices of cheese. Cook 2 minutes longer or until cheese is melted.

4. To serve, place toast, cheese side up, on a plate. Top with a burger, relish mixture, onion and remaining toast. **Yield:** 2 servings.

Southwestern Tomato Soup

(Pictured on page 46)

Sherri Jackson, Chillicothe, Ohio

This smooth, flavorful tomato soup is unbeatable when the season's ripest tomatoes are available and the weather starts to cool. Each delicious, fresh-tasting bowlful will warm you from the inside out.

    10 plum tomatoes, halved lengthwise
      1 to 2 Anaheim peppers, halved and seeded
  1/2 cup chopped onion
      2 garlic cloves, minced
      1 tablespoon olive oil
      2 cans (14-1/2 ounces *each*) chicken broth
      1 tablespoon minced fresh cilantro
      2 teaspoons ground cumin
  1/2 teaspoon sugar
  1/2 teaspoon salt
  1/4 teaspoon pepper
Vegetable oil for frying
      8 corn tortillas (6 inches), cut into 1/4-inch strips
Sour cream, optional

1. Place tomatoes cut side down on a broiler pan; broil 3-4 in. from the heat for 15-20 minutes. Peel and discard skins. Repeat with peppers, broiling for 5-10 minutes.

2. In a skillet, saute onion and garlic in oil until tender. Transfer to a blender or food processor; add the tomatoes and peppers. Cover and process until smooth. Pour into a large saucepan; cook and stir over medium heat for 2 minutes.

3. Press mixture through a strainer with a spoon; discard seeds. Return tomato mixture to the pan. Add broth, cilantro, cumin, sugar, salt and pepper. Cover and cook on low for 15-20 minutes or until heated through.

4. Meanwhile, heat 1/2 in. of oil in a skillet to 375°. Fry tortilla strips, in batches, for 3-5 minutes or until golden brown; drain on paper towels. Garnish bowls of soup with tortilla strips. Serve with sour cream if desired. **Yield:** 6 servings.

🎗🎗🎗
Garbanzo Gazpacho

Mary Ann Gomez, Lombard, Illinois

This chunky chilled soup is terrific in warm weather, but our family loves it so much I often prepare it in winter, too. I made some slight changes to the original recipe to suit our tastes, and the flavorful combination has been a favorite ever since.

✓ Uses less fat, sugar or salt. Includes Nutritional Analysis and Diabetic Exchanges.

- **1 can (15 ounces) garbanzo beans *or* chickpeas, rinsed and drained**
- **1 can (14-1/2 ounces) Italian diced tomatoes, undrained**
- **1-1/4 cups V8 juice**
- **1 cup beef broth**
- **1 cup quartered cherry tomatoes**
- **1/2 cup chopped seeded cucumber**
- **1/4 cup chopped red onion**
- **1/4 cup minced fresh cilantro**
- **3 tablespoons lime juice**
- **1 garlic clove, minced**
- **1/2 teaspoon salt**
- **1/4 teaspoon hot pepper sauce**

In a large bowl, combine all ingredients; cover and refrigerate until serving. **Yield:** 6 servings.

Nutritional Analysis: One serving (1 cup) equals 126 calories, 1 g fat (trace saturated fat), trace cholesterol, 993 mg sodium, 23 g carbohydrate, 4 g fiber, 6 g protein. **Diabetic Exchange:** 1-1/2 starch.

🎗🎗🎗
Slow-Cooked Chunky Chili

Margie Shaw, Greenbrier, Arkansas

Pork sausage, ground beef and plenty of beans make this chili a hearty meal-starter. I keep the versatile mixture in serving-size containers in my freezer at all times. I can quickly warm up bowls of it on cold days—or use it to fix chili dogs, chili tacos and more.

- **1 pound ground beef**
- **1 pound bulk pork sausage**
- **4 cans (16 ounces *each*) kidney beans, rinsed and drained**
- **2 cans (14-1/2 ounces *each*) diced tomatoes, undrained**
- **2 cans (10 ounces *each*) diced tomatoes and green chilies, undrained**
- **1 large onion, chopped**
- **1 medium green pepper, chopped**
- **1 envelope taco seasoning**
- **1/2 teaspoon salt**
- **1/4 teaspoon pepper**

1. In a skillet, cook beef and sausage over medium heat until meat is no longer pink; drain. Transfer to a 5-qt. slow cooker. Stir in the remaining ingredients.

2. Cover and cook on high for 4-5 hours or until vegetables are tender. Serve desired amount. Cool the remaining chili; transfer to freezer bags or containers. Freeze for up to 3 months. **Yield:** 3 quarts (12 servings).

To use frozen chili: Thaw in the refrigerator; place in a saucepan and heat through. Add water if desired.

Creamy White Chili

(Pictured on page 47)

Laura Brewer, Lafayette, Indiana

I received this wonderful recipe from my sister-in-law, who made a big batch and served a crowd one night. It was a hit. Plus, it's easy and quick, which is helpful since I'm a college student. In all my years of 4-H cooking, I've never had another dish get so many compliments.

   1 **pound skinless chicken breasts, cut into 1/2-inch cubes**
   1 **medium onion, chopped**
1-1/2 **teaspoons garlic powder**
   1 **tablespoon vegetable oil**
   2 **cans (15-1/2 ounces *each*) great northern beans, rinsed and drained**
   1 **can (14-1/2 ounces) chicken broth**
   2 **cans (4 ounces *each*) chopped green chilies**
   1 **teaspoon salt**
   1 **teaspoon ground cumin**
   1 **teaspoon dried oregano**
1/2 **teaspoon pepper**
1/4 **teaspoon cayenne pepper**
   1 **cup (8 ounces) sour cream**
1/2 **cup heavy whipping cream**

1. In a large saucepan, saute chicken, onion and garlic powder in oil until chicken is no longer pink. Add the beans, broth, chilies and seasonings. Bring to a boil.

2. Reduce heat; simmer, uncovered, for 30 minutes. Remove from the heat; stir in sour cream and heavy whipping cream. **Yield:** 7 servings.

Big Sandwich

Margaret Yost, Tipp City, Ohio

One look at this impressive sandwich and your family and friends will know their taste buds are in for a treat. I have served it many times for casual lunches and suppers. The tall layers prompt people to ask how they're supposed to eat it. I encourage them to simply dig in and enjoy!

   1 **unsliced round loaf of bread (8 inches)**
   2 **tablespoons horseradish**
1/2 **pound thinly sliced cooked roast beef**
   2 **tablespoons prepared mustard**
1/2 **pound thinly sliced fully cooked ham**
     ***or* turkey**
   4 **slices Swiss cheese**
   2 **tablespoons mayonnaise**
   1 **small tomato, thinly sliced**
   6 **bacon strips, cooked**
   4 **slices American cheese**
   1 **small onion, thinly sliced**
1/4 **cup butter, melted**
   1 **tablespoon sesame seeds**
1/2 **teaspoon onion salt**

1. Slice bread horizontally into five equal layers. Spread bottom layer with horseradish; top with roast beef. Place the next slice of bread over beef; spread with mustard and top with ham or turkey and Swiss cheese.

2. Add the next slice of bread; spread with mayonnaise and top with tomato and bacon. Add the next slice of bread; top with American cheese and onion. Cover with remaining bread. Combine butter, sesame seeds and onion salt; brush over top and sides of loaf.

3. Place on a baking sheet; loosely tent with heavy-duty foil. Bake at 400° for 15-20 minutes or until heated through. Carefully slice into eight wedges. **Yield:** 8 servings.

2 teaspoons celery seed
1 teaspoon coarsely ground pepper
1/4 to 1/2 teaspoon cayenne pepper
1 fresh beef brisket (3 to 4 pounds)
1 medium green pepper, chopped
1 small onion, chopped
1 bottle (12 ounces) chili sauce
1 cup ketchup
1/2 cup barbecue sauce
1/3 cup packed brown sugar
1/4 cup cider vinegar
1/4 cup Worcestershire sauce
1 teaspoon ground mustard
1 can (15-1/2 ounces) hot chili beans
1 can (15-1/2 ounces) great northern beans, rinsed and drained

1. Combine the first five ingredients; rub over brisket. Cut into eight pieces; place in a slow cooker. Combine the green pepper, onion, chili sauce, ketchup, barbecue sauce, brown sugar, vinegar, Worcestershire sauce and mustard; pour over meat. Cover and cook on high for 5-6 hours or until meat is tender.

2. Remove meat; cool slightly. Meanwhile, skim fat from cooking juices. Shred meat with two forks; return to slow cooker. Reduce heat to low. Stir in the beans. Cover and cook for 1 hour or until heated through. **Yield:** 12 servings.

Editor's Note: This is a fresh beef brisket, not corned beef.

🎖️ 🎖️ 🎖️

Barbecued Beef Chili

Phyllis Shyan, Elgin, Illinois

Served with a hot loaf of bread and a side salad, this slow-cooker chili makes a hearty meal. The recipe was inspired by two friends when we were talking about food at a potluck.

7 teaspoons chili powder
1 tablespoon garlic powder

🎖️ 🎖️ 🎖️

Roast Beef Sandwich Roll

(Pictured on page 46)

Shonda Haught, Wichita, Kansas

I'm a teacher and am always looking for quick and delicious recipes. I like how easily this sandwich roll comes together.

2 loaves (1 pound *each*) frozen bread dough, thawed
3/4 cup chopped sweet red pepper
1/2 cup chopped red onion
1 teaspoon garlic salt
1 teaspoon Italian seasoning
8 to 10 ounces thinly sliced deli roast beef, julienned
2 cups (8 ounces) finely shredded cheddar cheese
1 egg white
1 tablespoon water

1. Combine loaves of dough and shape into one ball. Place in a greased bowl, turning once to grease top. Cover and let rise in a warm place for 90 minutes.

2. In a microwave-safe bowl, combine the red pepper, onion, garlic salt and Italian seasoning. Cover and microwave on high for 1 minute or until vegetables are tender.

3. Punch dough down. On a lightly floured surface, roll into a 15-in. x 12-in. rectangle. Combine the beef, cheese and red pepper mixture; spread over the dough to within 1/2 in. of edges.

4. Roll up jelly-roll style, starting with a long edge; pinch seams and ends to seal. Place seam side down on a lightly greased baking sheet.

5. In a small bowl, beat egg white and water; brush over dough. Cut a slit with a sharp knife in top of dough. Bake at 400° for 30-35 minutes or until golden brown. Let stand for 10 minutes before slicing. **Yield:** 8 servings.

🎗🎗🎗
Pizza Hoagies

Barbara Mery, Bothell, Washington

My husband and three sons love these crispy sandwiches filled with a moist, pizza-flavored mixture. They're so popular, I often make them on a weekend and double the recipe.

> 1 pound ground beef
> 1/2 cup chopped onion
> 1 can (15 ounces) pizza sauce
> 1/4 cup chopped ripe olives
> 2 teaspoons dried basil
> 1 teaspoon dried oregano
> 8 hoagie *or* submarine sandwich buns
> 2 cups (8 ounces) shredded mozzarella cheese

1. In a skillet, cook beef and onion over medium heat until meat is no longer pink; drain. Stir in pizza sauce, olives, basil and oregano. Heat through.

2. Cut 1/4 in. off top of each roll; set aside. Carefully hollow out bottom of roll, leaving a 1/4-in. shell (discard removed bread or save for another use). Sprinkle 2 tablespoons cheese inside each shell. Fill each with about 1/2 cup meat mixture. Sprinkle with remaining cheese; gently press down to flatten. Replace bread tops.

3. If desired, individually wrap four sandwiches tightly in foil; freeze for up to 3 months. Place remaining sandwiches on a baking sheet. Bake at 375° for 15 minutes or until heated through. **Yield:** 8 servings.

To use frozen hoagies: Place foil-wrapped sandwiches on a baking sheet. Bake at 375° for 60-70 minutes or until heated through.

🎗🎗🎗
Bold Bean and Pork Chili

Natercia Yailaian, Somerville, Massachusetts

This tempting chili is big on flavor and simple to prepare. Sometimes on a Sunday, I'll get a good start on it—up to where it's time to add the beans. Then the next day, I'll take it out of the fridge and finish it off in just a few minutes. Voila—dinner is quickly served!

> 1 pork shoulder *or* butt roast (4 to 5 pounds), trimmed and cut into 3/4-inch cubes
> 3 tablespoons olive oil
> 2 large onions, chopped
> 8 garlic cloves, minced
> 4 cans (14-1/2 ounces *each*) chicken broth
> 1 can (28 ounces) crushed tomatoes
> 1/2 to 2/3 cup chili powder
> 3 tablespoons dried oregano
> 2 to 3 tablespoons ground cumin
> 4-1/2 teaspoons salt
> 2 teaspoons cayenne pepper
> 4 cans (15 ounces *each*) black beans, rinsed and drained
> Minced fresh cilantro, optional

1. In a Dutch oven, saute pork in oil until no longer pink; drain. Add onions; cook and stir for 3 minutes. Add garlic; cook 2 minutes longer. Stir in the broth, tomatoes and seasonings. Bring to a boil. Reduce heat; simmer, uncovered, for 1 hour, stirring several times.

2. Skim fat; stir in beans. Simmer 15-30 minutes longer or until chili reaches desired thickness. Garnish with cilantro if desired. **Yield:** 15 servings.

🎗🎗🎗
Meaty Mushroom Chili

Marjol Burr, Catawba, Ohio

Since our two daughters did not like beans in their chili, I adapted a recipe to suit our whole family's tastes. We all agree that mushrooms are an appealing alternative.

- **1 pound bulk Italian sausage**
- **1 pound ground beef**
- **1 cup chopped onion**
- **1 pound fresh mushrooms, sliced**
- **1 can (46 ounces) V8 juice**
- **1 can (6 ounces) tomato paste**
- **1 teaspoon sugar**
- **1 teaspoon salt**
- **1 teaspoon garlic powder**
- **1 teaspoon dried oregano**
- **1 teaspoon Worcestershire sauce**
- **1/2 teaspoon dried basil**
- **1/2 teaspoon pepper**
- **Sour cream, optional**

1. In a large saucepan, cook the sausage, beef and onion over medium heat until the meat is no longer pink; drain.

2. Stir in mushrooms, V8 juice, tomato paste and seasonings. Bring to a boil. Reduce heat; cover and simmer 1 hour. Garnish with sour cream if desired. **Yield:** 8 servings.

🎗🎗🎗
Grilled Beef Burgers

Lynda Ferguson, Sarnia, Ontario

I rely on a few common ingredients to put a new twist on a backyard barbecue staple. To make handling the patties even easier, let them firm up in the freezer a bit before grilling.

☑ Uses less fat, sugar or salt. Includes Nutritional Analysis and Diabetic Exchanges.

- **2 egg whites**
- **2/3 cup fat-free evaporated milk**
- **1 cup (4 ounces) shredded reduced-fat cheddar cheese**
- **1/2 cup dry bread crumbs**
- **1/4 cup chopped onion**
- **1 teaspoon prepared mustard**
- **1/4 teaspoon salt**
- **1/8 teaspoon pepper**
- **1-1/2 pounds lean ground beef**
- **8 multigrain hamburger buns, split**
- **8 lettuce leaves**
- **8 tomato slices**

1. In a bowl, combine the first eight ingredients. Crumble beef over mixture and mix well. Shape into eight patties.

2. Coat grill rack with nonstick cooking spray before starting the grill. Grill burgers, uncovered, over medium heat for 5-6 minutes on each side or until juices run clear and a meat thermometer reads 160°. Serve on buns with lettuce and tomato. **Yield:** 8 servings.

Nutritional Analysis: One serving (1 burger) equals 351 calories, 13 g fat (5 g saturated fat), 40 mg cholesterol, 530 mg sodium, 30 g carbohydrate, 2 g fiber, 29 g protein. **Diabetic Exchanges:** 4 lean meat, 2 starch.

Shrimp Patty Sandwiches

(Pictured on page 46)

Tina Jacobs, Hurlock, Maryland

Quite often when we eat at a restaurant, my husband will try something and tell me that I could make it better at home. That was the case with this shrimp patty. I made some improvements, and now it's one of my husband's favorites.

        4 eggs
        4 cans (6 ounces *each*) shrimp, rinsed and
           drained *or* 2 cups medium cooked shrimp,
           peeled and deveined
        8 ounces haddock, cooked and flaked
        1 cup plus 3 tablespoons pancake mix
        2 tablespoons cornmeal
    1/2 teaspoon dried parsley flakes
    1/2 teaspoon celery salt
    1/4 teaspoon ground mustard
    1/4 teaspoon paprika
    1/2 cup dry bread crumbs
        3 to 4 tablespoons vegetable oil
        8 hamburger buns
Lettuce leaves, tomato slices and onion slices,
    optional

1. In a large bowl, beat the eggs. Add the shrimp, haddock, pancake mix, cornmeal, parsley, celery salt, mustard and paprika; mix well. Shape into eight patties. Coat with bread crumbs.

2. In a skillet over medium-high heat, cook patties in oil for 2 minutes on each side or until golden brown. Serve on buns with lettuce, tomato and onion if desired. **Yield:** 8 servings.

Chili in Bread Bowls

Nancy Clancy, Standish, Maine

Some say you can have your cake and eat it, too…I say eat your chili and the bowl, too! I work the "graveyard shift" at the post office in Portland. During those hours, I often bring in dishes like this chili to share with co-workers.

        1 tablespoon all-purpose flour
    1/4 teaspoon salt
    1/8 teaspoon pepper
    1/2 pound *each* lean beef stew meat, boneless
           skinless chicken breast and boneless pork, cut
           into cubes
        1 tablespoon vegetable oil
        1 medium onion, chopped
        1 medium green pepper, chopped
        1 jalapeno pepper, seeded and chopped
        1 can (28 ounces) diced tomatoes, drained
        1 can (16 ounces) kidney beans, rinsed and
           drained
        1 can (15-1/2 ounces) navy beans *or* great
           northern beans, rinsed and drained
        1 can (8 ounces) tomato sauce
        1 tablespoon chili powder
        1 garlic clove, minced
  1-1/2 teaspoons ground cumin
    1/2 teaspoon dried basil
    1/4 to 1/2 teaspoon cayenne pepper
        9 large hard rolls
Sour cream, chopped green onions and sweet
    red pepper, optional

1. In a large resealable plastic bag, combine the flour, salt and pepper. Add meat in batches; toss to coat. In a

large skillet, brown meat in oil in batches. Transfer to a 5-qt. slow cooker with a slotted spoon.

2. Stir in onion, peppers, tomatoes, beans, tomato sauce and seasonings. Cover and cook on low for 7-8 hours or until the meat is tender.

3. Cut tops off rolls; carefully hollow out bottom halves. Spoon about 1 cup of chili into each roll. Garnish with sour cream, onions and red pepper if desired. **Yield:** 9 servings.

Editor's Note: When cutting or seeding hot peppers, use rubber or plastic gloves to protect your hands. Avoid touching your face.

🎖🎖🎖
Hearty Chicken Club

Debbie Johanesen, Missoula, Montana

I discovered the recipe for this sizable sandwich a while back and modified it to suit my family's tastes. We love it. The only problem is trying to open our mouths wide enough to take a bite!

1/4 cup mayonnaise
2 tablespoons salsa

4 slices seven-grain sandwich bread
2 lettuce leaves
4 slices tomato
8 ounces sliced cooked chicken *or* turkey
4 bacon strips, cooked
4 slices cheddar cheese
1 ripe avocado, sliced

Combine mayonnaise and salsa; spread on two slices of bread. Layer with lettuce, tomato, chicken or turkey, bacon, cheese and avocado. Top with remaining bread. **Yield:** 2 servings.

🎖🎖🎖
Vegetarian Chili

(Pictured on page 46)

Marilyn Barilleaux, Bothell, Washington

My husband and I try to have at least one vegetarian meal each week, and this is one of our favorites. The recipe makes a large pot of chili that's loaded with color and flavor. Once the chopping is done, it's quick to cook.

✓ Uses less fat, sugar or salt. Includes Nutritional Analysis and Diabetic Exchanges.

4 medium zucchini, chopped
2 medium onions, chopped
1 medium green pepper, chopped
1 medium sweet red pepper, chopped
4 garlic cloves, minced
1/4 cup canola oil
2 cans (28 ounces *each*) Italian stewed tomatoes, cut up
1 can (15 ounces) tomato sauce
1 can (15 ounces) pinto beans, rinsed and drained
1 can (15 ounces) black beans, rinsed and drained
1 jalapeno pepper, seeded and chopped
1/4 cup *each* minced fresh cilantro and parsley
2 tablespoons chili powder
1 tablespoon sugar
1 teaspoon salt
1 teaspoon ground cumin

1. In a Dutch oven, saute zucchini, onions, peppers and garlic in oil until tender. Stir in the tomatoes, tomato sauce, beans, jalapeno and seasonings.

2. Bring to a boil over medium heat. Reduce heat; cover and simmer for 30 minutes, stirring occasionally. **Yield:** 16 servings.

Nutritional Analysis: One serving (1 cup) equals 131 calories, 4 g fat (trace saturated fat), 0 cholesterol, 622 mg sodium, 18 g carbohydrate, 6 g fiber, 5 g protein. **Diabetic Exchanges:** 1 starch, 1 vegetable, 1 fat.

Editor's Note: When cutting or seeding hot peppers, use rubber or plastic gloves to protect your hands. Avoid touching your face.

✿✿✿ Unstuffed Pepper Soup

Evelyn Kara, Brownsville, Pennsylvania

One of my sisters gave me the recipe for this soup, which tastes just like stuffed green peppers. The thick mixture is chock-full of good stuff. The aroma while it's cooking is wonderful.

1-1/2 pounds ground beef
   3 large green peppers, chopped
   1 large onion, chopped
   2 cans (14-1/2 ounces *each*) beef broth
   2 cans (10-3/4 ounces *each*) condensed tomato
     soup, undiluted
   1 can (28 ounces) crushed tomatoes, undrained
   1 can (4 ounces) mushroom stems and pieces,
     drained
1-1/2 cups cooked rice

1. In a Dutch oven or large saucepan, cook the beef, green peppers and onion over medium heat until meat is no longer pink; drain.

2. Stir in broth, soup, tomatoes and mushrooms. Bring to a boil. Reduce heat; cover and simmer for at least 30 minutes, stirring occasionally. Add rice; heat through. **Yield:** 10 servings.

✿✿✿ Zippy Pork Chili

Michelle Beran, Claflin, Kansas

In addition to eating this chili the traditional way (with a spoon), my family likes to scoop bites onto tortilla chips. The leftovers are great rolled in tortillas and reheated, too.

   1 boneless pork roast (3 to 4 pounds), cut
     into 1-inch cubes
   1 medium onion, chopped
   1 *garlic* clove, minced
   2 tablespoons vegetable oil
   2 cans (15-1/2 ounces *each*) chili beans
   2 cans (10 ounces *each*) diced tomatoes and
     green chilies, undrained
   1 can (14-1/2 ounces) diced tomatoes,
     undrained
   1 cup water
   1 teaspoon beef bouillon granules
Chili powder, pepper and cayenne pepper to taste
Sour cream, tortilla chips and shredded cheddar
   cheese, optional

1. In a Dutch oven, cook pork, onion and garlic in oil over medium heat until meat is browned. Add the beans, tomatoes, water, bouillon and seasonings.

2. Bring to a boil. Reduce heat; cover and simmer for 2 hours or until meat is tender. If desired, serve with sour cream, tortilla chips and cheese. **Yield:** 10 servings.

🎗🎗🎗
Salmon Salad Sandwiches

(Pictured on page 47)

Yvonne Shust, Shoal Lake, Manitoba

These are perfect to pack in your kids' lunch boxes when they can't face another boring sandwich. We love the salmon, cream cheese and dill tucked inside a crusty roll. The carrots and celery add a nice crunch.

 1 package (3 ounces) cream cheese, softened
 1 tablespoon mayonnaise
 1 tablespoon lemon juice
 1 teaspoon dill weed
 1/4 to 1/2 teaspoon salt
 1/8 teaspoon pepper
 1 can (6 ounces) pink salmon, drained, skin and bones removed
 1/2 cup shredded carrot
 1/2 cup chopped celery
Lettuce leaves
 2 whole wheat buns, split

1. In a mixing bowl, beat the cream cheese, mayonnaise, lemon juice, dill, salt and pepper until smooth. Add the salmon, carrot and celery; mix well.

2. Place a lettuce leaf and about 1/2 cup salmon salad on each bun. **Yield:** 2 servings.

🎗🎗🎗
Ground Beef Chili

Shannon Wright, Erie, Pennsylvania

Everyone who tastes my chili comments that it is restaurant-quality. It's especially good with homemade corn bread. I have always loved to cook, and I enjoy developing original recipes like this one.

 3 pounds ground beef
 1 large onion, chopped
 1 medium green pepper, chopped
 2 celery ribs, chopped
 2 cans (16 ounces *each*) kidney beans, rinsed and drained
 1 can (29 ounces) tomato puree
 1 jar (16 ounces) salsa
 1 can (14-1/2 ounces) diced tomatoes, undrained
 1 can (10-1/2 ounces) condensed beef broth, undiluted
 1 to 2 cups water
 1/4 cup chili powder
 2 tablespoons Worcestershire sauce
 1 tablespoon dried basil
 2 teaspoons ground cumin
 2 teaspoons steak sauce
 1 teaspoon garlic powder
 1 teaspoon salt
 1 teaspoon coarsely ground pepper
1-1/2 teaspoons browning sauce, optional
Additional chopped onion, optional

1. In a Dutch oven, cook the beef, onion, green pepper and celery over medium heat until meat is no longer pink and vegetables are tender; drain.

2. Stir in the beans, tomato puree, salsa, tomatoes, broth, water, seasonings and browning sauce if desired. Bring to a boil. Reduce heat; simmer, uncovered, for 30 minutes or until chili reaches desired thickness. Garnish with chopped onion if desired. **Yield:** 16 servings.

Meatball Sandwiches

Sharon Simcizen, Bozeman, Montana

With all the cattle ranches in our state, these sandwiches are a great way to use ground beef. I've done a lot of traveling and tried a lot of recipes, but I think this is one of the best.

1/2 pound bulk Italian sausage
1/2 cup chopped onion
1/2 cup chopped green pepper
1-1/2 cups stewed tomatoes
1 can (12 ounces) tomato paste
2 cans (8 ounces *each*) tomato sauce

2 teaspoons brown sugar
1 teaspoon garlic powder
1/2 teaspoon dried oregano
1/2 teaspoon dried basil
MEATBALLS:
1 pound bulk Italian sausage
2 eggs, lightly beaten
1/2 cup dry bread crumbs
3 tablespoons milk
1 teaspoon dried basil
3/4 teaspoon salt
1/8 teaspoon pepper
1/8 teaspoon dried oregano
1/8 teaspoon rubbed sage
1 pound ground beef
3 tablespoons olive oil

Rolls
Sliced mozzarella cheese, optional

1. In a Dutch oven, cook sausage, onion and green pepper until the sausage is browned and the vegetables are tender; drain. Add the next seven ingredients; bring to a boil. Cover and simmer.

2. Meanwhile, in a bowl, combine the first 9 meatball ingredients. Crumble beef over mixture; mix well. Shape into 1-in. balls. Brown in oil; drain. Add to the sauce; cover and simmer for 2 hours. Serve on rolls. Top with cheese if desired. **Yield:** 10-12 servings.

Creamy Carrot Parsnip Soup

Phyllis Clinehens, Maplewood, Ohio

This creamy concoction tastes like it's fresh from the garden. A hint of horseradish and ginger sparks every steaming spoonful.

8 cups chopped carrots
6 cups chopped peeled parsnips
4 cups chicken broth
3 cups water
2 teaspoons sugar
1 teaspoon salt
1 medium onion, chopped
4 garlic cloves, minced
1 teaspoon grated fresh horseradish
1 teaspoon grated fresh gingerroot
3 tablespoons butter
2 cups buttermilk
2 tablespoons sour cream
Fresh dill sprigs, optional

1. In a Dutch oven or soup kettle, combine the carrots, parsnips, broth, water, sugar and salt; bring to a boil. Reduce heat; cover and cook for 25-30 minutes or until vegetables are tender.

2. In a skillet, saute onion, garlic, horseradish and ginger in butter until tender. Add to the carrot mixture.

3. Transfer soup to a blender in batches; cover and process until smooth. Return to the pan. Stir in buttermilk; heat through (do not boil). Garnish servings with sour cream and dill if desired. **Yield:** 12 servings (3 quarts).

🎗🎗🎗 Pepperoni Pizza Chili

Marilouise Wyatt, Cowen, West Virginia

I first made this recipe one day when I decided I didn't enjoy making pizza crust—I just put the pizza in a bowl instead!

- 1 pound ground beef
- 1 can (16 ounces) kidney beans, rinsed and drained
- 1 can (15 ounces) pizza sauce
- 1 can (14-1/2 ounces) Italian stewed tomatoes
- 1 can (8 ounces) tomato sauce
- 1-1/2 cups water
- 1 package (3-1/2 ounces) sliced pepperoni
- 1/2 cup chopped green pepper
- 1 teaspoon pizza seasoning *or* Italian seasoning
- 1 teaspoon salt
- Shredded mozzarella cheese, optional

1. In a large saucepan, cook beef over medium heat until no longer pink; drain. Stir in the beans, pizza sauce, tomatoes, tomato sauce, water, pepperoni, green pepper, pizza seasoning and salt. Bring to a boil.

2. Reduce heat; simmer, uncovered, for 30 minutes or until chili reaches desired thickness. Garnish with cheese if desired. **Yield:** 8 servings.

🎗🎗🎗 Greek Pork Wraps

Christine London, Kansas City, Missouri

If you like gyros, you'll love these strips of grilled pork wrapped in tortillas. It's a popular summer dish in my home.

- 1/4 cup lemon juice
- 2 tablespoons olive oil
- 1 tablespoon prepared mustard
- 1-3/4 teaspoons minced garlic, *divided*
- 1 teaspoon dried oregano
- 1 pork tenderloin (1 pound)
- 1 cup chopped peeled cucumber
- 1 cup plain yogurt
- 1/4 teaspoon salt
- 1/4 teaspoon dill weed
- 8 flour tortillas (6 inches)
- 1/2 cup chopped green onions

1. In a large resealable plastic bag, combine lemon juice, oil, mustard, 1-1/4 teaspoons garlic and oregano; add pork. Seal bag and turn to coat; refrigerate for 2 hours. In a bowl, combine the cucumber, yogurt, salt, dill and remaining garlic; cover and refrigerate until serving.

2. Drain and discard marinade. Coat grill rack with nonstick cooking spray before starting the grill for indirect medium-hot heat. Grill tenderloin, uncovered, over direct heat for 5 minutes, turning once. Move to indirect heat. Cover; cook 10-15 minutes longer or until a meat thermometer reads 160°. Let stand for 5 minutes.

3. Meanwhile, wrap tortillas in foil; place on grill for 2-3 minutes or until warmed, turning once. Slice tenderloin into strips; place on tortillas. Top each with 3 tablespoons yogurt sauce and 1 tablespoon green onions. **Yield:** 4 servings.

☆☆☆
Hearty Vegetable Soup

Janice Steinmetz, Somers, Connecticut

A friend gave me the idea to use V8 juice in soup because it provides more flavor. This soup is great to make on a crisp autumn afternoon.

8 medium carrots, sliced
2 large onions, chopped
4 celery ribs, chopped
1 large green pepper, seeded and chopped
1 garlic clove, minced
1 tablespoon olive oil
4 cups water
1 can (28 ounces) diced tomatoes, undrained
2 cups V8 juice
2 cups chopped cabbage
2 cups frozen cut green beans
2 cups frozen peas
1 cup frozen corn
1 can (15 ounces) garbanzo beans *or* chickpeas, rinsed and drained
2 teaspoons chicken bouillon granules
1-1/2 teaspoons dried parsley flakes
1 teaspoon salt
1 teaspoon dried marjoram

1 teaspoon dried thyme
1 bay leaf
1/2 teaspoon dried basil
1/4 teaspoon pepper

1. In a Dutch oven or soup kettle, saute the carrots, onions, celery, green pepper and garlic in oil until crisp-tender. Stir in remaining ingredients. Bring to a boil.

2. Reduce heat; cover and simmer for 1 to 1-1/2 hours or until vegetables are tender. Discard bay leaf before serving. **Yield:** 14-16 servings (4 quarts).

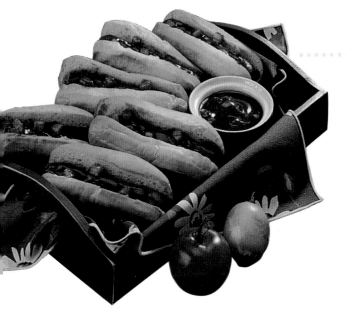

☆☆☆
Barbecued Hot Dogs

Joyce Koehler, Watertown, Wisconsin

I grew up in a family of eight kids, and we never complained if Mom made these terrific hot dogs often!

3/4 cup chopped onion
3 tablespoons butter
1-1/2 cups chopped celery
1-1/2 cups ketchup
3/4 cup water
1/3 cup lemon juice
3 tablespoons brown sugar
3 tablespoons vinegar
1 tablespoon Worcestershire sauce
1 tablespoon yellow mustard
2 packages (1 pound *each*) hot dogs
20 hot dog buns, split

1. In a saucepan over medium heat, saute onion in butter until tender. Add the celery, ketchup, water, lemon juice, sugar, vinegar, Worcestershire sauce and mustard; bring to a boil. Reduce the heat; cover and simmer for 30 minutes.

2. Cut three 1/4-in.-deep slits on each side of hot dogs; place in a 2-1/2-qt. baking dish. Pour the sauce over the hot dogs. Cover and bake at 350° for 40-45 minutes or until heated through. Serve on buns. **Yield:** 20 servings.

Dilly Turkey Melt

Henry Mujica, North Riverside, Illinois

This is a hearty grilled sandwich with a distinctive and delicious combination of ingredients. The pickle slices add a bit of fun, and the barbecue sauce provides a hint of sweetness.

> 2 medium onions, sliced
> 4 tablespoons butter, *divided*
> 4 tablespoons barbecue sauce
> 8 slices sourdough bread
> 8 slices Monterey Jack cheese
> 8 slices Canadian bacon
> 8 slices cooked turkey

Dill pickle slices

1. In a large skillet, saute onions in 1 tablespoon of butter until tender; remove and set aside. Spread barbecue sauce on four slices of bread. Layer each with one slice of cheese, bacon, turkey, pickles, onions and another slice

of cheese. Cover with remaining slices of bread.

2. In the same skillet over medium-low heat, melt remaining butter. Cook sandwiches on both sides until golden brown and cheese is melted (skillet may be covered the last few minutes to help melt cheese if necessary). **Yield:** 4 servings.

Italian Beef Sandwiches

Kristen Swihart, Perrysburg, Ohio

I'm a paramedic/firefighter, and slow-cooked recipes like this one suit my unpredictable schedule. My husband and children and the hungry bunch at the firehouse love these robust sandwiches, which have a little zip.

> 1 jar (11-1/2 ounces) pepperoncinis
> 1 boneless beef chuck roast (3-1/2 to 4 pounds)
> 1/4 cup water
> 1-3/4 teaspoons dried basil
> 1-1/2 teaspoons garlic powder
> 1-1/2 teaspoons dried oregano
> 1-1/4 teaspoons salt
> 1/4 teaspoon pepper
> 1 large onion, sliced and quartered
> 10 to 12 hard rolls, split

1. Drain pepperoncinis, reserving liquid. Remove and discard stems of peppers; set peppers aside. Cut roast into large chunks; place a third of the meat in a 5-qt. slow cooker. Add water.

2. In a small bowl, combine the basil, garlic powder, oregano, salt and pepper; sprinkle half over beef. Layer with half of the remaining meat, then onion, reserved peppers and liquid. Top with remaining meat and herb mixture.

3. Cover and cook on low for 8-9 hours or until meat is tender. Shred beef with two forks. Using a slotted spoon, serve the beef and peppers on rolls. **Yield:** 10-12 servings.

Editor's Note: Look for pepperoncinis (pickled peppers) in the pickle and olive section of your grocery store.

🎀 🎀 🎀
California Pepper Chili

Robyn Thompson, Los Angeles, California

In my opinion, this is the world's best chili! It features three meats in a peppery, eye-opening broth.

- **1/2 pound bacon, diced**
- **2-1/2 pounds beef stew meat, cut into 3/4-inch cubes**
- **1-1/2 pounds pork stew meat, cut into 3/4-inch cubes**
- **2 medium onions, chopped**
- **6 to 8 garlic cloves, minced**
- **1 to 2 tablespoons chopped seeded fresh serrano chili peppers**
- **1 to 2 tablespoons chopped seeded fresh poblano chili peppers**
- **1 to 2 tablespoons chopped seeded fresh jalapeno peppers**
- **2 to 3 teaspoons cayenne pepper**
- **1-1/2 teaspoons dried oregano**
- **1 teaspoon salt**
- **1 teaspoon ground cumin**
- **1 can (15 ounces) tomato puree**
- **1 can (14-1/2 ounces) beef broth**
- **7 plum tomatoes, chopped**
- **Shredded cheddar cheese, optional**

1. In a large saucepan, cook bacon over medium heat until crisp. Remove to paper towels to drain, reserving 3 tablespoons drippings.

2. In the drippings, cook the beef, pork and onions until meat is browned; drain. Add the garlic, peppers and seasonings; cook and stir for 1-2 minutes.

3. Stir in the tomato puree, broth and tomatoes. Bring to a boil. Reduce heat; cover and simmer for 1 to 1-1/2 hours or until meat is tender. Garnish with reserved bacon and cheese if desired. **Yield:** 8 servings.

Editor's Note: When cutting or seeding hot peppers, use rubber or plastic gloves to protect your hands. Avoid touching your face.

🎖🎖🎖
Bulgur Chili

Jeraldine Hall, Ravenden Springs, Arkansas

This vegetarian chili is zesty, but it also offers a slight hint of sweetness. Because it doesn't have to simmer for hours like other chili recipes, it's ideal for serving to drop-in visitors.

> ✓ Uses less fat, sugar or salt. Includes Nutritional Analysis and Diabetic Exchanges.

    3/4 cup bulgur
      2 cups boiling water
1-1/2 cups finely chopped green peppers
      1 large onion, chopped
      2 teaspoons canola oil
      2 cups reduced-sodium tomato juice
      1 can (16 ounces) kidney beans, rinsed and
        drained
      1 can (15 ounces) ranch-style beans, undrained
      1 can (14-1/2 ounces) diced tomatoes,
        undrained
      1 can (8 ounces) tomato sauce
      1 cup water
      2 to 3 tablespoons chili powder
      2 garlic cloves, minced
    1/2 teaspoon ground cumin
    1/8 to 1/4 teaspoon cayenne pepper
    3/4 cup shredded reduced-fat cheddar cheese

1. Place bulgur in a bowl; stir in boiling water. Cover and let stand for 30 minutes or until most of the liquid is absorbed. Drain and squeeze dry.

2. In a large saucepan, saute green peppers and onion in oil until tender. Stir in the bulgur, tomato juice, beans, tomatoes, tomato sauce, water, chili powder, garlic, cumin and cayenne. Bring to a boil. Reduce heat; cover and simmer for 20-25 minutes or until heated through. Garnish with cheese. **Yield:** 9 servings.

Nutritional Analysis: One serving (1 cup) equals 195 calories, 3 g fat (1 g saturated fat), 5 mg cholesterol, 657 mg sodium, 33 g carbohydrate, 7 g fiber, 11 g protein. **Diabetic Exchanges:** 2 vegetable, 1-1/2 starch, 1 very lean meat.

Cream of Wild Rice Soup

J. Beatrice Hintz, Neenah, Wisconsin

Tender cubes of chicken, fresh vegetables and wild rice make this soup hearty enough for a meal. You can't beat the comfort of a warm bowlful. I serve it with whole wheat rolls.

✓ Uses less fat, sugar or salt. Includes Nutritional Analysis and Diabetic Exchanges.

- 1 large onion, chopped
- 1 large carrot, shredded
- 1 celery rib, chopped
- 1/4 cup margarine
- 1/2 cup all-purpose flour
- 8 cups chicken broth
- 3 cups cooked wild rice
- 1 cup cubed cooked chicken breast
- 1/4 teaspoon salt
- 1/4 teaspoon pepper
- 1 cup fat-free evaporated milk
- 1/4 cup snipped chives

1. In a large saucepan, saute the onion, carrot and celery in margarine until tender. Stir in flour until blended. Gradually add broth.

2. Stir in the rice, chicken, salt and pepper. Bring to a boil over medium heat; cook and stir for 2 minutes or until thickened. Stir in milk; cook 3-5 minutes longer. Garnish with chives. **Yield:** 10 servings (2-1/2 quarts).

Nutritional Analysis: One serving (1 cup) equals 180 calories, 6 g fat (3 g saturated fat), 25 mg cholesterol, 899 mg sodium, 22 g carbohydrate, 2 g fiber, 11 g protein. **Diabetic Exchanges:** 1 starch, 1 very lean meat, 1 vegetable, 1 fat.

State Fair Subs

Christi Ross, Mill Creek, Oklahoma

My college roommate and I first ate these meaty sandwiches at the Iowa State Fair. After a little experimenting, we recreated the recipe. We ate the subs often because they were fast to fix between classes and didn't break our next-to-nothing grocery budget.

- 1 loaf (1 pound) unsliced French bread
- 2 eggs
- 1/4 cup milk
- 1/2 teaspoon pepper
- 1/4 teaspoon salt
- 1 pound bulk Italian sausage
- 1-1/2 cups chopped onion
- 2 cups (8 ounces) shredded mozzarella cheese

1. Cut bread in half lengthwise; carefully hollow out top and bottom of loaf, leaving a 1-in. shell. Cube removed bread. In a large bowl, beat the eggs, milk, pepper and salt. Add bread cubes and toss to coat; set aside.

2. In a skillet over medium heat, cook sausage and onion until the meat is no longer pink; drain. Add to the bread mixture. Spoon filling into bread shells; sprinkle with cheese. Wrap each in foil. Bake at 400° for 20-25 minutes or until cheese is melted. Cut into serving-size slices. **Yield:** 6 servings.

🎗️🎗️🎗️
Corn and Sausage Soup

Rebecca Clark, Hammond, Louisiana

I created this recipe years ago when I received an abundance of fresh sweet corn from friends. The soup is easy to make and has always been a big hit with family and friends. I usually serve it with bread and a tossed salad.

   2-1/2 cups chopped onions
     1/2 cup *each* chopped green pepper, sweet red pepper and celery
     6 tablespoons butter
  1-1/2 pounds fully cooked smoked sausage, cut into 1/4-inch pieces
     3 garlic cloves, minced
     4 cans (15 ounces *each*) Italian-style tomato sauce
     3 packages (16 ounces *each*) frozen corn
     2 cans (14-1/2 ounces *each*) Italian diced tomatoes, undrained
     2 cups water
     3 bay leaves
  1-1/2 teaspoons *each* dried basil, oregano and thyme
     1/2 teaspoon pepper
     1/4 teaspoon dried marjoram
     1/4 teaspoon hot pepper sauce, optional

1. In a Dutch oven or soup kettle, saute onions, peppers and celery in butter until tender. Add sausage and garlic; cook for 8-10 minutes or until heated through.

2. Stir in the remaining ingredients. Bring to a boil. Reduce heat; simmer, uncovered, for 1 hour, stirring occasionally. Discard bay leaves before serving. **Yield:** 16-18 servings (about 5 quarts).

🎗️🎗️🎗️
Bacon-Tomato Bagel Melts

Lindsay Orwig, Grand Terrace, California

My husband introduced me to this open-faced sandwich shortly after we got married, and it quickly became an all-time favorite. It's good made with plain or onion bagels.

  2 bagels, split and toasted
  8 tomato slices
  8 bacon strips, cooked
  1 cup (4 ounces) shredded mozzarella cheese
Prepared ranch salad dressing

1. Place bagel halves cut side up on a baking sheet. Top each with two tomato slices and two bacon strips. Sprinkle with cheese.

2. Broil 5 in. from the heat for 1-2 minutes or until cheese begins to brown. Serve with ranch dressing. **Yield:** 4 sandwiches.

🏅🏅🏅
Cowpoke Chili

Ramona Nelson, Fairbanks, Alaska

Many friends and relatives have requested my chili recipe, which I've been using for nearly 30 years. It actually won first place in a local contest, chosen from among 10 other entries. It always comes out delicious. Try it and enjoy!

- 1 pound ground beef
- 1 small onion, chopped
- 1 garlic clove, minced
- 1 can (10-1/2 ounces) condensed beef broth, undiluted
- 1 can (8 ounces) tomato sauce
- 1 can (6 ounces) tomato paste
- 1 can (15-1/2 ounces) hot chili beans
- 1 can (15 ounces) black beans, rinsed and drained
- 2 tablespoons sugar
- 1 tablespoon butter
- 1 teaspoon chili powder
- 1/4 teaspoon salt
- 1/4 teaspoon dried oregano
- 1/8 teaspoon ground cumin
- 1/8 teaspoon crushed red pepper flakes
- Dash cayenne pepper
- 2 cups frozen lima beans, thawed
- Cherry tomatoes, fresh oregano and small chili peppers, optional

1. In a large saucepan, cook the beef, onion and garlic over medium heat until meat is no longer pink; drain. Stir in the broth, tomato sauce and paste until blended. Add the next 10 ingredients, Bring to a boil. Reduce heat; cover and simmer for 30 minutes.

2. Add lima beans; cook 5-10 minutes longer or until beans are tender. Garnish with tomatoes, oregano and peppers if desired. **Yield:** 7 servings.

🎗🎗🎗
Cream Cheese Chicken Soup

Kathleen Rappleye, Mesa, Arizona

After tasting a similar soup in a restaurant, I went home and cooked up my own version. It's so soothing on a winter evening served with crusty French bread. For a change of pace, try substituting ham or turkey for the chicken.

- 1 small onion, chopped
- 1 tablespoon butter
- 3 cups chicken broth
- 3 medium carrots, cut into 1/4-inch slices
- 2 medium potatoes, peeled and cubed
- 2 cups cubed cooked chicken
- 2 tablespoons minced fresh parsley

  Salt and pepper to taste
- 1/4 cup all-purpose flour
- 1 cup milk
- 1 package (8 ounces) cream cheese, cubed

1. In a large saucepan, saute the onion in butter. Add broth, carrots and potatoes. Bring to a boil. Reduce heat; cover and simmer for 15 minutes or until vegetables are tender. Add the chicken, parsley, salt and pepper; heat through.

2. Combine flour and milk until smooth; add to the vegetable mixture. Bring to a boil; cook and stir for 2 minutes or until thickened. Reduce heat. Add the cream cheese; cook and stir until melted. **Yield:** 8 servings.

🎗🎗🎗
Grilled Ham and Egg Salad Sandwiches

Beverly Stiger, Wolf Creek, Montana

An aunt shared this recipe with me years ago when I was looking for some low-budget meals. The ham and toasted bread make it a deliciously different kind of egg salad sandwich.

- 6 hard-cooked eggs, chopped
- 1 cup diced fully cooked ham
- 1/2 cup finely chopped celery
- 1 tablespoon minced onion
- 1/2 cup mayonnaise
- 2 teaspoons prepared mustard
- 1/2 teaspoon salt
- 1/4 teaspoon pepper
- 12 slices whole wheat *or* white bread

Vegetable oil for frying
BATTER:
- 1/2 cup cornmeal
- 1/2 cup all-purpose flour
- 1 teaspoon baking powder
- 1 teaspoon salt
- 2 cups milk
- 2 eggs, lightly beaten

1. Combine eggs, ham, celery, onion, mayonnaise, mustard, salt and pepper; spread on six slices of bread. Top with remaining bread and set aside. In a bowl, whisk batter ingredients until well blended.

2. Heat about 1/2 in. of oil in a large deep skillet. Dip sandwiches into batter. Fry in hot oil for 3 minutes on each side or until golden brown. Drain on paper towels. **Yield:** 6 servings.

🎗🎗🎗
Rock'n and Roast'n Chili

Rob Via, Charlotte, North Carolina

I got the basics of this recipe from a friend at a Super Bowl party and tweaked it. I have to tone it down a bit for my wife, and my mom once asked if I was trying to get my inheritance early! People who like spicy food really go for it.

- 2 pounds beef stew meat, cut into 3/4-inch cubes
- 1 medium onion, chopped
- 2 to 3 garlic cloves, minced
- 2 tablespoons vegetable oil
- 1 jar (16 ounces) hot banana peppers
- 2 cans (14-1/2 ounces *each*) diced tomatoes, undrained
- 1 can (10 ounces) diced tomatoes and green chilies, undrained
- 1 can (6 ounces) tomato paste
- 1 can (16 ounces) kidney beans, rinsed and drained
- 1 can (4 ounces) chopped green chilies
- 1 fresh jalapeno *or* banana pepper, seeded and chopped
- 2 tablespoons chili powder
- 1 to 2 tablespoons hot pepper sauce
- 1 teaspoon salt
- 1/8 teaspoon ground cumin

Additional banana peppers, optional

1. In a large saucepan, cook beef, onion and garlic in oil over medium heat until meat is no longer pink; drain. Remove stems and seeds of 10 hot banana peppers; chop (refrigerate remaining peppers for another use). Add peppers, tomatoes, tomato paste, beans, chilies, jalapeno and seasonings to beef mixture.

2. Bring to a boil. Reduce heat; cover and simmer for 2 hours or until meat is tender. Uncover; simmer until chili reaches desired thickness. Garnish with peppers if desired. **Yield:** 8 servings.

Editor's Note: When cutting or seeding hot peppers, use rubber or plastic gloves to protect your hands. Avoid touching your face.

Maple Toast and Eggs, p. 79

Strawberry Banana Crepes, p. 72

Wild Rice Mushroom Omelet, p. 76

Breakfast & Brunch

When is breakfast food a good choice for supper? Any time you prepare one of the delicious dishes in this chapter. They all make great day-starters, but they're also hearty enough for a family-pleasing dinner.

Three-Cheese Souffles, p. 80

True Belgian Waffles, p. 75

it's an easy-to-reheat meal for lunch or dinner, too. The recipe makes two casseroles, so you can serve one right away and freeze the second one for later.

4-1/2 cups seasoned croutons
2 cups (8 ounces) shredded cheddar cheese
1 medium onion, chopped
1/4 cup chopped sweet red pepper
1/4 cup chopped green pepper
1 jar (4-1/2 ounces) sliced mushrooms, drained
8 eggs
4 cups milk
1 teaspoon salt
1 teaspoon ground mustard
1/8 teaspoon pepper
8 bacon strips, cooked and crumbled

1. Sprinkle croutons, cheese, onion, peppers and mushrooms into two greased 8-in. square baking dishes. In a bowl, combine the eggs, milk, salt, mustard and pepper. Slowly pour over vegetables. Sprinkle with bacon.

2. Cover and freeze one casserole for up to 3 months. Bake the second casserole, uncovered, at 350° for 45-50 minutes or until a knife inserted near the center comes out clean. **Yield:** 2 casseroles (6-8 servings each).

To use frozen casserole: Completely thaw in the refrigerator for 24-36 hours. Remove from the refrigerator 30 minutes before baking. Bake, uncovered, at 350° for 50-60 minutes or until a knife inserted near the center comes out clean.

🎗 🎗 🎗
Breakfast Bake

Kim Weaver, Olathe, Kansas

This light, fluffy egg casserole, sprinkled with tasty bacon, retains its fresh flavor after freezing. While it's great for breakfast,

🎗 🎗 🎗
Strawberry Banana Crepes

(Pictured on page 70)

Shelly Soule, Las Vegas, Nevada

My family often has company over for breakfast or brunch, and these light, fruit-topped crepes are our favorite. The sweet sensations are as fast to make as they are fabulous. You can cook the crepes the night before, refrigerate them with waxed paper in between, then fill and top them in the morning.

1 cup all-purpose flour
1 tablespoon sugar
1/2 teaspoon ground cinnamon
1-1/2 cups milk
2 eggs
1 to 2 tablespoons butter
FILLING:
1 package (8 ounces) cream cheese, softened
1 carton (8 ounces) frozen whipped topping, thawed

1/2 cup confectioners' sugar
TOPPING:
2 cups sliced fresh strawberries
2 medium firm bananas, sliced
1/4 cup sugar, optional

1. In a mixing bowl, combine the flour, sugar, cinnamon, milk and eggs; mix well. Cover and refrigerate for 1 hour.

2. In an 8-in. nonstick skillet, melt 1 teaspoon butter. Stir batter; pour about 2 tablespoons into the center of skillet. Lift and tilt pan to evenly coat bottom. Cook until top appears dry; turn and cook 15-20 seconds longer. Remove to a wire rack.

3. Repeat with remaining batter, adding butter to skillet as needed. When cool, stack crepes with waxed paper or paper towels in between.

4. In a mixing bowl, combine the filling ingredients. Spread 2 rounded tablespoonfuls on each crepe; roll up. Combine topping ingredients; spoon over crepes. **Yield:** 18 crepes.

✿✿✿ Sheepherder's Breakfast

Pauletta Bushnell, Albany, Oregon

My sister-in-law always made this delicious breakfast dish when we were camping. Served with toast, juice and milk or coffee, it's a sure hit with the breakfast crowd! One-dish casseroles like this were a big help while I was raising my nine children. Now I've passed this recipe on to them.

1 pound sliced bacon, diced
1 medium onion, chopped
32 ounces frozen shredded hash brown
   potatoes, thawed
10 eggs
Salt and pepper to taste
2 cups (8 ounces) shredded cheddar cheese,
   optional
Chopped fresh parsley

1. In a large skillet, cook bacon and onion until bacon is crisp. Drain the drippings, reserving 1/2 cup. Add hash browns and reserved drippings to skillet; mix well.

2. Cook over medium heat for 10 minutes, turning when browned. Make 10 "wells" evenly spaced in the hash browns. Place one egg in each well. Sprinkle with salt and pepper. Sprinkle with cheese if desired.

3. Cover and cook over low heat for about 10 minutes or until eggs are set. Garnish with parsley; serve immediately. **Yield:** 10 servings.

✿✿✿ Broccoli Ham Quiche

Marilyn Day, North Fort Myers, Florida

This rich quiche recipe is featured in a family cookbook I compiled. It's attractive enough to serve for a company brunch...and it tastes terrific. My husband is proof that quiche can satisfy even a man-sized appetite!

1 unbaked deep-dish pastry shell (9 inches)
1 cup water
1/2 cup chopped fresh broccoli

1 cup (4 ounces) shredded Swiss cheese
1 cup (4 ounces) shredded mozzarella cheese
2 tablespoons all-purpose flour
4 eggs
1-1/4 cups milk
2 tablespoons chopped green onion
1/4 teaspoon salt
1/8 teaspoon pepper
1/8 teaspoon dried thyme
1/8 teaspoon dried rosemary, crushed
1/2 cup diced fully cooked ham

1. Line unpricked pastry shell with a double thickness of heavy-duty foil. Bake at 450° for 8 minutes. Remove foil; bake 5 minutes longer. Cool on a wire rack.

2. Meanwhile, in a saucepan, bring water to a boil. Add broccoli; cover and cook for 2 minutes. Drain and immediately place broccoli in ice water. Drain and pat dry with paper towels.

3. Toss cheeses with flour; set aside. In a bowl, beat the eggs. Add the milk, onion and seasonings; mix well. Stir in the ham, broccoli and cheese mixture. Pour into prepared crust.

4. Bake at 350° for 40-45 minutes or until a knife inserted near the center comes out clean. Let stand for 10 minutes before cutting. **Yield:** 6-8 servings.

🎗 🎗 🎗
Amish Baked Oatmeal

Colleen Butler, Inwood, West Virginia

The first time I had this treat was at a bed-and-breakfast in Lancaster, Pennsylvania. To me, it tasted just like a big warm-from-the-oven oatmeal cookie!

1-1/2 cups quick-cooking oats
1/2 cup sugar
1/2 cup milk
1/4 cup butter, melted
1 egg
1 teaspoon baking powder
3/4 teaspoon salt
1 teaspoon vanilla extract
Warm milk
Fresh fruit *and/or* brown sugar, optional

1. Combine the first eight ingredients; mix well. Spread evenly in a greased 13-in. x 9-in. x 2-in. baking pan.

2. Bake at 350° for 25-30 minutes or until the edges are golden brown. Immediately spoon into bowls; add milk. Top with fruit and/or brown sugar if desired. **Yield:** 6 servings.

🎗 🎗 🎗
Breakfast Pockets

Dolores Jantzen, Plymouth, Nebraska

With these, I like being able to serve a complete breakfast inside a tidy pocket of dough. Just add fresh fruit or purchased juice or yogurt on the side.

2 packages (1/4 ounce *each*) active dry yeast
1/2 cup warm water (110° to 115°)
3/4 cup warm evaporated milk (110° to 115°)

1/2 cup vegetable oil
1/4 cup sugar
1 egg
1 teaspoon salt
3 to 4 cups all-purpose flour
FILLING:
1 pound bulk pork sausage
1/2 cup chopped onion
2-1/2 cups frozen shredded hash browns, thawed
7 eggs, lightly beaten
3 tablespoons milk
1/2 teaspoon salt
1/2 teaspoon pepper
1/2 teaspoon garlic salt
Pinch cayenne pepper
3 cups (12 ounces) shredded cheddar cheese

1. In a mixing bowl, dissolve yeast in water. Add evaporated milk, oil, sugar, egg, salt and 2 cups flour; beat until smooth. Add enough remaining flour to form a soft dough (do not knead). Cover and let rise in a warm place until doubled, about 1 hour.

2. Meanwhile, in a skillet, cook the sausage and onion over medium heat until sausage is no longer pink; drain. Add hash browns, eggs, milk and seasonings. Cook and stir until the eggs are completely set. Sprinkle with cheese; keep warm.

3. Punch dough down; divide into 14 pieces. On a floured surface, roll out dough into 7-in. circles. Top each with about 1/3 cup filling; fold dough over filling and pinch the edges to seal. Place on greased baking sheets. Bake at 350° for 15-20 minutes or until golden brown. **Yield:** 14 servings.

★★★
True Belgian Waffles

(Pictured on page 71)

Rose Delemeester, St. Charles, Michigan

It was on a visit to my husband's relatives in Belgium that I was given this recipe. Back in the U.S., I served the waffles to his Belgian-born grandmother. She said they tasted just like home. The grandkids love these waffles with about any kind of topping—blueberries, strawberries, raspberries, fried apples, powdered sugar or whipped topping.

- 2 cups all-purpose flour
- 3/4 cup sugar
- 3-1/2 teaspoons baking powder
- 2 eggs, *separated*
- 1-1/2 cups milk
- 1 cup butter, melted
- 1 teaspoon vanilla extract
- Sliced fresh strawberries *or* syrup

1. In a bowl, combine flour, sugar and baking powder. In another bowl, lightly beat egg yolks. Add milk, butter and vanilla; mix well. Stir into dry ingredients just until combined. Beat egg whites until stiff peaks form; fold into batter.

2. Bake in a preheated waffle iron according to manufacturer's directions until golden brown. Serve with strawberries or syrup. **Yield:** 10 waffles (about 4-1/2 inches).

★★★
Brunch Berry Pizza

Maria Schuster, Wolf Point, Montana

This beautiful berry-topped pizza tastes as good as it looks! It's impossible to resist the pecan shortbread crust, rich cream cheese layer, glossy berry topping and sprinkling of luscious fresh berries. It's so convenient to make the night before and serve the next morning.

- 1 cup all-purpose flour
- 1/4 cup confectioners' sugar
- 1/2 cup cold butter
- 1/2 cup chopped pecans
- 1 package (8 ounces) cream cheese, softened
- 1 egg
- 1/3 cup sugar

TOPPING:
- 1-3/4 cups frozen mixed berries, thawed
- 1/2 cup sugar
- 2 tablespoons cornstarch
- 1/4 cup water
- 2-1/2 cups fresh strawberries, sliced
- 2 cups fresh blackberries
- 2 cups fresh raspberries
- 1 cup fresh blueberries

1. In a bowl, combine flour and confectioners' sugar. Cut in butter until crumbly. Stir in pecans. Press into an ungreased 12-in. pizza pan. Bake at 350° for 12-14 minutes or until crust is set and edges are lightly browned.

2. Meanwhile, in a mixing bowl, beat cream cheese, egg and sugar until smooth. Spread over the crust. Bake 8-10 minutes longer or until set. Cool to room temperature.

3. For topping, process mixed berries and sugar in a blender or food processor until blended. In a saucepan, combine cornstarch and water until smooth. Add mixed berry mixture. Bring to a boil; cook and stir for 2 minutes or until thickened. Set saucepan in ice water for 15 minutes, stirring several times.

4. Spread berry mixture over the cream cheese layer. Arrange fresh fruit on top. Refrigerate for at least 2 hours before slicing. **Yield:** 10-12 servings.

⚜ ⚜ ⚜
Broccoli-Ham Puff Pancake

Edna Hoffman, Hebron, Indiana

You won't have to pay a pretty penny to prepare this special-looking Sunday supper. The golden brown puff pancake makes a tasty main dish for brunch, lunch or dinner when filled with a creamy ham and broccoli mixture.

  1/4 cup butter
    1 cup all-purpose flour
    4 eggs
    1 cup milk
FILLING:
    3 tablespoons butter
    3 tablespoons all-purpose flour
    1 cup plus 2 tablespoons milk
    1 package (16 ounces) frozen chopped broccoli, thawed
1-1/2 cups cubed fully cooked ham
  1/3 cup sour cream
1-1/2 teaspoons lemon juice
  1/8 teaspoon hot pepper sauce

1. Place butter in a 10-in. ovenproof skillet; place in a 425° oven for 3-4 minutes or until melted.

2. In a mixing bowl, beat flour, eggs and milk until smooth. Pour into prepared skillet. Bake at 425° for

22-25 minutes or until puffed and golden brown.

3. Meanwhile, in a saucepan, melt butter. Stir in flour until smooth; gradually add milk. Bring to a boil; cook and stir for 2 minutes or until thickened. Reduce heat; add the remaining filling ingredients. Cook for 10 minutes or until heated through. Spoon into center of puff pancake. Cut into wedges; serve immediately. **Yield:** 6 servings.

⚜ ⚜ ⚜
Wild Rice Mushroom Omelet

(Pictured on page 70)

Bonnie Bourdeau, Akeley, Minnesota

Since wild rice is plentiful here, I love to create recipes starring that crunchy staple. Pork sausage helps spice up the mild rice flavor in this hearty omelet, which is draped with a silky-smooth cheese sauce. You can easily serve it to guests with little last-minute fuss.

  1/2 pound bulk pork sausage
    1 medium onion, chopped
    1 celery rib, finely chopped
    2 tablespoons butter
    1 can (4 ounces) mushroom stems and pieces, drained
1-1/2 cups cooked wild rice
    1 teaspoon dried parsley flakes
   14 eggs
  1/2 cup water
  1/4 teaspoon salt
  1/8 teaspoon pepper
CHEESE SAUCE:
    2 tablespoons butter
    1 teaspoon chicken bouillon granules
    2 tablespoons all-purpose flour
    1 cup milk
  1/4 cup cubed process cheese, (Velveeta)
Minced fresh parsley, optional

1. In a skillet, cook sausage over medium heat until no longer pink; drain. Remove and set aside. In the skillet, saute onion and celery in butter until tender. Add mushrooms; heat through. Stir in sausage, rice and parsley.

2. In a bowl, whisk eggs, water, salt and pepper. Heat an 8-in. nonstick skillet coated with nonstick cooking spray over medium heat. Add 1/2 cup egg mixture. As eggs set, lift edges, letting uncooked portion flow underneath. When nearly set, spoon 1/2 cup of sausage-rice mixture over one side of eggs; fold in half and press down lightly for about 30 seconds. Remove and keep warm. Repeat to make six more omelets.

3. For cheese sauce, melt butter in a saucepan over medium heat. Stir in bouillon until dissolved. Stir in flour until smooth. Gradually add milk. Bring to a boil; cook and stir for 2 minutes or until thickened. Reduce heat to low; stir in cheese until melted. Drizzle over omelets. Sprinkle with parsley if desired. **Yield:** 7 omelets.

🎀🎀🎀
Apple Pecan Crepes

Carolyn Hayes, Marion, Illinois

This is a very easy, quick and delicious brunch item. When they taste the nutty apple pie filling tucked inside and the vanilla sauce draped over the tender crepes, everyone oohs and aahs between bites. Prepare a big batch—people tend to go back for seconds and even thirds!

  1 **can (21 ounces) apple pie filling**
1/2 **cup coarsely chopped pecans**
1/2 **teaspoon ground cinnamon**
 12 **prepared crepes (7 inches *each*)**
  1 **egg, beaten**
3/4 **cup half-and-half cream**
  2 **tablespoons sugar**
1/2 **teaspoon vanilla extract**
1/4 **teaspoon almond extract**

1. In a bowl, combine pie filling, pecans and cinnamon; mix well. Spread 2 rounded tablespoonfuls down the center of each crepe; roll up tightly.

2. Place in a greased 13-in. x 9-in. x 2-in. baking dish. Bake, uncovered, at 375° for 10-14 minutes or until heated through.

3. Meanwhile, in a microwave-safe bowl, combine the egg, cream, sugar and extracts. Cover and microwave at 50% power for 5-6 minutes or until thickened, stirring every 2 minutes. Cool. Serve over crepes. **Yield:** 6 servings.

   Editor's Note: This recipe was tested in an 850-watt microwave.

🎀🎀🎀
Baked Stuffed Eggs

Lorraine Bylsma, Eustis, Florida

Lucky for me, the man I married was patient. As a young bride, I could hardly boil water! This make-ahead egg dish is wonderful for potlucks.

STUFFED EGGS:
  8 **hard-cooked eggs**
  3 **to 4 tablespoons sour cream**
  2 **teaspoons prepared mustard**
1/2 **teaspoon salt**
SAUCE:
1/2 **cup chopped onion**
  2 **tablespoons butter**
  1 **can (10-3/4 ounces) condensed cream of**
     mushroom soup, undiluted
  1 **cup (8 ounces) sour cream**
1/2 **cup shredded cheddar cheese**
1/2 **teaspoon paprika**

1. Slice eggs in half lengthwise; remove yolks and set whites aside. In a bowl, mash yolks with a fork. Add sour cream, mustard and salt; mix well. Fill egg whites; set aside.

2. In a saucepan, saute onion in butter until tender. Add soup and sour cream; mix well. Pour half into an ungreased 11-in. x 7-in. x 2-in. baking pan. Arrange stuffed eggs over the sauce. Spoon remaining sauce on top. Sprinkle with cheese and paprika. Cover and refrigerate overnight.

3. Remove from refrigerator 30 minutes before baking. Bake, uncovered, at 350° for 25-30 minutes or until heated through. Serve immediately. **Yield:** 6-8 servings.

🎗 🎗 🎗
Cajun Corned Beef Hash

Del Mason, Martensville, Saskatchewan

Neither the flavor nor the texture is "mushy" when you whip up a skillet of this tongue-tingling hash. This is an all-time favorite of mine. I created it after eating a similar variation in Texas.

- 6 cups frozen shredded hash brown potatoes, thawed
- 1/4 cup butter
- 1/2 cup *each* finely chopped green onions, sweet red pepper and green pepper
- 1 teaspoon seasoned salt
- 3/4 teaspoon Cajun seasoning
- 3/4 teaspoon chili powder
- 1/2 teaspoon pepper
- 1-1/2 cups chopped cooked corned beef
- 1 tablespoon white vinegar
- 8 eggs

Additional Cajun seasoning and hot pepper sauce, optional

1. In a large skillet, cook hash browns in butter until almost tender. Stir in onions, peppers and seasonings. Cook until hash browns are lightly browned and peppers are tender. Add corned beef; heat through.

2. Meanwhile, in a skillet with high sides, bring vinegar and 2 to 3 in. of water to a boil. Reduce heat; simmer gently. Break cold eggs, one at a time, into a custard cup or saucer. Holding the cup close to the surface of the water, slip eggs, one at a time, into simmering water. Cook, uncovered, until whites are completely set and yolks begin to thicken, about 3-4 minutes.

3. With a slotted spoon, lift poached eggs out of the water. Serve over hash mixture. Sprinkle with additional Cajun seasoning and serve with hot pepper sauce if desired. **Yield:** 4 servings.

🎗 🎗 🎗
Pasta Frittata

Penny McBride, Decatur, Illinois

This well-seasoned frittata, starring ham, eggs, cheese and pasta, is always popular on a buffet. It bakes up a lovely golden brown and slices like a dream. Folks can bring their appetites when this dish is served and walk away satisfied!

- 1 large onion, chopped
- 1 tablespoon vegetable oil
- 12 ounces sliced deli ham, finely chopped
- 4 garlic cloves, minced
- 6 eggs
- 3 egg whites
- 1/2 cup shredded mozzarella cheese
- 1/2 cup shredded Colby cheese
- 2 tablespoons minced fresh parsley
- 1 to 1-1/2 teaspoons Italian seasoning
- 1/2 teaspoon salt
- 1/2 teaspoon pepper

Dash cayenne pepper
- 2 cups cooked angel hair pasta

1. In an ovenproof skillet, saute onion in oil. Add ham and garlic; saute 1 minute longer. Remove and set aside. In a large bowl, whisk the eggs and egg whites. Add cheeses, parsley and seasonings. Add the ham mixture and pasta.

2. Coat the same skillet with cooking spray if necessary. Add pasta mixture. Cover and cook over medium heat for 3 minutes. Uncover.

3. Bake at 400° for 13 minutes or until set. Let stand for 5 minutes before cutting. **Yield:** 6 servings.

🎗🎗🎗
Maple Toast and Eggs

(Pictured on page 70)

Susan Buttel, Plattsburgh, New York

My home's in the country, right next door to my sister and brother-in-law's. They and their two children all enjoy this dish each time I serve it as a special evening meal—although it can also be made for breakfast or lunch.

        12 **bacon strips, diced**
    1/2 **cup maple syrup**
    1/4 **cup butter**
        12 **slices firm-textured white bread**
        12 **eggs**
Salt and pepper to taste

1. In a large skillet, cook bacon until crisp; remove to paper towels to drain.

2. In a small saucepan, heat syrup and butter until butter is melted; set aside. Trim crusts from bread; flatten slices with a rolling pin. Brush one side generously with syrup mixture; press each slice into an ungreased muffin cup with syrup side down.

3. Divide bacon among muffin cups. Carefully break one egg into each cup. Sprinkle with salt and pepper. Cover with foil. Bake at 400° for 18-20 minutes or until eggs reach desired doneness. Serve immediately. **Yield:** 12 servings.

🎗🎗🎗
Creamed Chicken in a Basket

Sue Bolsinger, Anchorage, Alaska

Chunks of tender chicken in a creamy sauce are spooned into puff pastry shells in this delicious dish, which has long been one of our family's favorites. I served it to my husband and our five children for years. It is now a "must" for our Easter brunch.

        6 **bone-in chicken breast halves (about 4 pounds)**
        1 **small onion, quartered**
        2 **celery ribs with leaves, cut into chunks**
    2-1/2 **cups water**
        2 **teaspoons salt,** *divided*
        6 **whole peppercorns**
        8 to 10 **frozen puff pastry shells**
    1/2 **cup butter**
    1/2 **cup all-purpose flour**
    1/4 **teaspoon ground nutmeg**
    1/8 **teaspoon pepper**
    1/2 **pound fresh mushrooms, sliced**
        1 **can (5 ounces) sliced water chestnuts, drained**
        1 **jar (2 ounces) diced pimientos, drained**
        1 **tablespoon lemon juice**
        2 **cups heavy whipping cream**

1. Place the chicken, onion, celery, water, 1 teaspoon salt and peppercorns in a large saucepan. Bring to a boil; skim foam. Reduce heat; cover and simmer 35-40 minutes or until juices run clear. Remove chicken with a slotted spoon; set aside until cool enough to handle. Bake pastry shells according to package directions.

2. Remove chicken from bones; cut into cubes and set aside. Discard skin and bones. Strain broth, discarding vegetables and peppercorns. Set aside 2 cups broth (save remaining broth for another use).

3. In a saucepan, melt butter. Stir in flour until smooth. Gradually add reserved broth, nutmeg, pepper and remaining salt. Bring to a boil; cook and stir 2 minutes. Remove from heat; stir in the mushrooms, water chestnuts, pimientos, lemon juice and chicken. Return to heat. Gradually stir in cream and heat through (do not boil). Spoon into pastry shells. **Yield:** 8-10 servings.

1-1/4 cups all-purpose flour
   2 teaspoons baking powder
1/2 teaspoon salt
1/2 teaspoon dried basil
1/2 cup shortening
1/2 cup sour cream
FILLING:
3/4 cup mayonnaise
   1 cup (4 ounces) shredded cheddar cheese
   1 can (4-1/2 ounces) mushroom stems and pieces, drained
   8 bacon strips, cooked and crumbled
   1 tablespoon chopped green pepper
   1 tablespoon chopped onion
   3 medium tomatoes, peeled and sliced

1. In a bowl, combine the first four ingredients. Cut in shortening until crumbly. Stir in sour cream. Cover and refrigerate for 30 minutes. Press pastry into a 9-in. pie plate; flute edges if desired. Bake at 375° for 10 minutes. Cool completely.

2. In a bowl, combine the mayonnaise, cheddar cheese, mushrooms, bacon, green pepper and onion. Layer half of the tomatoes in crust; top with half of the mayonnaise mixture. Repeat layers. Bake at 350° for 30-35 minutes or until golden brown. Refrigerate leftovers. **Yield:** 6-8 servings.

   Editor's Note: Reduced-fat or fat-free sour cream and mayonnaise may not be substituted for regular sour cream and mayonnaise.

🎀 🎀 🎀

BLT Brunch Pie

Shara Walvoort, Oostburg, Wisconsin

My boys can't wait to pick the first ripe tomatoes in our garden to be used in this terrific pie. It has a tempting filling and tomatoes layered in a melt-in-your-mouth crust. And the tasty crust is so easy to make—you just pat the dough into the pan!

🎀 🎀 🎀

Three-Cheese Souffles

(Pictured on page 71)

Jean Ference, Sherwood Park, Alberta

No matter when I've made these—for breakfast, brunch or lunch—they have never failed. I have not had them fall once. I often get asked for the recipe.

1/3 cup butter
1/3 cup all-purpose flour
   2 cups milk
   1 teaspoon Dijon mustard
1/4 teaspoon salt
Dash hot pepper sauce
1-1/2 cups (6 ounces) shredded Swiss cheese
   1 cup (4 ounces) shredded cheddar cheese
1/4 cup shredded Parmesan cheese
   6 eggs, *separated*
1/2 teaspoon cream of tartar

1. Melt butter in a medium saucepan. Stir in flour; cook for 1 minute or until bubbly. Gradually add milk, mustard, salt and hot pepper sauce; cook and stir until thickened and bubbly. Add cheeses; stir until melted. Remove from the heat and set aside.

2. In a small mixing bowl, beat egg yolks until thick and lemon-colored, about 3-4 minutes. Add 1/3 cup cheese mixture and mix well. Return all to the saucepan; return to the heat and cook for 1-2 minutes. Cool completely, about 30-40 minutes.

3. In another mixing bowl, beat egg whites until soft peaks form. Add cream of tartar; continue beating until stiff peaks form. Fold into cheese mixture.

4. Pour into ungreased 1-cup souffle dishes or custard cups. Place in a shallow pan. Pour warm water into larger pan to a depth of 1 in. Bake, uncovered, at 325° for 40-45 minutes or until tops are golden browned. Serve immediately. **Yield:** 8 servings.

   Editor's Note: Souffles can be made ahead and frozen. Cover each dish or cup with foil and freeze. To bake, remove foil and place unthawed souffles in a shallow pan; add warm water to a depth of 1 in. Bake at 325° for 60-65 minutes or until tops are golden brown.

🎀🎀🎀
Morning Mix-Up

Kim Scholting, Springfield, Nebraska

This filling dish is super to serve for breakfast or supper. It's one of my family's favorites—even our daughter, Amanda, eats a hearty helping. The eggs, cheese, hash browns and ham go well together.

> **2 cups frozen hash brown potatoes**
> **1 cup chopped fully cooked ham**
> **1/2 cup chopped onion**
> **2 tablespoons vegetable oil**
> **6 eggs**
> **Salt and pepper to taste**
> **1 cup (4 ounces) shredded cheddar cheese**
> **Minced fresh chives**

1. In a large skillet, saute potatoes, ham and onion in oil for 10 minutes or until potatoes are tender. In a small bowl, beat eggs, salt and pepper.

2. Add to the skillet; cook, stirring occasionally, until eggs are set. Remove from the heat and gently stir in

cheese. Spoon onto a serving platter; sprinkle with chives. **Yield:** 4 servings.

🎀🎀🎀
Baked Breakfast Burritos

Carol Towey, Pasadena, California

Every week, I try a minimum of three new recipes. This is one I clipped from the paper. When I served it to my five grown children, not a morsel was left!

> **6 to 8 bacon strips**
> **8 fresh mushrooms, sliced**
> **6 green onions, sliced**
> **1/3 cup chopped green pepper**
> **1 garlic clove, minced**
> **8 eggs**
> **1/4 cup sour cream**
> **3/4 cup shredded cheddar or Monterey Jack cheese, *divided***
> **3 tablespoons enchilada *or* taco sauce**
> **1 tablespoon butter**
> **4 large flour tortillas (9 inches)**
> **Sour cream and additional enchilada *or* taco sauce, optional**

1. In a skillet, cook bacon until crisp; remove to paper towel to drain. Reserve 1 tablespoon of drippings. Saute mushrooms, onions, green pepper and garlic in drippings until tender; set aside and keep warm.

2. In a bowl, beat eggs and sour cream. Stir in 1/4 cup cheese and enchilada sauce.

3. In a skillet, melt butter; add egg mixture. Cook over low heat, stirring occasionally until eggs are set. Remove from the heat. Crumble the bacon; add to eggs with mushroom mixture. Spoon down center of tortillas; roll up.

4. Place, seam side down, in an 11-in. x 7-in. x 2-in. baking dish. Sprinkle with remaining cheese. Bake at 350° for 5 minutes or until cheese melts. Serve with sour cream and enchilada sauce if desired. **Yield:** 4 servings.

❦ ❦ ❦
Blueberry Sour Cream Pancakes

Paula Hadley, Forest Hill, Louisiana

Serve these light pancakes as is with blueberries inside and out. Or prepare them as simple, classic pancakes without the blueberries and serve with butter and warm maple syrup.

      1/2 cup sugar
        2 tablespoons cornstarch
        1 cup water
        4 cups fresh *or* frozen blueberries
PANCAKES:
        2 cups all-purpose flour
      1/4 cup sugar
        4 teaspoons baking powder
      1/2 teaspoon salt
        2 eggs
    1-1/2 cups milk
        1 cup (8 ounces) sour cream
      1/3 cup butter, melted
        1 cup fresh *or* frozen blueberries

1. In a medium saucepan, combine sugar and cornstarch. Gradually stir in water. Add blueberries; bring to a boil over medium heat. Boil for 2 minutes, stirring constantly. Remove from heat; cover and keep warm.

2. Combine first four pancake ingredients in a bowl. In another bowl, beat the eggs. Add milk, sour cream and butter; mix well. Stir into dry ingredients just until moistened. Fold in the blueberries.

3. Pour batter by 1/4 cupfuls onto a greased hot griddle; turn when bubbles form on top of pancakes. Cook until the second side is golden brown. Serve with blueberry topping. **Yield:** about 20 pancakes (3-1/2 cups topping).

❦ ❦ ❦
Creamed Ham on Toast

Robin Morton, Ripley, Mississippi

Whether for breakfast or brunch—or lunch or supper—this recipe has been popular in our family for many years. It is one that my grandmother passed down.

        1 cup chopped fully cooked ham
      1/3 cup chopped green pepper
      1/4 cup sliced celery
        2 tablespoons butter
        3 tablespoons all-purpose flour
    1-1/2 cups milk
      1/4 teaspoon pepper
      1/4 teaspoon celery seed
        1 hard-cooked egg, chopped
        5 slices process American cheese, quartered
        3 slices toast, cut into triangles

1. In a skillet, saute the ham, green pepper and celery in butter for 4-5 minutes. Sprinkle with flour; stir until smooth and bubbly. Add the milk, pepper and celery seed; bring to a boil. Cook and stir for 2 minutes.

2. Remove from the heat. Add egg and cheese; stir until cheese melts. Serve over toast. **Yield:** 2-3 servings.

Gran's Granola Parfaits

Angela Keller, Newburgh, Indiana

When my mother-in-law (Gran to our kids) had us over for brunch, I especially enjoyed her yogurt parfaits. They were refreshing, light and wholesome. I made a few changes to her recipe and came up with this sweet, crunchy and nutty variation. Yum!

- 2 cups old-fashioned oats
- 1 cup Wheaties
- 1 cup whole almonds
- 1 cup pecan halves
- 1 cup flaked coconut
- 4-1/2 teaspoons wheat germ
- 1 tablespoon sesame seeds, toasted
- 1 teaspoon ground cinnamon
- 1/4 cup butter, melted
- 2 tablespoons maple syrup
- 2 tablespoons honey
- 1 can (20 ounces) pineapple tidbits, drained
- 1 can (15 ounces) mandarin oranges, drained
- 1 cup halved green grapes
- 2 to 3 medium firm bananas, sliced
- 1 cup sliced fresh strawberries
- 1 carton (32 ounces) vanilla yogurt

1. In a bowl, combine the first eight ingredients. Combine the butter, syrup and honey; drizzle over oat mixture and stir until well coated.

2. Pour into a greased 13-in. x 9-in. x 2-in. baking pan. Bake, uncovered, at 350° for 30 minutes, stirring every 10 minutes. Cool on a wire rack; crumble into pieces.

3. Combine the fruits in a large bowl. For each parfait, layer 2 tablespoons yogurt, 2 tablespoons of granola and 3 rounded tablespoons fruit in a parfait glass or dessert bowl. Repeat layers. Sprinkle with remaining granola. Serve immediately. **Yield:** 16 servings.

🎗🎗🎗
Best-of-Show Tomato Quiche

Dorothy Swanson, Affton, Missouri

I knew this delicious recipe was a "keeper" when I first tried it back in the 1970s as a new bride—it impressed my in-laws when I made it for them! Now I sometimes substitute Mexican or Cajun seasoning for the basil. No matter how it's seasoned, it's wonderful.

  3/4 cup all-purpose flour
  1/2 cup cornmeal
  1/2 teaspoon salt
  1/8 teaspoon pepper
  1/3 cup shortening
    4 to 5 tablespoons cold water
FILLING:
    2 cups chopped plum tomatoes
    1 teaspoon salt
  1/2 teaspoon dried basil
  1/8 teaspoon pepper

  1/2 cup chopped green onions
  1/2 cup shredded cheddar cheese
  1/2 cup shredded Swiss cheese
    2 tablespoons all-purpose flour
    1 cup evaporated milk
    2 eggs

1. In a bowl, combine the first four ingredients. Cut in shortening until crumbly. Add water, tossing with a fork until dough forms a ball. Refrigerate for 30 minutes.

2. On a lightly floured surface, roll out dough to fit a 9-in. pie plate; transfer pastry to plate. Trim to 1/2 in. beyond edge of plate; flute edges. Bake at 375° for 10 minutes. Cool completely.

3. Place tomatoes in the crust; sprinkle with salt, basil, pepper, onions and cheeses. In a bowl, whisk flour, milk and eggs until smooth. Pour over filling.

4. Bake at 375° 40-45 minutes or until a knife inserted near the center comes out clean. Let stand for 10 minutes before cutting. **Yield:** 6-8 servings.

🎀🎀🎀 BLT Egg Bake

Priscilla Detrick, Catoosa, Oklahoma

BLTs are a favorite at my house, so I created this recipe to combine those flavors in a "dressier" dish. It was such a hit, I served it to my church ladies' group at a brunch I hosted. I received lots of compliments and wrote out the recipe many times.

- 1/4 cup mayonnaise
- 5 slices bread, toasted
- 4 slices process American cheese
- 12 bacon strips, cooked and crumbled
- 4 eggs
- 1 medium tomato, halved and sliced
- 2 tablespoons butter
- 2 tablespoons all-purpose flour
- 1/4 teaspoon salt
- 1/8 teaspoon pepper
- 1 cup milk
- 1/2 cup shredded cheddar cheese
- 2 green onions, thinly sliced

Shredded lettuce

1. Spread mayonnaise on one side of each slice of toast and cut into small pieces. Arrange toast, mayonnaise side up, in a greased 8-in. square baking dish. Top with cheese slices and bacon.

2. In a skillet, fry eggs over medium heat until completely set; place over bacon. Top with tomato slices; set aside.

3. In a saucepan, melt butter. Stir in flour, salt and pepper until smooth. Gradually add milk. Bring to a boil; cook and stir for 2 minutes or until thickened. Pour over tomato. Sprinkle with cheddar cheese and onions.

4. Bake, uncovered, at 325° for 10 minutes. Cut into squares; serve with lettuce. **Yield:** 4 servings.

🎀🎀🎀 Breakfast Ham Ring

Betty Becker, Columbus, Wisconsin

This recipe is a dandy one to have on hand! You can make it ahead or make it and freeze it. It can also bake while you're attending church, then be ready for a brunch with friends or family afterward.

- 10 eggs
- 1 pound ground fully cooked ham
- 1 pound bulk pork sausage
- 1-1/2 cups soft bread crumbs
- 1/2 cup milk
- 2 tablespoons dried parsley flakes
- 1 tablespoon prepared horseradish

1. In a large bowl, lightly beat 2 eggs. Add the ham, sausage, bread crumbs, milk, parsley and horseradish; mix well. Press into a greased 6-cup ring mold.

2. Bake at 350° for 1-1/4 hours. Toward the end of the baking time, prepare scrambled eggs with remaining eggs, seasoning as desired.

3. Remove ring from oven and drain juices; unmold onto a serving platter. Fill the center with scrambled eggs. Serve immediately. **Yield:** 8 servings.

Cheesy O'Brien Egg Scramble

Margaret Edmondson, Red Oak, Iowa

This breakfast bake is a snap to prepare. It's perfect for a brunch buffet or when out-of-town guests stay the night. Full of bacon, cheese, hash browns and eggs, the all-in-one dish is a hearty crowd-pleaser.

- 1 package (28 ounces) frozen O'Brien hash brown potatoes
- 1/2 teaspoon garlic salt
- 1/4 teaspoon pepper
- 1 can (10-3/4 ounces) condensed cheddar cheese soup, undiluted
- 1 pound sliced bacon, cooked and crumbled
- 12 eggs, lightly beaten
- 2 tablespoons butter
- 2 cups (8 ounces) shredded cheddar cheese

1. In a large skillet, prepare hash browns according to package directions. Sprinkle with garlic salt and pepper. Transfer to a greased 2-1/2-qt. baking dish. Top with soup. Set aside 1/2 cup of bacon; sprinkle remaining bacon over soup.

2. In another skillet, scramble eggs in butter until nearly set. Spoon over bacon. Sprinkle with cheese and reserved bacon. Bake, uncovered, at 350° for 20-25 minutes or until cheese is melted. **Yield:** 10-12 servings.

Garlic Cheese Grits

Bobbie Jo Yokley, Franklin, Kentucky

My dad prepared this family favorite every Christmas morning. Grits are a true Southern specialty. The garlic and cheese add a tasty touch.

- 1 cup quick-cooking grits
- 1 cup (4 ounces) shredded process cheese, (Velveeta)
- 1/2 cup butter
- 1 teaspoon garlic salt
- 1 egg
- 1/4 to 1/3 cup milk
- Additional cheese, optional

1. Cook grits according to package directions. Add cheese, butter and garlic salt; stir until cheese and butter are melted. In a measuring cup, beat egg; add milk to measure 1/2 cup. Stir into grits.

2. Pour into a greased 1-1/2-qt. baking dish. Bake, uncovered, at 350° for 20-25 minutes or until bubbly around the edges. Sprinkle with additional cheese if desired. **Yield:** 4-6 servings.

🎗 🎗 🎗
Croissant French Toast

June Dickenson, Philippi, West Virginia

More like a scrumptious dessert than a main dish, this rich French toast is topped with a tangy raspberry sauce and a vanilla sauce that includes ice cream. I cut the croissants into shapes with a cookie cutter for my young grandson, Patrick. He even asks for the "ice cream sauce" on pancakes!

VANILLA SAUCE:
> 1 tablespoon all-purpose flour
> 4 egg yolks
> 1 tablespoon vanilla extract
> 2 cups heavy whipping cream
> 1/2 cup sugar
> 2 scoops vanilla ice cream

BERRY SAUCE:
> 2 cups unsweetened raspberries
> 2 tablespoons sugar

FRENCH TOAST:
> 3 eggs
> 4 croissants, split
> 2 tablespoons butter

1. In a bowl, combine flour, egg yolks and vanilla; set aside. In a saucepan over medium-high heat, bring the whipping cream and sugar to a boil; remove from the heat. Stir a small amount of hot cream into egg yolk mixture; return all to the pan, stirring constantly. Bring to a gentle boil; cook and stir for 2 minutes. Remove from the heat; stir in ice cream until melted. Set aside.

2. For berry sauce, combine raspberries and sugar in a saucepan. Simmer, uncovered, for 2–3 minutes. Remove from the heat; set aside.

3. In a shallow bowl, beat eggs. Dip both sides of croissants in egg mixture. On a griddle, brown croissants on both sides in butter. Serve with vanilla and berry sauces. **Yield:** 4 servings.

🎀 🎀 🎀
Cherry Almond Granola

Deborah Purdue, Freeland, Michigan

Skim milk turns this crunchy snack into a healthy breakfast cereal, while a dollop of low-fat yogurt makes it a delicious dessert. Try adding a little baking cocoa to the brown sugar for a flavor twist.

✓ Uses less fat, sugar or salt. Includes Nutritional Analysis and Diabetic Exchanges.

- 1 **cup packed brown sugar**
- 1/2 **cup nonfat dry milk powder**
- 1/2 **cup honey**
- 1/3 **cup unsweetened apple juice concentrate**
- 2 **tablespoons canola oil**
- 3 **teaspoons almond extract**
- 6 **cups old-fashioned oats**
- 1-1/2 **cups dried cherries *or* cranberries**
- 1 **cup slivered almonds**
- **Fat-free vanilla yogurt, optional**

1. In a saucepan, combine the brown sugar, milk powder, honey, apple juice concentrate and oil. Cook and stir over medium heat until the sugar is dissolved; stir in extract.

2. In a large bowl, combine the oats, cherries and almonds. Drizzle with sugar mixture and mix well.

3. Spread in a thin layer in two 15-in. x 10-in. x 1-in. baking pans coated with nonstick cooking spray. Bake at 375° for 15-20 minutes or until golden brown, stirring occasionally. Cool completely. Serve with yogurt if desired. Store in an airtight container. **Yield:** 3 quarts.

Nutritional Analysis: One serving (1/2 cup granola) equals 222 calories, 5 g fat (1 g saturated fat), trace cholesterol, 15 mg sodium, 38 g carbohydrate, 3 g fiber, 5 g protein. **Diabetic Exchanges:** 1-1/2 fruit, 1 starch, 1 fat.

🎖️🎖️🎖️
Bacon and Cheese Breakfast Pizza

Dina Davis, Madison, Florida

An area firefighter shared this recipe with me. It's good for breakfast and even a light dinner. When I was a busy college student, I was a big fan of this easy recipe.

Pastry for single-crust pie (9 inches)
  1/2 **pound bacon, cooked and crumbled**
    2 **cups (8 ounces) shredded Swiss cheese**
    4 **eggs**
1-1/2 **cups (12 ounces) sour cream**
    2 **tablespoons chopped fresh parsley**

Roll pastry to fit into a 12-in. pizza pan. Bake at 425° for 5 minutes. Sprinkle bacon and cheese evenly over crust. In a bowl, beat eggs, sour cream and parsley until smooth; pour over pizza. Bake for 20-25 minutes or until pizza is puffy and lightly browned. **Yield:** 6 main-dish or 18 appetizer servings.

🎖️🎖️🎖️
Ham 'n' Cheese Omelet Roll

Nancy Daugherty, Cortland, Ohio

This brunch dish has wonderful ingredients and an impressive look all rolled into one! I love hosting brunch, and this special omelet roll is one of my favorite items to prepare and share. A platter of these pretty swirled slices always disappears in no time.

    4 **ounces cream cheese, softened**
  3/4 **cup milk**
    2 **tablespoons all-purpose flour**
  1/4 **teaspoon salt**
  12 **eggs**
    2 **tablespoons Dijon mustard**
2-1/4 **cups shredded cheddar or Swiss cheese, divided**
    2 **cups finely chopped fully cooked ham**
  1/2 **cup thinly sliced green onions**

1. Line the bottom and sides of a greased 15-in. x 10-in. x 1-in. baking pan with parchment paper; grease the paper and set aside.

2. In a small mixing bowl, beat cream cheese and milk until smooth. Add flour and salt; mix until combined. In a large mixing bowl, beat the eggs until blended. Add cream cheese mixture; mix well. Pour into prepared pan.

3. Bake at 375° for 30-35 minutes or until eggs are puffed and set. Remove from the oven. Immediately spread with mustard and sprinkle with 1 cup cheese. Sprinkle with ham, onions and 1 cup cheese.

4. Roll up from a short side, peeling parchment paper away while rolling. Sprinkle top of roll with the remaining cheese; bake 3-4 minutes longer or until cheese is melted. **Yield:** 12 servings.

Flavorful Swedish Meatballs, p. 96

Vegetarian Cabbage Rolls, p. 100

Spinach-Beef Spaghetti Pie, p. 92

Caesar Salmon Fillets, p. 94

Main Dishes

This chapter is chock-full of enticing entree choices for weeknight dinners, Sunday suppers and special occasions. You have your pick of beef, pork, chicken or seafood.

Yankee Pot Roast, p. 99

I like to keep a batch of these tender chicken rolls in the freezer. Coated with golden crumbs, they seem fancy enough for company. I've substituted mozzarella cheese for the provolone and pastrami for the ham with equally delicious results.

> 8 boneless skinless chicken breast halves (2 pounds)
> 8 thin slices (4 ounces) deli ham
> 4 slices provolone cheese, halved
> 2/3 cup seasoned bread crumbs
> 1/2 cup grated Romano *or* Parmesan cheese
> 1/4 cup minced fresh parsley
> 1/2 cup milk

1. Flatten chicken to 1/4-in. thickness. Place a slice of ham and half slice of cheese on each piece of chicken. Roll up from a short side and tuck in ends; secure with a toothpick. In a shallow bowl, combine crumbs, grated cheese and parsley. Pour milk into another bowl. Dip chicken rolls in milk, then roll in crumb mixture.

2. Wrap and freeze four chicken roll-ups for up to 2 months. Place the remaining roll-ups, seam side down, on a greased baking sheet. Spritz chicken with non-stick cooking spray. Bake, uncovered, at 425° for 25 minutes or until juices run clear. Remove toothpicks. **Yield:** 8 servings.

To use frozen chicken: Completely thaw in the refrigerator. Unwrap roll-ups and place on a greased baking sheet. Spritz with nonstick cooking spray. Bake, uncovered, at 425° for 30 minutes or until juices run clear.

🎗 🎗 🎗
Italian Chicken Roll-Ups

Barbara Wobser, Sandusky, Ohio

🎗 🎗 🎗
Spinach-Beef Spaghetti Pie

(Pictured on page 90)

Carol Hicks, Pensacola, Florida

With its angel hair pasta crust, this cheesy ground beef, tomato and spinach pie is always a hit when I serve it. Each neat slice has layers of pasta, cream cheese filling and spinach topping.

> 6 ounces uncooked angel hair pasta
> 2 eggs, lightly beaten
> 1/3 cup grated Parmesan cheese
> 1 pound ground beef
> 1/2 cup chopped onion
> 1/4 cup chopped green pepper
> 1 jar (14 ounces) meatless spaghetti sauce
> 1 teaspoon Creole seasoning
> 3/4 teaspoon garlic powder
> 1/2 teaspoon dried basil
> 1/2 teaspoon dried oregano
> 1 package (8 ounces) cream cheese, softened
> 1 package (10 ounces) frozen chopped spinach, thawed and squeezed dry
> 1/2 cup shredded mozzarella cheese

1. Cook pasta according to package directions; drain. Add eggs and Parmesan cheese. Press onto the bottom and up the sides of a greased 9-in. deep-dish pie plate. Bake at 350° for 10 minutes.

2. Meanwhile, in a skillet, cook beef, onion and green pepper over medium heat until meat is no longer pink; drain. Stir in spaghetti sauce and seasonings. Bring to a boil. Reduce heat; cover and simmer for 10 minutes.

3. Between two pieces of waxed paper, roll out cream cheese into a 7-in. circle. Place in the crust. Top with spinach and meat sauce. Sprinkle with mozzarella cheese. Bake at 350° for 20-30 minutes or until set. **Yield:** 6-8 servings.

🏅🏅🏅
Tomato-Onion Phyllo Pizza

Neta Cohen, Bedford, Virginia

With a delicate crust and lots of lovely tomatoes on top, this dish is a special one to serve to guests. I make it often when fresh garden tomatoes are in season. It freezes well unbaked, so I can keep one on hand to pop in the oven for a quick dinner.

- **5 tablespoons butter, melted**
- **7 sheets phyllo dough (18 inches x 14 inches)**
- **7 tablespoons grated Parmesan cheese, *divided***
- **1 cup (4 ounces) shredded mozzarella cheese**
- **1 cup thinly sliced onion**
- **7 to 9 plum tomatoes (about 1-1/4 pounds), sliced**
- **1-1/2 teaspoons minced fresh oregano *or* 1/2 teaspoon dried oregano**
- **1 teaspoon minced fresh thyme *or* 1/4 teaspoon dried thyme**

Salt and pepper to taste

1. Brush a 15-in. x 10-in. x 1-in. baking pan with some of the melted butter. Lay a sheet of phyllo in pan, folding edges in to fit (keep remaining dough covered with waxed paper to avoid drying out). Brush dough with butter and sprinkle with 1 tablespoon Parmesan cheese. Repeat layers five times, folding edges for each layer.

2. Top with remaining dough, folding edges to fit pan; brush with remaining butter. Sprinkle with mozzarella

cheese; arrange onion and tomatoes over the cheese. Sprinkle with oregano, thyme, salt, pepper and remaining Parmesan. Bake at 375° for 20-25 or until edges are golden brown. **Yield:** 28 slices.

🏅🏅🏅
Trout Baked in Cream

Ann Nace, Perkasie, Pennsylvania

Here's a quick and tasty way to serve trout. It's definitely one of our family's favorites.

- **6 trout fillets (about 3-1/2 ounces *each*)**
- **2 tablespoons lemon juice**
- **1 teaspoon dill weed**
- **1/2 teaspoon salt**
- **1/8 teaspoon pepper**
- **1 cup heavy whipping cream**
- **2 tablespoons seasoned bread crumbs**

Place trout in a greased 13-in. x 9-in. x 2-in. baking dish. Sprinkle with lemon juice, dill, salt and pepper. Pour cream over all. Sprinkle with bread crumbs. Bake, uncovered, at 350° for 11-15 minutes or until fish flakes easily with a fork. **Yield:** 4-6 servings.

🎀🎀🎀
Caesar Salmon Fillets

(Pictured on page 90)

Joan Garneau, Ellenton, Florida

Not only is this my husband's favorite meal, but it's a dish dinner guests enjoy as well. The delicate taste is a wonderful reminder that it is as tasty as it is healthy.

✓ Uses less fat, sugar or salt. Includes Nutritional Analysis and Diabetic Exchanges.

> 4 salmon fillets (6 ounces *each*)
> 1/2 cup fat-free Caesar salad dressing
> 1/4 cup reduced-sodium soy sauce
> 1 garlic clove, minced

1. Place salmon fillets in a large resealable plastic bag; add the salad dressing. Seal bag and turn to coat; refrigerate for at least 2 hours.

2. Drain and discard marinade. Coat grill rack with nonstick cooking spray before starting the grill. Place salmon skin side down on grill rack. Grill, covered, over medium heat for 5 minutes.

3. In a small bowl, combine soy sauce and garlic; brush over salmon. Grill 10-15 minutes longer or until fish flakes easily with a fork, basting occasionally. **Yield:** 4 servings.

Nutritional Analysis: One serving (1 fillet) equals 322 calories, 18 g fat (4 g saturated fat), 112 mg cholesterol, 880 mg sodium, 2 g carbohydrate, trace fiber, 35 g protein. **Diabetic Exchange:** 5 lean meat.

🎀🎀🎀
Chicken Roll-Ups With Cherry Sauce

Margaret Scott, Traverse City, Michigan

Since I grew up on a cherry farm, I have many recipes featuring that delightful fruit. This one is a delicious way that I like to use chicken.

> 8 boneless skinless chicken breast halves
> 8 slices Swiss *or* Brie cheese
> 1 egg
> 1 tablespoon water
> 1 tablespoon Dijon mustard
> 3/4 cup dry bread crumbs
> 1/2 teaspoon dried thyme
> 1/4 teaspoon salt
> Dash pepper
> 1/4 cup all-purpose flour
> 1/4 cup vegetable oil
> **CHERRY SAUCE:**
> 2 cups canned pitted tart red cherries
> 3/4 cup sugar
> 2 tablespoons cornstarch
> 1 teaspoon lemon juice
> 1/4 teaspoon almond extract
> 3 drops red food coloring, optional

1. Flatten chicken breasts to 1/4-in. thickness. Place a slice of cheese on each; roll up and secure with toothpicks. In a shallow dish, beat egg, water and mustard. In another shallow dish, combine bread crumbs, thyme, salt and pepper. Lightly coat chicken with flour, then dip in egg mixture and roll in bread crumb mixture.

2. In a large skillet, heat oil. Add roll-ups; cook until golden brown, turning often. Transfer to an ungreased 13-in. x 9-in. x 2-in. baking dish. Bake, uncovered, at 350° for 20-25 minutes or until chicken juices run clear.

3. Meanwhile, drain cherries, reserving juice. Add enough water to juice to measure 1 cup. In a saucepan, combine sugar and cornstarch. Stir in cherry juice until smooth. Add cherries. Bring to a boil; cook and stir for 2 minutes or until thickened. Remove from the heat. Stir in lemon juice, extract and food coloring if desired.

4. Discard toothpicks from roll-ups; serve with cherry sauce. **Yield:** 8 servings.

This is a wonderfully elegant entree to serve at a cozy dinner party for four. Your guests will think you spent hours in the kitchen preparing the tender hens and perfecting the full-flavored basting sauce.

4 Cornish game hens (22 ounces *each*)
1/4 cup butter, melted
1 teaspoon salt
1/2 teaspoon pepper
3/4 cup orange juice
1/2 cup packed brown sugar
1/2 cup Madeira wine, sherry *or* chicken broth
2 tablespoons lemon juice
1 teaspoon ground mustard
1/4 teaspoon ground allspice

1. Tie legs of each hen together; turn wing tips under backs. Place on a greased rack in a roasting pan. Brush with butter; sprinkle with salt and pepper. Bake, uncovered, at 350° for 1 hour.

2. In a saucepan, combine the remaining ingredients; bring to a boil. Reduce heat; simmer, uncovered, for 15 minutes. Spoon over hens. Bake 15 minutes longer or until a meat thermometer reads 180°. **Yield:** 4 servings.

🎗🎗🎗
Orange-Glazed Cornish Hens
Laurie Bartley, Lake Hiawatha, New Jersey

🎗🎗🎗
Meat Loaf Miniatures
Joyce Wegmann, Burlington, Iowa

I don't usually like meat loaf, but my family and I can't get enough of these little muffins topped with a sweet ketchup sauce. This recipe requires no chopping, so it's quick and easy to make a double batch and have extras for another day. They're great to give to new moms, too.

1 cup ketchup
3 to 4 tablespoons packed brown sugar
1 teaspoon ground mustard
2 eggs, beaten
4 teaspoons Worcestershire sauce
3 cups Crispix cereal, crushed
3 teaspoons onion powder
1/2 to 1 teaspoon seasoned salt
1/2 teaspoon garlic powder
1/2 teaspoon pepper
3 pounds lean ground beef

1. In a large bowl, combine ketchup, brown sugar and mustard. Remove 1/2 cup for topping; set aside. Add eggs, Worcestershire sauce, cereal and seasonings to remaining ketchup mixture; mix well. Let stand for 5 minutes. Crumble beef over cereal mixture and mix well.

2. Press meat mixture into 18 muffin cups (about 1/3 cup each). Bake at 375° for 18-20 minutes. Drizzle with

reserved ketchup mixture; bake 10 minutes longer or until meat is no longer pink and a meat thermometer reads 160°. Serve desired number of meat loaves. Cool remaining loaves; freeze. Transfer to freezer bags; freeze for up to 3 months. **Yield:** 1-1/2 dozen.

To use frozen meat loaves: Completely thaw in the refrigerator. Place loaves in a greased baking dish. Bake at 350° for 30 minutes or until heated through, or cover and microwave on high for 1 minute or until heated through.

★ ★ ★
Taco-Filled Pasta Shells

Marge Hodel, Roanoke, Illinois

I've been stuffing pasta shells with different fillings for years, but my family enjoys this version with taco-seasoned meat the most. The frozen shells are so convenient, because you can take out only the number you need for a single-serving lunch or family dinner. Just add zippy taco sauce and bake.

> **2 pounds ground beef**
> **2 envelopes taco seasoning**
> **1 package (8 ounces) cream cheese, cubed**

> **24 uncooked jumbo pasta shells**
> **1/4 cup butter, melted**
> **ADDITIONAL INGREDIENTS (for each casserole):**
> **1 cup salsa**
> **1 cup taco sauce**
> **1 cup (4 ounces) shredded cheddar cheese**
> **1 cup (4 ounces) shredded Monterey Jack or mozzarella cheese**
> **1-1/2 cups crushed tortilla chips**
> **1 cup (8 ounces) sour cream**
> **3 green onions, chopped**

1. In a skillet, cook beef over medium heat until no longer pink; drain. Add taco seasoning; prepare according to package directions. Add cream cheese; cover and simmer for 5-10 minutes or until melted. Transfer to a bowl; chill for 1 hour. Cook pasta according to package directions; drain. Gently toss with butter. Fill each shell with about 3 tablespoons meat mixture.

2. Place 12 shells in a greased 9-in. square baking dish. Cover and freeze for up to 3 months. To prepare remaining shells, spoon salsa into a greased 9-in. square baking dish. Top with stuffed shells and taco sauce.

3. Cover and bake at 350° for 30 minutes. Uncover; sprinkle with cheeses and chips. Bake 15 minutes longer or until heated through. Serve with sour cream and onions. **Yield:** 2 casseroles (6 servings each).

To use frozen shells: Thaw in the refrigerator for 24 hours (shells will be partially frozen). Remove from dish. Add salsa to dish; top with shells and taco sauce. Cover and bake at 350° for 40 minutes. Uncover; continue as above.

★ ★ ★
Flavorful Swedish Meatballs

(Pictured on page 90)

Stacy Thomas, Anchorage, Alaska

Our kids love to roll the ground beef and pork mixture into these moist meatballs. We like them prepared in a creamy gravy. But the meatballs also are great additions to soups and stews or to stir into spaghetti sauce and serve over pasta.

> **2 eggs, lightly beaten**
> **1/4 cup ketchup**
> **3/4 cup dry bread crumbs**
> **2 tablespoons dried parsley flakes**
> **2 tablespoons Worcestershire sauce**
> **1 teaspoon onion powder**
> **1 teaspoon garlic powder**
> **1 teaspoon pepper**
> **1/2 teaspoon salt**
> **1/2 teaspoon chili powder**
> **2 pounds ground beef**

> **1 pound ground pork**
> **ADDITIONAL INGREDIENTS (for each batch):**
> **1 envelope brown gravy mix**
> **1/2 cup sour cream**
> **Dash each nutmeg and pepper**
> **Hot cooked noodles**

1. In a bowl, combine the first 10 ingredients. Crumble meat over mixture and mix well. Shape into 1-in. balls (about 6 dozen). Place in a single layer in ungreased 15-in. x 10-in. x 1-in. baking pans. Bake at 400° for 20 minutes or until no longer pink, turning often. Cool.

2. Place about 35 meatballs each into freezer containers. May be frozen for up to 3 months. **Yield:** 2 batches (35 meatballs, which is 7 servings, per batch).

To prepare Swedish meatballs: Completely thaw in the refrigerator. In a large skillet, prepare gravy according to package directions. Add meatballs; cover and cook for 10 minutes or until heated through. Remove from the heat; stir in the sour cream, nutmeg and pepper. Serve over noodles.

✿✿✿
Stroganoff-Style Pork Chops
Kim Alpers, Traverse City, Michigan

Topped with a mustard and mushroom sauce, these tender, moist pork chops are Sunday-special. They're wonderful served with noodles and are a welcome change from grilled or fried chops.

        4 boneless butterfly pork loin chops (1 inch thick)
        2 tablespoons vegetable oil
        1 large onion, chopped
        8 medium fresh mushrooms, sliced
    1/4 cup water
        2 teaspoons prepared mustard
    1/2 teaspoon salt
        1 tablespoon all-purpose flour
    1/2 cup sour cream
Hot cooked noodles

1. In a large skillet over medium heat, brown pork chops in oil for 5-6 minutes on each side. Remove and keep warm. In the drippings, saute onion and mushrooms until tender.

2. Stir in the water, mustard and salt; bring to a boil. Return chops to pan. Reduce heat; cover and simmer for 15-20 minutes or until pork is tender. Remove chops and keep warm.

3. Combine flour and sour cream until smooth; add to the skillet. Bring to a boil; cook and stir for 1-2 minutes or until slightly thickened. Serve pork chops and mustard-mushroom sauce with noodles. **Yield:** 4 servings.

✿✿✿
Spicy Chicken Linguine
Tracy Haroldson, Aztec, New Mexico

Our state is famous for its green chilies. Naturally, my husband and I included them in this linguine dish we invented. The sauce is also excellent with spaghetti or fettuccine noodles. All of our five children love it.

    1/4 cup butter
        3 tablespoons all-purpose flour
        2 teaspoons garlic powder
        1 teaspoon pepper
    2-1/2 cups milk
        1 package (8 ounces) cream cheese, cubed
        1 cup (4 ounces) shredded Parmesan cheese
      12 ounces uncooked linguine
        3 cups cubed cooked chicken
        1 can (4 ounces) diced green chilies

1. In a saucepan, melt butter. Stir in flour, garlic powder and pepper until smooth. Gradually add milk. Bring to a boil; cook and stir for 2 minutes or until thickened. Reduce heat; add cream cheese and Parmesan cheese. Cook and stir for 8-10 minutes or until cheese is melted.

2. Meanwhile, cook linguine according to package directions. Add chicken and chilies to cheese sauce; cook 5 minutes longer or until heated through. Drain linguine; top with chicken mixture. **Yield:** 6 servings.

🎀🎀🎀
Green Bean Chicken Casserole

DeLissa Mingee, Warr Acres, Oklahoma

My husband, who claims to be strictly a meat-and-potatoes man, asked for seconds the first time I threw together this comforting all-in-one meal. My daughter and several guests raved about it, too.

- 1 package (6 ounces) long grain and wild rice mix
- 4 cups cubed cooked chicken
- 1-3/4 cups frozen French-style green beans
- 1 can (10-3/4 ounces) condensed cream of mushroom soup, undiluted
- 1 can (10-3/4 ounces) condensed cream of chicken and broccoli soup, undiluted
- 1 can (4 ounces) mushroom stems and pieces, drained
- 2/3 cup chopped onion
- 2/3 cup chopped green pepper
- 1 envelope onion soup mix
- 3/4 cup shredded Colby cheese

ADDITIONAL INGREDIENT (for each casserole):
- 2/3 cup french-fried onions

1. Prepare wild rice according to package directions. Stir in chicken, beans, soups, mushrooms, onion, green pepper and soup mix. Spoon into two greased 1-1/2-qt. baking dishes. Sprinkle with cheese.

2. Cover and freeze one casserole for up to 3 months. Cover and bake the second casserole at 350° for 25-30 minutes or until heated through. Uncover and sprinkle with french-fried onions; bake 5 minutes longer or until onions are golden. **Yield:** 2 casseroles (4-6 servings each).

To use frozen casserole: Completely thaw in the refrigerator. Remove from the refrigerator 30 minutes before baking. Cover and bake at 350° for 60-65 minutes or until heated through. Uncover and sprinkle with french-fried onions; bake 5 minutes longer.

🎀🎀🎀
Mom's Oven-Barbecued Ribs

Yvonne White, Williamson, New York

My mom made these tender ribs for special Sunday suppers when we were growing up. A few common ingredients are all you need to make the zesty sauce that coats them. My family's eyes light up when I bring these ribs to the table.

- 3 to 4 pounds country-style pork ribs
- 1-1/2 cups water
- 1 cup ketchup
- 1/3 cup Worcestershire sauce
- 1 teaspoon salt
- 1 teaspoon chili powder
- 1/2 teaspoon onion powder
- 1/8 teaspoon hot pepper sauce

1. Place ribs in a greased roasting pan. Bake, uncovered, at 350° for 45 minutes. Meanwhile, in a saucepan, combine the remaining ingredients. Bring to a boil; cook for 1 minute. Drain ribs. Spoon sauce over ribs.

2. Cover and bake for 1-1/2 hours. Uncover; bake 30 minutes longer, basting once. **Yield:** 4-6 servings.

🎀🎀🎀 Yankee Pot Roast

(Pictured on page 91)

Vera Burke, West Pittston, Pennsylvania

Here's a traditional main dish that's tested and true. It's been a favorite with my family for many years.

- 1 boneless beef chuck roast (4 to 5 pounds)
- 1 tablespoon vegetable oil
- 2 large onions, coarsely chopped
- 2 cups sliced carrots
- 2 celery ribs, sliced
- 2 cans (14-1/2 ounces *each*) Italian stewed tomatoes
- 1-3/4 cups water
- 1 teaspoon salt
- 1/2 teaspoon dried thyme
- 1/4 teaspoon pepper
- 4 medium potatoes, peeled and cut into eighths

1. In a large deep skillet over medium-high heat, brown roast on all sides in oil. Remove roast. Add onions, carrots, celery, tomatoes, water, salt, thyme and pepper to the skillet. Bring to a boil.

2. Return roast to skillet. Reduce heat; cover and simmer for 2 hours. Add potatoes; cover and cook 40 minutes longer or until meat and vegetables are tender. **Yield:** 12-14 servings.

🎀🎀🎀 Taco Chili Pie

Liza Taylor, Seattle, Washington

This zesty pie combines ground beef, stewed tomatoes, kidney and pinto beans with zippy seasonings, all tucked into a flaky golden crust. It slices so nicely, you can easily dish it up for a crowd.

- 1 pound ground beef
- 2 cups sliced fresh mushrooms
- 1 cup chopped onion
- 4 cups torn fresh spinach
- 1 can (16 ounces) kidney beans, rinsed and drained
- 1 can (15 ounces) pinto beans, rinsed and drained
- 1 can (15 ounces) tomato sauce
- 1 can (14-1/2 ounces) stewed tomatoes, undrained
- 2 tablespoons taco seasoning
- 1 tablespoon sugar
- 1 tablespoon molasses

CRUST:
- 4-1/2 cups all-purpose flour
- 4 teaspoons sugar
- 2 teaspoons salt
- 2 cups cold butter
- 12 to 14 tablespoons cold water

1. In a skillet, cook the beef, mushrooms and onion over medium heat until meat is no longer pink; drain. Stir in the next eight ingredients. Bring to a boil. Reduce heat; simmer, uncovered, for 20-30 minutes.

2. Meanwhile, combine the flour, sugar and salt in a bowl. Cut in butter until crumbly. Gradually add water, tossing with a fork until dough forms a ball. Divide into fourths; flatten each portion into a circle. Cover with plastic wrap. Refrigerate for 30 minutes.

3. Line two 9-in. pie plates with pastry. Divide beef mixture between crusts. Roll out remaining pastry to fit tops of pies; place over filling. Trim, seal and flute edges. Cut slits in top.

4. Bake at 400° for 20 minutes. Reduce heat to 375°; bake 30-35 minutes longer or until golden brown. Let stand for 10-15 minutes before cutting. **Yield:** 2 pies (6-8 servings each).

Caribbean Chicken

Rusty Collins, Orlando, Florida

You'd be hard-pressed to find a marinade that's this flavorful from any store!

✓ Uses less fat, sugar or salt. Includes Nutritional Analysis and Diabetic Exchanges.

1/2 cup lemon juice
1/3 cup honey
3 tablespoons canola oil
6 green onions, sliced
3 jalapeno peppers, seeded and chopped
3 teaspoons dried thyme
3/4 teaspoon salt
1/4 teaspoon ground allspice
1/4 teaspoon ground nutmeg
6 boneless skinless chicken breast halves (1-1/2 pounds)

1. Place the first nine ingredients in a blender or food processor; cover and process until smooth. Pour 1/2 cup into a small bowl for basting; cover and refrigerate. Pour remaining marinade into a large resealable plastic bag; add chicken. Seal bag and turn to coat; refrigerate for up to 6 hours.

2. Drain and discard marinade. Coat grill rack with nonstick cooking spray before starting the grill. Grill chicken, covered, over medium heat for 4-6 minutes on each side or until juices run clear, basting frequently with the reserved marinade. **Yield:** 6 servings.

Editor's Note: When cutting or seeding hot peppers, use rubber or plastic gloves to protect your hands. Avoid touching your face.

Nutritional Analysis: One serving (1 chicken breast half) equals 205 calories, 6 g fat (1 g saturated fat), 66 mg cholesterol, 272 mg sodium, 11 g carbohydrate, trace fiber, 27 g protein. **Diabetic Exchanges:** 3 lean meat, 1/2 starch.

Vegetarian Cabbage Rolls

(Pictured on page 90)

Michelle Dougherty, Lewiston, Idaho

This marvelous meatless entree comes from my grandmother, who cooks a lot with grains, particularly bulgur.

✓ Uses less fat, sugar or salt. Includes Nutritional Analysis and Diabetic Exchanges.

1-1/2 cups chopped fresh mushrooms
1 cup diced zucchini
3/4 cup chopped green pepper
3/4 cup chopped sweet red pepper
3/4 cup vegetable broth
1/2 cup bulgur
1 teaspoon dried basil
1/2 teaspoon dried marjoram
1/2 teaspoon dried thyme
1/4 teaspoon pepper
1 large head cabbage
6 tablespoons shredded Parmesan cheese, *divided*
2 teaspoons lemon juice
1 can (8 ounces) tomato sauce
1/8 teaspoon hot pepper sauce

1. In a large saucepan, combine the first 10 ingredients. Bring to a boil over medium heat. Reduce heat; cover and simmer for 5 minutes. Remove from the heat; let stand for 5 minutes.

2. Meanwhile, cook cabbage in boiling water just until leaves fall off head. Set aside eight large leaves for rolls (refrigerate remaining cabbage for another use). Cut out the thick vein from each leaf, making a V-shaped cut. Overlap cut ends before filling. Stir 4 tablespoons cheese and lemon juice into vegetable mixture.

3. Place a heaping 1/3 cupful on each cabbage leaf; fold in sides. Starting at an unfolded edge, roll to completely enclose filling.

4. Combine tomato sauce and hot pepper sauce; pour 1/3 cup into a 2-qt. baking dish. Place cabbage rolls in dish; spoon remaining sauce over top. Cover and bake at 400° for 15 minutes or until heated through. Sprinkle with remaining cheese. **Yield:** 4 servings.

Nutritional Analysis: One serving (2 cabbage rolls) equals 142 calories, 3 g fat (1 g saturated fat), 5 mg cholesterol, 675 mg sodium, 25 g carbohydrate, 6 g fiber, 8 g protein. **Diabetic Exchanges:** 2 vegetable, 1 starch.

🎀🎀🎀 Sweet 'n' Sour Pot Roast

Taryn Daniels, Maple City, Michigan

Just a whiff of this pot roast reminds me of my grandmother. She's been making this family favorite for over 45 years. For variety, try it with a whole chicken, or add potatoes, carrots and onions or Chinese vegetables to the pot.

    1 teaspoon garlic salt
1/2 teaspoon ground mustard
1/4 teaspoon pepper
    1 boneless beef chuck roast (4-1/2 to 5 pounds)
    2 tablespoons vegetable oil
    2 cups water
1/2 cup soy sauce
    2 tablespoons white vinegar
    2 tablespoons honey
    1 tablespoon celery seed
    2 tablespoons minced fresh gingerroot
    6 tablespoons cornstarch
1/2 cup cold water
Hot cooked brown rice, optional

1. Combine garlic salt, mustard and pepper; rub over entire roast. In a Dutch oven, brown roast on all sides in oil over medium-high heat; drain. Combine the water, soy sauce, vinegar, honey, celery seed and ginger; pour over roast. Bring to a boil. Reduce heat; cover and simmer for 3 to 3-1/2 hours or until meat is tender.

2. Remove roast from pan and keep warm. Pour pan drippings and loosened brown bits into a measuring cup. Skim fat, reserving drippings. Add enough water, if needed, to measure 5 cups. Return to Dutch oven.

3. Combine cornstarch and cold water until smooth; gradually add to drippings. Bring to a boil; cook and stir for 2 minutes or until thickened. Slice roast; serve with gravy and brown rice if desired. **Yield:** 12-16 servings.

🎀🎀🎀 French Canadian Meat Pie

Diane Davies, Indian Trail, North Carolina

This hearty meat pie was traditionally served on Christmas Eve by my mother's family in Quebec. The recipe has been passed down through at least four generations and has been translated from my grandmother's original recipe in French.

    1 pound ground beef
3/4 pound ground pork
3/4 cup chopped onion
    2 celery ribs, chopped
    2 garlic cloves, minced
    6 cups hot mashed potatoes (prepared without milk and butter)
1/4 cup chicken broth
1/2 teaspoon dried rosemary, crushed
1/2 teaspoon rubbed sage
1/2 teaspoon dried thyme
1/4 teaspoon dried marjoram
Salt and pepper to taste
Pastry for two double-crust pies (9 inches)
Milk, optional

1. In a large skillet, cook the beef, pork, onion, celery and garlic over medium heat until meat is no longer pink and vegetables are tender; drain. Remove from the heat. Stir in potatoes, broth and seasonings.

2. Line two 9-in. pie plates with pastry. Divide meat mixture between crusts. Top with remaining pastry; trim, seal and flute edges. Cut slits in top. Brush with milk if desired. Bake at 375° for 30-35 minutes or until golden brown. **Yield:** 2 pies (6-8 servings each).

🎀🎀🎀
Roast Pork with Raspberry Sauce

Carolyn Zimmerman, Fairbury, Illinois

Want to treat your guests to a spectacular meal? Plan this pork as the centerpiece of your menu. The fruity sauce enhances the meat's flavor and looks so pretty! I decorate the platter with red spiced apples and fresh parsley.

- 1 teaspoon salt
- 1 teaspoon rubbed sage
- 1 teaspoon pepper
- 1 boneless pork loin roast (3-1/2 to 4 pounds)

SAUCE:
- 1 package (10 ounces) frozen sweetened raspberries, thawed
- 1-1/2 cups sugar
- 1/4 cup white vinegar
- 1/4 teaspoon *each* ground ginger, nutmeg and cloves
- 1/4 cup cornstarch
- 1 tablespoon butter, melted
- 1 tablespoon lemon juice
- 3 to 4 drops red food coloring, optional

1. Combine the salt, sage and pepper; rub over entire roast. Place roast fat side up on a rack in a shallow roasting pan. Bake, uncovered, at 350° for 70-80 minutes or until a meat thermometer reads 160°.

2. For the sauce, drain raspberries, reserving liquid. Set berries aside. Add enough water to juice to measure 3/4 cup. In a saucepan, combine the sugar, vinegar, spices and 1/2 cup raspberry juice. Bring to a boil. Reduce heat; simmer, uncovered, for 10 minutes.

3. Combine cornstarch and remaining raspberry juice until smooth; stir into the saucepan. Bring to a boil; cook and stir for 2 minutes or until thickened. Remove from the heat. Stir in the butter, lemon juice, food coloring if desired and reserved raspberries.

4. Let roast stand for 10-15 minutes before slicing. Serve with raspberry sauce. **Yield:** 8-10 servings.

🎀🎀🎀
Honey-Dijon Chicken

Barbara Leventhal, Hauppauge, New York

These tender chicken breasts are nicely browned, then covered in a sauce that gets its sweetness from honey and pineapple juice.

- 12 boneless skinless chicken breast halves (3 pounds)
- 4 garlic cloves, minced
- 2 teaspoons dried thyme

Salt and pepper to taste
- 1 tablespoon vegetable oil
- 2 tablespoons cornstarch
- 1-1/2 cups pineapple juice
- 1/2 cup water
- 1/2 cup Dijon mustard
- 1/3 cup honey

Hot cooked rice *or* noodles

1. Rub chicken with garlic and thyme. Sprinkle with salt and pepper. In a skillet, cook chicken in oil until no longer pink. In a bowl, combine cornstarch, pineapple juice and water until smooth. Stir in mustard and honey. Add to the skillet. Bring to a boil; cook and stir for 2 minutes or until thickened.

2. Spoon half of chicken and sauce into a greased 11-in. x 7-in. x 2-in. baking dish; cool. Cover and freeze for up to 3 months. Serve remaining chicken and sauce over rice or noodles. **Yield:** 2 casseroles (6 servings each).

To use frozen chicken: Completely thaw in refrigerator. Remove from refrigerator 30 minutes before baking. Cover; bake at 350° for 35 minutes or until heated through.

🏵 🏵 🏵
Shrimp Kabobs

Cheryl Williams, Evington, Virginia

My family always asks me to prepare these tangy and juicy kabobs during our beach getaways.

✓ Uses less fat, sugar or salt. Includes Nutritional Analysis and Diabetic Exchanges.

- **1 can (8 ounces) tomato sauce**
- **1 cup chopped onion**
- **1/2 cup water**
- **1/4 cup packed brown sugar**
- **1/4 cup lemon juice**
- **3 tablespoons Worcestershire sauce**
- **2 tablespoons canola oil**
- **2 tablespoons prepared mustard**
- **1/2 teaspoon salt**
- **1/2 teaspoon pepper**
- **1 can (20 ounces) unsweetened pineapple chunks**
- **1 pound uncooked medium shrimp, peeled and deveined (about 32)**
- **1 medium green pepper, cut into chunks**
- **1 medium onion, cut into chunks**
- **3 cups hot cooked rice**

1. In a saucepan, combine first 10 ingredients. Bring to a boil. Reduce heat and simmer, uncovered, for 15 minutes.

2. Drain pineapple, reserving 2 tablespoons juice (save remaining juice for another use); set pineapple aside. Stir reserved juice into sauce. Pour half into a bowl for basting; cover and refrigerate. Pour remaining sauce into a large resealable plastic bag; add shrimp. Seal bag and turn to coat; refrigerate for 2-3 hours.

3. Drain and discard marinade. Alternately thread shrimp, pineapple, green pepper and onion on eight metal or soaked wooden skewers.

4. Coat grill rack with nonstick cooking spray before starting the grill. Grill kabobs, covered, over medium heat for 5 minutes on each side or until shrimp turn pink, basting occasionally with reserved sauce. Serve over rice. **Yield:** 4 servings.

Nutritional Analysis: One serving (2 kabobs with 3/4 cup rice) equals 428 calories, 6 g fat (1 g saturated fat), 161 mg cholesterol, 775 mg sodium, 71 g carbohydrate, 4 g fiber, 23 g protein. **Diabetic Exchanges:** 3 lean meat, 2-1/2 starch, 2 vegetable, 1 fruit, 1 fat.

🎗 🎗 🎗
Farmer's Market Sausage Pie

Teri Schuman, Oregon, Wisconsin

Our son named this savory pie for the Saturday morning farmer's market that's held near our state capitol. Most of the fresh ingredients called for in the recipe can be found there and baked into this deliciously different entree.

- 4 Italian sausage links, casings removed, halved and cut into 1/2-inch pieces
- 1 medium tomato, cut into chunks
- 1 small yellow tomato, cut into chunks
- 1 cup thinly sliced zucchini
- 1 cup thinly sliced yellow summer squash
- 1/2 cup julienned green pepper
- 1/2 cup julienned sweet red pepper
- 1 tablespoon Italian salad dressing mix
- 1/2 teaspoon garlic powder
- 1/4 to 1/2 teaspoon fennel seed, crushed
- Pastry for double-crust pie (9 inches)
- 1 cup (4 ounces) shredded cheddar cheese
- 1 cup (4 ounces) shredded mozzarella cheese

1. In a large skillet, cook sausage over medium heat until no longer pink; drain. Stir in the tomatoes, squash, peppers, salad dressing mix, garlic powder and fennel seed. Cook and stir for 10 minutes; drain. Cool for 10 minutes.

2. Line a 9-in. pie plate with bottom pastry; trim even with edge. Fill with the sausage mixture. Sprinkle with cheeses. Roll out remaining pastry to fit top of pie; place over filling. Trim, seal and flute edges. Cut slits in top.

3. Bake at 375° for 35–40 minutes or until filling is bubbly and crust is golden brown. Let stand for 10 minutes before cutting. **Yield:** 8 servings.

🎀 🎀 🎀
Orange-Ginger Pork Chops

Lynette Randleman, Cheyenne, Wyoming

Basting chops with this tangy sauce makes them extremely tender and savory. My family requests this dish for the terrific taste.

     4 teaspoons minced fresh gingerroot
     1 garlic clove, minced
     1 tablespoon canola oil

 1/2 cup sherry *or* chicken broth
 1/4 cup honey
 1/4 cup soy sauce
     1 tablespoon sesame seeds
     1 tablespoon grated orange peel
 3/4 teaspoon hot pepper sauce
     4 bone-in pork loin chops (6 ounces *each*)
     1 teaspoon cornstarch
     2 tablespoons water

1. In a saucepan, cook ginger and garlic in oil for 1 minute; remove from the heat. Stir in the sherry or broth, honey, soy sauce, sesame seeds, orange peel and hot pepper sauce; mix well.

2. Pour 1/2 cup into a small bowl; set aside. Pour remaining marinade into a large resealable plastic bag; add pork chops. Seal bag and turn to coat; refrigerate for at least 1 hour.

3. Meanwhile, in a saucepan, combine cornstarch and water until smooth; add reserved marinade. Bring to a boil; cook and stir for 1 minute or until thickened.

4. Drain and discard marinade from the pork. Coat grill rack with nonstick cooking spray before starting the grill. Grill chops, covered, over medium heat for 4 minutes. Turn; baste with sauce. Grill 15-20 minutes longer or until juices run clear, basting occasionally. Serve with any remaining sauce. **Yield:** 4 servings.

🎀 🎀 🎀
Special Scallops and Chicken

Sheila Vail, Long Beach, California

I make this main course when I want to wow company. It tastes heavenly, and guests always love it.

 1/2 cup all-purpose flour
 1/2 teaspoon salt
 1/2 teaspoon pepper
     6 boneless skinless chicken breast halves
 1/2 pound bay scallops
 1/4 cup olive oil
 1-1/2 cups sliced fresh mushrooms
     1 medium onion, chopped
 1/4 cup white wine *or* chicken broth
     2 teaspoons cornstarch
 1/2 cup heavy whipping cream
     1 teaspoon dried tarragon
 1/2 cup shredded Swiss cheese

1. In a large resealable plastic bag, combine the flour, salt and pepper. Add chicken and scallops in batches; shake to coat. In a large skillet, saute chicken and scallops in oil until lightly browned. Transfer to a greased 13-in. x 9-in. x 2-in. baking dish.

2. In the pan drippings, saute mushrooms and onion. Add wine or broth. Bring to a boil; cook until liquid is reduced to 2 tablespoons. Combine cornstarch, cream and tarragon until blended; add to skillet. Bring to a boil; cook and stir for 1 minute or until thickened. Spoon over chicken and scallops. Sprinkle with cheese.

3. Bake, uncovered, at 375° for 18-20 minutes or until chicken juices run clear. **Yield:** 6 servings.

✿ ✿ ✿
Picante Chicken

Karen Stattelman, Effingham, Kansas

My husband used to claim this entree as his specialty until I made it and discovered how quick and easy it is. Our two sons love the juicy chicken while my husband and I enjoy the twist that brown sugar and mustard give the picante sauce.

- **4 boneless skinless chicken breast halves (1 pound)**
- **1 jar (16 ounces) picante sauce**
- **3 tablespoons brown sugar**
- **1 tablespoon prepared mustard**

Hot cooked rice, optional

Place chicken in a greased shallow 2-qt. baking dish. In a small bowl, combine the picante sauce, brown sugar and mustard; pour over chicken. Bake, uncovered, at 400° for 30-35 minutes or until chicken juices run clear. Serve over rice if desired. **Yield:** 4 servings.

✿ ✿ ✿
Meatball Stroganoff With Noodles

Carol Schurvinske, Geneseo, Illinois

Instead of cake, my great-nephews and great-niece ask me to whip up this Stroganoff as their special birthday treat.

- **2 cups all-purpose flour**
- **1 teaspoon salt**
- **3 egg yolks**
- **1 egg**
- **6 tablespoons water**

MEATBALLS:
- **1 egg, lightly beaten**
- **2 tablespoons ketchup**
- **1/4 cup quick-cooking oats**
- **1 tablespoon finely chopped onion**
- **1/2 teaspoon salt**
- **1 pound ground beef**

SAUCE:
- **2 cans (10-3/4 ounces *each*) condensed cream of mushroom soup, undiluted**
- **1 cup (8 ounces) sour cream**
- **1 cup milk**
- **1 tablespoon paprika**
- **2 quarts water**
- **1 teaspoon salt**
- **1 tablespoon butter**
- **1 tablespoon minced parsley**

1. In a bowl, combine flour and salt; make a well. Beat yolks, egg and water; pour into well and stir. Turn onto a floured surface; knead 8-10 times. Divide into thirds; roll out each as thin as possible. Let stand 20 minutes or until partially dried. Cut into 1/4-in. strips, then into 2-in. pieces; set aside.

2. In a bowl, combine egg, ketchup, oats, onion and salt. Add beef; mix well. Shape into 1-1/2-in. balls. Place in a greased 11-in. x 7-in. x 2-in. baking dish. Bake, uncovered, at 400° for 10-15 minutes or until no longer pink.

3. In a large saucepan, combine first four sauce ingredients; heat through. Add meatballs. Cover; cook until heated through, stirring frequently. In another saucepan, bring water and salt to a boil; add noodles. Cook for 12-15 minutes or until tender; drain. Toss with butter and parsley. Serve with meatballs. **Yield:** 6 servings.

★★★
Beef Stew Pie

Karol Sprague, Gobles, Michigan

This tastes just like beef stew in a pie crust! My daughter and I serve it to our families often, and everyone loves it. The pie is especially good made the day before so the flavors can blend. I sometimes double the recipe so we're sure to have leftovers.

      6 tablespoons all-purpose flour, *divided*
1-1/2 teaspoons salt
  1/2 teaspoon pepper
      1 pound boneless beef round steak, cut into 1-inch pieces
      2 tablespoons vegetable oil
  1/2 cup chopped onion
      2 garlic cloves, minced
2-1/4 cups water, *divided*
      1 tablespoon tomato paste
  1/2 teaspoon Italian seasoning
  1/2 teaspoon dried basil
      1 bay leaf
      2 cups cubed cooked potatoes
1-1/2 cups sliced cooked carrots
      2 tablespoons minced fresh parsley
Pastry for single-crust pie (9 inches)

1. In a large resealable plastic bag, combine 3 tablespoons flour, salt and pepper. Add beef in batches; shake to coat. In a large skillet, saute beef in oil until browned. Add onion and garlic; cook and stir until onion is tender. Add 1/4 cup water, stirring to scrape browned bits.

2. Combine 1-1/2 cups water, tomato paste, Italian seasoning and basil; stir into skillet. Add bay leaf. Bring to a boil. Reduce heat; cover and simmer for 1-1/4 to 1-1/2 hours or until meat is tender.

3. Combine the remaining flour and water until smooth; gradually stir into skillet. Bring to a boil; cook and stir for 2 minutes or until thickened and bubbly. Discard bay leaf. Stir in potatoes, carrots and parsley. Transfer to a greased 2-qt. baking dish.

4. On a floured surface, roll out pastry to fit dish. Place over filling; flute edges. Cut slits in top. Bake at 425° for 25-30 minutes or until golden brown. Let stand for 10 minutes. **Yield:** 4-6 servings.

★★★
Sweet and Savory Brisket

Chris Snyder, Boulder, Colorado

I like this recipe because it makes such tender beef and takes advantage of a slow cooker. It's wonderful to come home from work and have this mouth-watering dish waiting for you.

      1 beef brisket (3 to 3-1/2 pounds), cut in half
      1 cup ketchup
  1/4 cup grape jelly
      1 envelope onion soup mix
  1/2 teaspoon pepper

1. Place half of the brisket in a slow cooker. In a bowl, combine the ketchup, jelly, soup mix and pepper; spread half over meat. Top with the remaining meat and ketchup mixture.

2. Cover and cook on low for 8-10 hours or until meat is tender. Slice brisket; serve with cooking juices. **Yield:** 8-10 servings.

Editor's Note: This is a fresh beef brisket, not corned beef.

🎀🎀🎀
Steak on a Stick

Jennifer Schwerin, Rockford, Illinois

I combine molasses, mustard and soy sauce to make these the most robust kabobs you've ever tasted. You'll never miss the oil in this hearty marinade.

- 1 **beef flank steak (1-1/2 pounds)**
- 1/2 **cup soy sauce**
- 1/4 **cup water**
- 2 **tablespoons molasses**
- 2 **teaspoons ground mustard**
- 1 **teaspoon ground ginger**
- 1/2 **teaspoon garlic powder**

1. Freeze steak for 1-1/2 hours. Cut diagonally into 1/4-in. slices. In a bowl, combine the remaining ingredients. Pour 1/4 cup into a small bowl for basting; cover and refrigerate. Pour remaining marinade into a large resealable plastic bag; add the beef. Seal bag and turn to coat; refrigerate for at least 4 hours.

2. Drain and discard marinade. Coat grill rack with nonstick cooking spray before starting the grill. Thread beef ribbon-style on 12 metal or soaked wooden skewers. Grill, uncovered, over medium heat for 3-4 minutes on each side or until meat reaches desired doneness, basting frequently with reserved marinade. **Yield:** 6 servings.

🎀🎀🎀
Chicken Cordon Bleu Calzones

Kathy Gounaud, Warwick, Rhode Island

This recipe combines the delicate flavor of chicken cordon bleu with the impressive look of beef Wellington.

- 4 **boneless skinless chicken breasts (1 pound)**
- 1 **cup sliced fresh mushrooms**
- 1/2 **medium onion, chopped**
- 2 **tablespoons butter**
- 3 **tablespoons cornstarch**
- 1-1/4 **cups milk**
- 1 **tablespoon minced fresh basil *or* 1 teaspoon dried basil**
- 1 **teaspoon salt**
- 1/4 **teaspoon pepper**
- 1 **package (17-1/4 ounces) frozen puff pastry, thawed**
- 8 **thin slices deli ham**
- 4 **slices provolone cheese**

Additional milk, optional

1. Place chicken in a greased 2-qt. baking dish; cover with water. Cover and bake at 350° for 30 minutes or until juices run clear.

2. Meanwhile, in a skillet, saute mushrooms and onion in butter until tender. Combine cornstarch and milk until smooth; stir into skillet. Add seasonings. Bring to a boil; cook and stir for 2 minutes or until thickened.

3. Drain chicken. Cut pastry sheets in half widthwise. On one side of each half, place a chicken breast, 1/4 cup mushroom mixture, two ham slices and one cheese slice. Fold pastry over filling and seal edges.

4. Place on a greased baking sheet. Brush tops with milk if desired. Bake at 400° for 15-20 minutes or until puffed and golden. **Yield:** 4 servings.

Cheese-Stuffed Pork Roast

Kara Holtkamp, West Point, Iowa

I first served this roast for a Christmas dinner. My family raved about it, so I make it often.

      1 tablespoon all-purpose flour
  1/4 teaspoon lemon-pepper seasoning
      2 tablespoons butter, melted
      2 tablespoons heavy whipping cream
      1 cup (4 ounces) shredded Swiss cheese
      1 boneless pork loin roast (2 to 2-1/2 pounds),
         trimmed
      6 ounces thinly sliced deli ham
      1 teaspoon paprika
  1/2 teaspoon *each* dried marjoram, oregano and
         basil
CREAM SAUCE:
      1 small onion, finely chopped
      1 tablespoon butter
      1 tablespoon cornstarch
      1 cup heavy whipping cream
  1/4 cup chicken broth
      1 teaspoon sour cream
Salt to taste

1. In a bowl, combine the flour, lemon-pepper, butter and cream until smooth. Stir in the cheese; set aside. Cut a lengthwise slit down the center of the roast to within 1/2 in. of the bottom. Open roast so it lies flat; cover with plastic wrap. Flatten to 3/4-in. thickness.

2. Remove plastic; place ham slices over roast. Spread cheese mixture lengthwise down the center of one side of roast to within 1-1/2 in. of ends. Roll up, jelly-roll style, starting with the long side with cheese filling. Tie several times with kitchen string; secure ends with toothpicks.

3. Combine paprika, marjoram, oregano and basil; rub over roast. Place on a rack in a shallow roasting pan. Bake, uncovered, at 325° for 1-1/4 to 1-1/2 hours or until a meat thermometer reads 160°. Let stand for 10 minutes.

4. Meanwhile, in a skillet, saute onion in butter until tender. Stir in the cornstarch until blended. Whisk in cream and broth. Bring to a boil; cook and stir for 2 minutes or until thickened. Remove from the heat; stir in sour cream and salt. Slice roast; serve with cream sauce. **Yield:** 8-10 servings.

Mexican Chicken Manicotti

Keely Jankunas, Corvallis, Montana

Our family of five enjoys trying different ethnic cuisines. This Italian specialty has a little Mexican zip. Be very careful not to overcook the manicotti. If the filled shells happen to break, just place them in the pan seam-side down.

- 1 package (8 ounces) manicotti shells
- 2 cups cubed cooked chicken
- 2 cups (8 ounces) shredded Monterey Jack cheese, *divided*
- 1-1/2 cups (6 ounces) shredded cheddar cheese
- 1 cup (8 ounces) sour cream
- 1 small onion, diced, *divided*
- 1 can (4 ounces) chopped green chilies, *divided*
- 1 can (10-3/4 ounces) condensed cream of chicken soup, undiluted
- 1 cup salsa
- 2/3 cup milk

1. Cook manicotti according to package directions. Meanwhile, in a large bowl, combine the chicken, 1-1/2 cups Monterey Jack cheese, cheddar cheese, sour cream, half of the onion and 6 tablespoons chilies. In another bowl, combine the soup, salsa, milk and remaining onion and chilies. Spread 1/2 cup in a greased 13-in. x 9-in. x 2-in. baking dish.

2. Drain manicotti; stuff each with about 1/4 cup chicken mixture. Arrange over sauce in baking dish. Pour remaining sauce over shells.

3. Cover and bake at 350° for 30 minutes. Uncover; sprinkle with remaining Monterey Jack cheese. Bake for 10 minutes longer or until cheese is melted. **Yield:** 7 servings.

Mushroom Shrimp Creole

Shirlee Vader, Hensley, Arkansas

We especially enjoy this hearty main dish on chilly or stormy days. The tomatoes, mushrooms, onions, green peppers and shrimp are nicely spiced with seasonings.

- 6 bacon strips, diced
- 2 large onions, chopped
- 1-1/2 cups chopped green peppers
- 1 garlic clove, minced
- 1 can (29 ounces) diced tomatoes, undrained
- 1 can (6 ounces) tomato paste
- 4-1/2 teaspoons brown sugar
- 1 tablespoon Worcestershire sauce
- 1 teaspoon salt
- 1/2 teaspoon pepper
- 1/2 teaspoon dried basil
- 1 bay leaf
- 1-1/2 pounds cooked medium shrimp, peeled and deveined
- 1 jar (4-1/2 ounces) whole mushrooms, drained
- 2 tablespoons butter
- 1 tablespoon lemon juice
- 1/4 teaspoon dried savory

Hot cooked rice

1. In a large skillet, cook bacon over medium heat until crisp. Remove to paper towels to drain. In the drippings, saute onions, green peppers and garlic. Add the next eight ingredients. Bring to a boil. Reduce heat; cover and simmer for 30-45 minutes.

2. Add the shrimp, mushrooms, butter, lemon juice and savory. Cook 5-10 minutes longer or until heated through. Discard bay leaf. Stir in bacon. Serve over rice. **Yield:** 6-8 servings.

🎗️🎗️🎗️
Salmon Stuffed Peppers

Kathleen Bowman, Sun Valley, Nevada

These colorful stuffed peppers are a nice change from the usual ground beef versions.

6 medium green, sweet yellow *or* red peppers
1-1/4 pounds salmon fillets *or* steaks
3/4 cup chicken broth
1 medium leek (white portion only), chopped
1 to 3 medium jalapeno peppers, minced
2 tablespoons minced fresh cilantro
1 teaspoon Worcestershire sauce
1/2 teaspoon dried tarragon
1/2 teaspoon dried oregano
1/4 teaspoon salt
1/8 teaspoon pepper
2 cups hot cooked rice
1/2 cup tartar sauce
1/2 cup sour cream
2 tablespoons shredded Parmesan cheese

1. Cut tops off peppers and remove seeds. Cook peppers in boiling water for 3-5 minutes or until tender. Drain and rinse in cold water; set aside. Broil salmon 4-6 in. from the heat for 4-5 minutes on each side or until fish flakes easily with a fork. Discard bones and skin. Flake fish with a fork; set aside.

2. In a large skillet, combine the broth, leek, jalapenos, cilantro, Worcestershire sauce, tarragon, oregano, salt and pepper. Bring to a boil. Reduce heat; simmer, uncovered, for 10 minutes or until the liquid has evaporated.

3. Stir in hot rice, tartar sauce and sour cream. Fold in salmon. Spoon into peppers. Place in an ungreased shallow baking dish. Sprinkle with Parmesan cheese. Cover and bake at 350° for 25-30 minutes or until peppers are tender and filling is hot. **Yield:** 6 servings.

Editor's Note: When cutting or seeding hot peppers, use rubber or plastic gloves to protect your hands. Avoid touching your face.

🎗️🎗️🎗️
New Haven Clam Pizza

Susan Seymour, Valatie, New York

This appetizer is the perfect start to any meal. It's always a big hit with our family and friends.

1 package (1/4 ounce) active dry yeast
1 cup warm water (110° to 115°)
1 teaspoon sugar
2-1/2 cups all-purpose flour
1 teaspoon salt
2 tablespoons vegetable oil
2 cans (6-1/2 ounces *each*) chopped clams, drained
4 bacon strips, cooked and crumbled
3 garlic cloves, minced
2 tablespoons grated Romano *or* Parmesan cheese
1 teaspoon dried oregano
1 cup (4 ounces) shredded mozzarella cheese

1. In a mixing bowl, dissolve yeast in water. Add sugar; let stand 5 minutes. Add flour, salt and oil; beat until smooth. Cover; let rise in a warm place until doubled, about 15-20 minutes.

2. Punch dough down. Press onto the bottom and up the sides of a greased 14-in. pizza pan; build up edges slightly. Prick dough several times with a fork.

3. Bake at 425° for 6-8 minutes. Sprinkle remaining ingredients over crust in order listed. Bake for 13-15 minutes or until crust is golden and cheese is melted. Cut into wedges. **Yield:** 8 servings.

🎗🎗🎗
Spiced Pork Potpie

Kay Krause, Sioux Falls, South Dakota

Chock-full of cranberries, apple, sweet potatoes, cinnamon and cloves, this scrumptious meat pie smells just like autumn as it bakes! The original recipe called for a pastry crust, but I prefer the fuss-free batter crust on top.

1-1/2 pounds cubed pork shoulder roast
  1/2 cup butter, *divided*
    2 cups apple cider *or* juice
    1 cup water
    1 cup chopped peeled tart apple
  1/2 cup dried cranberries
  1/2 cup dried pitted prunes, chopped
    2 teaspoons ground cinnamon
1-1/2 teaspoons ground ginger
    2 whole cloves
    6 tablespoons all-purpose flour
    1 can (15 ounces) sweet potatoes, drained and cubed

CRUST:
    1 cup all-purpose flour
1-1/2 teaspoons baking powder
  1/2 teaspoon salt
  3/4 cup milk
  1/2 cup butter, melted

1. In a Dutch oven, cook pork in 2 tablespoons butter until no longer pink. Add the cider and water; bring to a boil. Reduce heat; simmer for 10 minutes. Stir in the fruit and seasonings; simmer 10 minutes longer.

2. Melt remaining butter; stir in flour until smooth. Slowly add to meat mixture. Bring to a boil; cook for 1-2 minutes or until thickened. Discard cloves. Stir in sweet potatoes. Pour into a greased 3-qt. baking dish.

3. For crust, combine the flour, baking powder and salt in a bowl. Combine the milk and butter; stir into dry ingredients until smooth. Spread over filling. Bake at 400° for 28-32 minutes or until crust is browned.
Yield: 6 servings.

🎀🎀🎀
Marinated Beef Tenderloin

Connie Scheffer, Salina, Kansas

My three grown children and grandkids enjoy this tempting tenderloin. Leftovers make wonderful sandwiches with fresh bread and Dijon mustard. I sometimes substitute a marinated eye of round roast…and it turns out fine.

    1 cup soy sauce
  3/4 cup beef broth
  1/2 cup olive oil
    2 tablespoons red wine vinegar
    4 to 5 garlic cloves, minced
    1 teaspoon coarsely ground pepper
    1 teaspoon dried thyme
  1/2 teaspoon salt
  1/2 teaspoon hot pepper sauce
    1 bay leaf
    1 whole beef tenderloin (3-1/2 to 4 pounds)

1. In a bowl, combine the first nine ingredients; mix well. Cover and refrigerate 1 cup for basting. Pour remaining marinade into a large resealable plastic bag; add bay leaf and tenderloin. Seal bag and turn to coat; refrigerate overnight.

2. Drain and discard marinade and bay leaf. Place tenderloin on a rack in a shallow roasting pan. Bake, uncovered, at 425° for 55-60 minutes or until meat reaches desired doneness (for medium-rare, a meat thermometer should read 145°; medium, 160°; well-done, 170°), basting often with reserved marinade. Let stand for 15 minutes before slicing. **Yield:** 6-8 servings.

🎀🎀🎀
Pepperoni Pasta Bake

Delores Marie Kolosovsky, Dodgeville, Wisconsin

Here's my version of a family-favorite Italian restaurant entree. For a change of pace, I substitute hamburger for pepperoni, add Italian seasonings and use a mix of fun pasta shapes.

    3 cups uncooked wagon wheel *or* spiral pasta
    1 can (4 ounces) mushroom stems and pieces, undrained
    1 package (3-1/2 ounces) sliced pepperoni, quartered
  3/4 cup chopped green pepper
    1 medium onion, chopped
    1 jar (14 ounces) spaghetti sauce
    1 can (8 ounces) tomato sauce
    1 can (6 ounces) tomato paste
    1 cup (4 ounces) shredded cheddar cheese
    2 cups (8 ounces) shredded mozzarella cheese

1. Cook pasta according to package directions; drain and place in a large bowl. Add mushrooms, pepperoni, green pepper and onion. Stir in spaghetti sauce, tomato sauce, tomato paste and cheddar cheese; mix well.

2. Transfer to a greased 3-qt. baking dish. Cover and bake at 350° for 50 minutes. Uncover; sprinkle with mozzarella cheese. Bake 10 minutes longer or until cheese is melted. **Yield:** 6 servings.

🎖🎖🎖
Busy Day Beef Stew

Beth Wyatt, Paris, Kentucky

Here's a classic, old-fashioned beef stew that simmers for hours in the slow cooker. I call it my "lazy" stew because it's so easy to make on busy days.

- 1 boneless beef chuck roast (1 to 1-1/2 pounds)
- 1 envelope onion soup mix
- 2 teaspoons browning sauce, optional
- 1/2 teaspoon salt
- 1/2 teaspoon pepper
- 6 cups water
- 2 cups cubed peeled potatoes (1/2-inch pieces)
- 6 to 8 medium carrots, cut into chunks
- 1 medium onion, chopped
- 1 cup frozen peas, thawed
- 1 cup frozen corn, thawed, optional
- 5 tablespoons cornstarch
- 6 tablespoons cold water

1. Place roast in a slow cooker; sprinkle with soup mix, browning sauce if desired, salt and pepper. Pour water over meat. Cover and cook on low for 8 hours.

2. Remove roast to a cutting board; let stand for 5 minutes. Add vegetables to slow cooker. Cube beef and return to slow cooker. Cover and cook on low for 1-1/2 hours or until vegetables are tender.

3. Combine cornstarch and cold water until smooth; stir into stew. Cover and cook on high for 30-45 minutes or until thickened. **Yield:** 8-10 servings.

🎖🎖🎖
Meaty Chili Lasagna

Melba NeSmith, Corsicana, Texas

My mother-in-law has been gone for years, but her recipe is still in great demand at family gatherings and potluck suppers. Serve this lasagna with salad, bread and a light dessert to satisfy the heartiest appetites.

- 12 uncooked lasagna noodles
- 1-1/2 pounds ground beef
- 1 medium onion, chopped
- 1 medium green pepper, chopped
- 2 to 3 jalapeno peppers, seeded and chopped
- 1 to 2 tablespoons chili powder
- 1 garlic clove, minced
- 1 can (10-3/4 ounces) condensed cream of mushroom soup, undiluted
- 1 cup frozen corn
- 1 can (8 ounces) tomato sauce
- 3 tablespoons tomato paste
- 1 can (2-1/4 ounces) sliced ripe olives, drained
- 4 cups (16 ounces) shredded cheddar cheese

1. Cook noodles according to package directions. Meanwhile, in a large skillet, cook beef, onion, peppers, chili powder and garlic over medium heat until meat is no longer pink; drain. Add the soup, corn, tomato sauce, tomato paste and olives; simmer until heated through.

2. Drain noodles. Spread 1/2 cup meat sauce in a greased 13-in. x 9-in. x 2-in. baking dish. Layer with four noodles, half of the remaining sauce and a third of the cheese. Repeat layers once. Top with remaining noodles and cheese. Cover and bake at 350° for 30 minutes. Uncover; bake 15 minutes longer or until cheese is melted. Let stand for 15 minutes before cutting. **Yield:** 12 servings.

Editor's Note: When cutting or seeding hot peppers, use rubber or plastic gloves to protect your hands. Avoid touching your face.

Sausage Spaghetti Pie

Linda Remillard, Bonaire, Georgia

I have made freezer meals for years now, and this is by far my most requested. In fact, I like to make several of these Italian pies at one time so we can have one every week for more than a month! With its lasagna-like flavor, this dish is very tasty when it's hot from the oven.

- 1 package (1 pound) spaghetti
- 4 eggs, beaten
- 2/3 cup grated Parmesan cheese
- 1 cup chopped onion
- 1/4 cup butter
- 2 cups (16 ounces) sour cream
- 2 teaspoons Italian seasoning
- 2 pounds bulk pork sausage
- 2 cups water
- 1 can (12 ounces) tomato paste
- 1 cup (4 ounces) shredded mozzarella cheese
- 1/2 cup shredded cheddar cheese

1. Cook spaghetti according to package directions; drain and place in a large bowl. Add eggs and Parmesan cheese. Transfer to three greased 9-in. pie plates; press mixture onto the bottom and up the sides to form a crust. Set aside.

2. In a saucepan, saute onion in butter until tender. Remove from the heat; stir in sour cream and Italian seasoning. Spoon into the crusts. In a skillet, cook the sausage over medium heat until no longer pink; drain. Stir in water and tomato paste. Simmer, uncovered, for 5-10 minutes or until thickened. Spoon over sour cream mixture. Sprinkle with mozzarella and cheddar cheeses.

3. Cover and freeze two pies for up to 1 month. Cover and bake third pie at 350° for 35-40 minutes or until heated through. **Yield:** 3 pies (6 servings each).

To use frozen pies: Completely thaw in the refrigerator. Remove from the refrigerator 30 minutes before baking. Bake as directed.

Zesty Mustard Chicken

Michael Everidge, Morristown, Tennessee

Whether you're grilling a broiler chicken or chicken breasts, consider this lip-smacking glaze. There are only four ingredients in the honey-mustard sauce, so you can whip it up in minutes.

- 1/2 cup prepared mustard
- 1/2 cup honey
- 1 tablespoon salt-free seasoning blend
- 1 tablespoon Worcestershire sauce
- 1 broiler/fryer chicken (3 pounds), cut in half

1. In a bowl, combine the first four ingredients; mix well. Carefully loosen the skin of the chicken; spoon some of the mustard sauce under the skin.

2. Coat grill rack with nonstick cooking spray before starting the grill. Place chicken skin side up on grill rack. Grill, covered, over indirect medium heat for 20 minutes. Turn; grill 20-30 minutes longer or until juices run clear, basting occasionally with remaining mustard sauce. Remove chicken skin; cut into serving-size pieces. **Yield:** 6 servings.

Ravioli with Shrimp Tomato Sauce

Nettie Smith, Loveland, Colorado

I came up with this recipe after I sampled a similar dish when my husband and I went out to dinner to celebrate our 25th anniversary. Now I make it at home often.

1/2 cup chopped onion
2 tablespoons butter
2 tablespoons all-purpose flour
1 can (14-1/2 ounces) Italian stewed tomatoes
1 tablespoon brown sugar
1 bay leaf
1 whole clove
1/2 teaspoon dried basil
1/2 teaspoon salt
1/8 to 1/4 teaspoon pepper

2 packages (9 ounces *each*) fresh *or* frozen small cheese ravioli
1-1/2 cups heavy whipping cream, warmed
1/2 pound cooked medium shrimp, peeled and deveined
1 tablespoon grated Parmesan cheese
1 tablespoon minced chives

1. In a skillet, saute onion in butter until tender. Stir in flour until blended. Bring to a boil; cook and stir until thickened. Puree the tomatoes in a blender or food processor; add to onion mixture. Stir in the brown sugar, bay leaf, clove, basil, salt and pepper. Bring to a boil. Reduce heat; cover and simmer for 10 minutes.

2. Meanwhile, cook ravioli according to package directions. Remove and discard bay leaf and clove from the sauce. Reduce heat; gradually stir in cream. Add shrimp; heat through. Drain ravioli; top with sauce, Parmesan cheese and chives. **Yield:** 5 servings.

Pork Chops with Apples And Stuffing

Joan Hamilton, Worcester, Massachusetts

The heartwarming taste of cinnamon and apples is the perfect accompaniment to these tender pork chops.

- 6 boneless pork loin chops (1 inch thick)
- 1 tablespoon vegetable oil
- 1 package (6 ounces) crushed stuffing mix
- 1 can (21 ounces) apple pie filling with cinnamon

1. In a skillet, brown pork chops in oil over medium-high heat. Meanwhile, prepare stuffing according to package directions. Spread pie filling into a greased 13-in. x 9-in. x 2-in. baking dish. Place the pork chops on top; spoon stuffing over chops.

2. Cover and bake at 350° for 35 minutes. Uncover; bake 10 minutes longer or until a meat thermometer reads 160°. **Yield:** 6 servings.

Pasta Crab Casserole

Georgia Mountain, Tampa, Florida

This is an easy dish to freeze ahead for company. A yummy combination of spiral pasta, crab and sauteed veggies is coated with a buttery sauce, then covered with cheddar cheese. All that's needed to complete the meal is warm garlic bread and a tossed green salad.

- 8 ounces uncooked spiral pasta
- 2 large onions, chopped
- 1/2 pound fresh mushrooms, sliced
- 1/2 cup chopped green pepper
- 2 garlic cloves, minced
- 1/2 cup butter
- 2 packages (8 ounces *each*) imitation crabmeat, chopped
- 1/2 cup sour cream
- 2 teaspoons salt
- 1-1/2 teaspoons dried basil
- 1-1/2 cups (6 ounces) shredded cheddar cheese

1. Cook pasta according to package directions. Meanwhile, in a skillet, saute onions, mushrooms, green pepper and garlic in butter until crisp-tender. Remove from the heat. Drain pasta; add to vegetable mixture. Stir in the crab, sour cream, salt and basil.

2. Transfer to two greased 8-in. square baking dishes. Sprinkle with cheese. Cover and freeze one casserole for up to 1 month. Cover and bake the second casserole at 350° for 20 minutes. Uncover and bake 5 minutes longer. **Yield:** 2 casseroles (4-6 servings each).

To use frozen casserole: Thaw in the refrigerator for 24 hours. Remove from the refrigerator 30 minutes before baking. Cover and bake at 350° for 55-60 minutes or until heated through.

🎀 🎀 🎀
Greek Shepherd's Pie

Sharon Ann McCray, San Francisco, California

It's hard to resist a big scoop of this comforting casserole with its fluffy mashed potato topping. Eggplant, lamb and ground turkey complement each other nicely in the filling.

- 4 large potatoes, peeled and cubed
- 1/2 cup sour cream
- 1/4 cup butter

5-1/2 cups cubed eggplant (about 1 large)
- 2 teaspoons salt
- 2 tablespoons all-purpose flour
- 1/4 cup vegetable oil
- 1 pound ground lamb
- 1/2 pound ground turkey
- 1 jar (26 ounces) meatless spaghetti sauce
- 2 tablespoons dried minced onion
- 2 tablespoons minced fresh parsley
- 1 teaspoon garlic powder
- 1/2 teaspoon dried rosemary, crushed
- 1/2 teaspoon dried basil
- 1/2 teaspoon pepper
- 1 cup (4 ounces) crumbled feta cheese

1. In a large saucepan, cook potatoes in boiling water until tender; drain. Mash potatoes with sour cream and butter; set aside. In a bowl, combine eggplant and salt. Let stand for 10 minutes; drain. Add flour and toss to coat. In a skillet, cook eggplant in oil over medium heat until browned and oil is absorbed. Transfer to a greased 3-qt. baking dish.

2. In the same skillet, cook lamb and turkey over medium heat until no longer pink; drain. Stir in spaghetti sauce, onion, parsley and seasonings. Cook until heated through, about 5 minutes. Pour over eggplant; sprinkle with feta cheese. Spread mashed potatoes over top.

3. Bake, uncovered, at 350° for 35-45 minutes or until top begins to brown. Let stand for 10-15 minutes before serving. **Yield:** 6 servings.

🎀 🎀 🎀
Cider-Baked Country Ham

Marion Lowery, Medford, Oregon

This is the best ham I've ever made. I serve it often to family and friends, and each time I get requests for the recipe.

- 1/2 bone-in fully cooked ham (5 to 7 pounds)
- 2 quarts apple cider or apple juice
- 1-1/2 teaspoons whole peppercorns
- 1 bay leaf
- Whole cloves
- 1 cup applesauce
- 1 tablespoon prepared horseradish
- 2 teaspoons ground mustard

1. Place ham in a Dutch oven or large kettle. Add cider, peppercorns and bay leaf. Add enough water just to cover; bring to a boil. Reduce heat; cover and simmer for 1 hour.

2. Drain, reserving 3 cups cooking liquid; discard peppercorns and bay leaf. Remove skin from ham if desired; score the surface with shallow cuts, making diamond shapes. Insert whole cloves in the center of each dia-

mond. Combine applesauce, horseradish and mustard; rub over ham.

3. Place ham on a rack in a shallow roasting pan; pour reserved liquid into pan. Bake, uncovered, at 350° for 1 hour or until a meat thermometer reads 140°. Remove from the oven; cover with foil and let stand for 10-15 minutes before slicing. **Yield:** 16-20 servings.

🎀 🎀 🎀
Spaghetti 'n' Meatballs

Marilou Krumm, Stanhope, Iowa

My mom's Italian friend taught her the secret to this saucy spaghetti dish. Our whole family is grateful!

  2 eggs
  1 cup dry bread crumbs
  1/2 cup grated Parmesan cheese
  1/2 cup tomato juice, milk *or* beef broth
  1/4 cup finely chopped green pepper
  1/4 cup finely chopped onion
  1 teaspoon Italian seasoning
  1/2 teaspoon *each* salt, poultry seasoning and garlic powder
  2 pounds bulk pork sausage
SAUCE:
  4 cups water
  2 cans (11-1/2 ounces *each*) tomato juice
  3 cans (6 ounces *each*) tomato paste
  1 jar (1/2 ounce) dried celery flakes
  1 bay leaf
  1 teaspoon Italian seasoning
  1 teaspoon salt
  1/2 teaspoon pepper
  1/2 cup finely chopped green pepper
  1/2 cup finely chopped onion
  2 garlic cloves, minced
Hot cooked spaghetti

1. In a large bowl, combine eggs, bread crumbs, Parmesan cheese, tomato juice, green pepper, onion and seasonings. Crumble sausage over mixture and mix well. Shape into 1-in. balls. In a skillet, brown meatballs over medium heat; drain.

2. In a large saucepan, combine first eight sauce ingredients. Add green pepper, onion and garlic. Bring to a boil. Reduce heat; simmer, uncovered, for 30-45 minutes or until thickened, stirring occasionally. Discard bay leaf.

3. Add meatballs to sauce; simmer for 1 hour or until meat is no longer pink. Serve over spaghetti. **Yield:** 10 servings.

🎀 🎀 🎀
Sausage Spinach Turnovers

Vicky Henry, Aurora, Colorado

One Christmas, I gave these tasty meat pies to our neighbors as gifts instead of sweets—they loved them! I freeze leftovers and reheat them later in the microwave when I need a quick meal.

  1 pound bulk pork sausage
  1/3 cup chopped onion
  1 package (10 ounces) frozen chopped spinach, thawed and squeezed dry
1-1/2 cups (6 ounces) shredded sharp cheddar cheese
  2 teaspoons prepared mustard
  1 teaspoon dried marjoram
Salt and pepper to taste
  1 loaf (16 ounces) frozen bread dough, thawed
  1 egg white, beaten

1. In a skillet, cook sausage and onion over medium heat until meat is no longer pink; drain. Stir in the spinach, cheese, mustard, marjoram, salt and pepper. Cook and stir until cheese is melted. Remove from the heat; cool slightly.

2. Divide dough into eight portions; roll each into a

6-in. circle. Spoon about 1/2 cup meat mixture on half of each circle. Brush edges with egg white; fold dough over filling and press edges with a fork to seal. Place on greased baking sheets. Cover and let rise in a warm place for 20 minutes.

3. Brush tops with egg white; cut slits in the top of each. Bake at 350° for 20 minutes or until golden brown. **Yield:** 8 turnovers.

1/2 cup ketchup, *divided*
  1 egg
1/4 cup dry bread crumbs
  1 teaspoon onion powder
  1 pound lean ground beef
  2 teaspoons prepared mustard
  2 teaspoons dill pickle relish
  6 slices process American cheese

1. In a bowl, combine 1/4 cup ketchup, egg, bread crumbs and onion powder. Crumble beef over mixture and mix well. On a large piece of waxed paper, pat beef mixture into a 10-in. x 6-in. rectangle. Spread remaining ketchup over meat to within 1/2 in. of long sides and 1-1/2 in. of short sides. Top with mustard and relish.

2. Place four cheese slices on top; set remaining cheese aside. Roll up loaf, jelly-roll style, starting with a short side and pulling away waxed paper while rolling. Seal seams and ends well. Place loaf, seam side down, in a greased 11-in. x 7-in. x 2-in. baking pan.

3. Bake at 350° for 45 minutes or until meat is no longer pink and a meat thermometer reads 160°. Cut the reserved cheese slices in half diagonally; place on top of loaf. Return to the oven for 5 minutes or until cheese is melted. Let stand for 10 minutes before slicing. **Yield:** 6 servings.

🎗🎗🎗

Cheeseburger Meat Loaf

Paula Sullivan, Barker, New York

I created this meat loaf one day when I wanted to make cheeseburgers but it was too chilly to grill outside. I've served it numerous times since then, and it never fails to get rave reviews. Even your most finicky eater will enjoy this oven-baked main dish.

🎗🎗🎗

Slow-Cooked Rump Roast

Mimi Walker, Palmyra, Pennsylvania

I enjoy a good pot roast, but I was tired of the same old thing…so I started experimenting. Cooking the beef in horseradish sauce gives it a tangy flavor. Even my kids love this roast with its tender veggies and gravy.

  1 boneless beef rump roast (3 to 3-1/2 pounds)
  2 tablespoons vegetable oil
  4 medium carrots, halved lengthwise and cut into 2-inch pieces
  3 medium potatoes, peeled and cut into chunks
  2 small onions, sliced
1/2 cup water
  6 to 8 tablespoons horseradish sauce
1/4 cup red wine vinegar
1/4 cup Worcestershire sauce
  2 garlic cloves, minced
1-1/2 to 2 teaspoons celery salt
  3 tablespoons cornstarch
1/3 cup cold water

1. Cut roast in half. In a large skillet, brown meat on all sides in oil over medium-high heat; drain. Place carrots and potatoes in a 5-qt. slow cooker. Top with meat and onions. Combine the water, horseradish sauce, vinegar, Worcestershire sauce, garlic and celery salt. Pour over meat. Cover and cook on low for 10-11 hours or until meat and vegetables are tender.

2. Combine cornstarch and cold water until smooth; stir into slow cooker. Cover and cook on high for 30 minutes or until gravy is thickened. **Yield:** 6-8 servings.

🏅🏅🏅
Bruschetta Chicken

Carolin Cattoi-Demkiw, Lethbridge, Alberta

My husband and I enjoy serving this to company as well as family. It looks like we fussed, but it's fast and easy to fix.

✓ Uses less fat, sugar or salt. Includes Nutritional Analysis and Diabetic Exchanges.

- **1/2 cup all-purpose flour**
- **2 eggs, lightly beaten**
- **4 boneless skinless chicken breast halves (1 pound)**
- **1/4 cup grated Parmesan cheese**
- **1/4 cup dry bread crumbs**
- **1 tablespoon butter, melted**
- **2 large tomatoes, seeded and chopped**
- **3 tablespoons minced fresh basil**
- **2 garlic cloves, minced**
- **1 tablespoon olive oil**
- **1/2 teaspoon salt**
- **1/4 teaspoon pepper**

1. Place flour and eggs in separate shallow bowls. Dip chicken in flour, then in eggs; place in a greased 13-in. x 9-in. x 2-in. baking dish. Combine the Parmesan cheese, bread crumbs and butter; sprinkle over chicken. Loosely cover baking dish with foil.

2. Bake at 375° for 20 minutes. Uncover; bake 5-10 minutes longer or until top is browned.

3. Meanwhile, in a bowl, combine the remaining ingredients. Spoon over the chicken. Return to the oven for 3-5 minutes or until tomato mixture is heated through. **Yield:** 4 servings.

Nutritional Analysis: One serving (prepared with 1/2 cup egg substitute) equals 358 calories, 13 g fat (5 g saturated fat), 86 mg cholesterol, 623 mg sodium, 22 g carbohydrate, 2 g fiber, 36 g protein. **Diabetic Exchanges:** 4-1/2 lean meat, 1 starch, 1 vegetable.

1-1/2 cups beef broth
   2 celery ribs, chopped
   2 large carrots, cut into 1/4-inch slices
   1 medium onion, chopped
   1 can (46 ounces) V8 juice
   1 can (14-1/2 ounces) Italian diced tomatoes, undrained
   2 cans (6 ounces *each*) Italian tomato paste
   1 tablespoon dried oregano
1-1/2 teaspoons pepper
  1/4 teaspoon garlic powder
  3/4 pound ground pork
  3/4 cup canned kidney beans, rinsed and drained
  3/4 cup canned great northern beans, rinsed and drained
   1 cup medium shell pasta, cooked and drained
Shredded Parmesan cheese

1. In a large saucepan, combine the broth, celery, carrots and onion. Bring to a boil. Reduce heat; cover and simmer for 5-7 minutes or until vegetables are crisp-tender. Stir in the V8 juice, tomatoes, tomato paste, oregano, pepper and garlic powder. Cover and simmer for 40-45 minutes.

2. Meanwhile, in a skillet, cook pork over medium heat until no longer pink; drain. Add meat and beans to soup; cover and simmer 30-45 minutes longer or until heated through. Stir in pasta just before serving. Garnish with Parmesan cheese. **Yield:** 8 servings.

🎗🎗🎗
Peasant Pasta Stew

Eileen Snider, Cincinnati, Ohio

When I was trying to duplicate a favorite restaurant recipe, I came up with this hearty stew. Pork, pasta, vegetables and beans in a thick tomato broth make it a comforting meal. My husband and I love the savory Italian flavor.

🎗🎗🎗
Chicken Carrot Fried Rice

Peggy Spieckermann, Joplin, Missouri

A dear friend shared this colorful stir-fry when my children were small. It quickly won over those picky eaters! To cut down on prep time, I make the rice ahead and often marinate the chicken beforehand.

  3/4 pound boneless skinless chicken breasts, cubed
    4 tablespoons soy sauce, *divided*
    2 garlic cloves, minced
1-1/2 cups chopped fresh broccoli
    3 green onions, sliced
    2 tablespoons vegetable oil, *divided*
    3 large carrots, shredded
    4 cups cold cooked rice
  1/4 teaspoon pepper

1. In a bowl, combine the chicken, 1 tablespoon soy sauce and garlic; set aside. In a large skillet or wok, stir-fry the broccoli and green onions in 1 tablespoon oil for 5 minutes. Add carrots; stir-fry 4 minutes longer or until crisp-tender. Remove and set aside.

2. In the same skillet, stir-fry chicken in remaining oil until no longer pink and juices run clear. Add the rice, pepper, vegetables and remaining soy sauce. Stir-fry until heated through. **Yield:** 4-6 servings.

❧❧❧
Cheesy Veal Pie

Grace Epperson, Richmond, Michigan

This pie tastes just like veal Parmesan in a savory pastry crust. My daughter often asked me to make it for her birthday dinner. I've also made it with chicken, and it's just as tasty.

    1/2 cup all-purpose flour
      1 pound veal *or boneless skinless chicken
        breasts, cubed*
    1/4 cup butter
      1 can (14-1/2 ounces) diced tomatoes, undrained
      1 can (8 ounces) tomato sauce
    1/4 cup chopped onion

      1 teaspoon dried basil
    1/2 teaspoon garlic salt
    1/2 teaspoon dried oregano
    1/8 teaspoon pepper
      3 tablespoons grated Parmesan cheese
HERB-CHEESE CRUST:
  1-1/2 cups all-purpose flour
    1/4 cup grated Parmesan cheese
      1 teaspoon garlic salt
      1 teaspoon dried oregano
    1/2 cup cold butter
      4 to 6 tablespoons cold water
    1/2 cup shredded cheddar cheese

1. Place flour in a large resealable bag; add veal in batches and shake to coat. In a skillet, cook veal in butter until no longer pink. Add tomatoes, tomato sauce, onion and seasonings. Bring to a boil. Reduce heat; cover and simmer for 30 minutes or until meat is tender. Stir in Parmesan cheese.

2. In a bowl, combine the first four crust ingredients. Cut in butter until crumbly. Gradually add water, tossing with a fork until dough forms a ball. Divide in half. Roll out one portion to fit a 9-in. pie plate; place in plate. Trim pastry to 1/2 in. beyond edge of plate; flute edges. Add filling. Top with cheddar cheese.

3. Roll out remaining pastry to 1/8-in. thickness. With a 2-in. biscuit cutter, cut out circles; place over cheese, overlapping slightly. Bake at 400° for 35-40 minutes or until golden brown. **Yield:** 6-8 servings.

❧❧❧
Glazed Holiday Pork Roast

Sherry Kreiger, York, Pennsylvania

With its sweet and tangy fruit glaze, this pretty pork roast is perfect for a holiday meal. But don't save it for special occasions! My husband and son love this warm and satisfying supper whenever I serve it.

      1 pork rib roast (4 to 4-1/2 pounds)
      1 cup mixed dried fruit, *divided*
    2/3 cup water
    2/3 cup honey
      1 envelope onion soup mix
    1/4 cup ketchup
      2 tablespoons lemon juice
      2 teaspoons grated lemon peel

1. Make 15-20 slits, about 1 to 1-1/2 in. deep, in the roast; place some fruit in each slit. In a bowl, combine the water, honey, soup mix, ketchup, lemon juice, peel and remaining fruit; mix well.

2. Place roast fat side up in a roasting pan. Pour fruit mixture over the top. Cover and bake at 325° for 3 to

3-1/2 hours or until a meat thermometer reads 160°. Let stand for 10-15 minutes before carving. **Yield:** 6-8 servings.

🎗 🎗 🎗

Beef-Stuffed Sopaipillas

Lara Pennell, Irving, Texas

After my brothers' football games when we were kids, we'd descend on a local restaurant for their wonderful Southwestern stuffed sopaipillas. This recipe takes me back to that delicious childhood memory. Even my Canadian husband raves about these!

   2 **cups all-purpose flour**
   1 **teaspoon salt**
   1 **teaspoon baking powder**
1/2 **cup water**
1/4 **cup evaporated milk**
1-1/2 **teaspoons vegetable oil**
Additional oil for frying
FILLING:
   1 **pound ground beef**
3/4 **cup chopped onion**
1/2 **teaspoon salt**
1/2 **teaspoon garlic powder**
1/4 **teaspoon pepper**

SAUCE:
   1 **can (10-3/4 ounces) condensed cream of chicken soup, undiluted**
1/2 **cup chicken broth**
   1 **can (4 ounces) chopped green chilies**
1/2 **teaspoon onion powder**
   2 **cups (8 ounces) shredded cheddar cheese**

1. In a bowl, combine the flour, salt and baking powder. Stir in water, milk and oil with a fork until a ball forms. On a lightly floured surface, knead dough gently for 2-3 minutes. Cover and let stand for 15 minutes. Divide into four portions; roll each into a 6-1/2-in. circle.

2. In an electric skillet or deep-fat fryer, heat oil to 375°. Fry circles, one at a time, for 2-3 minutes on each side or until golden brown. Drain on paper towels.

3. In a skillet, cook beef and onion over medium heat until meat is no longer pink; drain. Stir in the salt, garlic powder and pepper. In a saucepan, combine soup, broth, chilies and onion powder; cook for 10 minutes or until heated through. Cut a slit on one side of each sopaipilla; fill with 1/2 cup of meat mixture. Top with cheese. Serve with sauce. **Yield:** 4 servings.

🏅🏅🏅
Stuffed Pork Tenderloin

Dale Ann Glover, Strathroy, Ontario

I combined part of one recipe and part of another to come up with this extra-special roast.

- 2 **pork tenderloins (1 pound** *each*)
- 2 **tablespoons vegetable oil**
- 2 **tablespoons soy sauce**
- 2 **tablespoons lemon juice**
- 1/4 **cup finely chopped celery**
- 2 **tablespoons finely chopped onion**
- 2 **tablespoons butter**
- 2 **cups soft bread crumbs**
- 1/2 **cup chopped apple**
- 2 **tablespoons raisins**
- 2 **tablespoons red currant** *or* **raspberry jelly**
- 3/4 **teaspoon salt**
- 1/4 **teaspoon poultry seasoning**

Dash pepper
Dash dried rosemary, crushed
- 6 **bacon strips**

1. Cut a lengthwise slit down the center of each tenderloin to within 1/2 in. of bottom; open tenderloins so they lie flat. Cover with plastic wrap; pound to flatten to 3/4-in. thickness. Remove plastic wrap.

2. In a large resealable plastic bag, combine the oil, soy sauce and lemon juice; add tenderloins. Seal bag and turn to coat; refrigerate for 8 hours or overnight.

3. In a skillet, saute celery and onion in butter until tender. Remove from the heat. Stir in bread crumbs, apple, raisins, jelly, salt, poultry seasoning, pepper and rosemary. Remove tenderloins from marinade; discard marinade.

4. Spread stuffing down the center of one tenderloin; top with second tenderloin. Tie several times with kitchen string and secure ends with toothpicks. Arrange bacon over the top.

5. Place on a rack in a shallow roasting pan. Bake, uncovered, at 350° for 1 hour or until a meat thermometer reads 160°. Broil 4-6 in. from the heat for 4-5 minutes or until bacon is browned and crisp. Let stand for 10-15 minutes before slicing. **Yield:** 4-6 servings.

🏅 🏅 🏅
Spanish Noodles 'n' Ground Beef

Kelli Jones, Perris, California

Bacon adds flavor to this stovetop supper my mom made when we were growing up. Now I prepare it for my family.

- 1 **pound ground beef**
- 1 **small green pepper, chopped**
- 1 **small onion, chopped**
- 3-1/4 **cups uncooked medium** *egg* **noodles**
- 1 **can (14-1/2 ounces) diced tomatoes, undrained**
- 1 **cup water**
- 1/4 **cup chili sauce**
- 1 **teaspoon salt**
- 1/8 **teaspoon pepper**
- 4 **bacon strips, cooked and crumbled**

1. In a large skillet over medium heat, cook beef, green pepper and onion until meat is no longer pink; drain.

2. Stir in noodles, tomatoes, water, chili sauce, salt and pepper; mix well. Cover and cook over low heat for 15-

20 minutes or until the noodles are tender, stirring frequently. Add bacon. **Yield:** 5 servings.

Mandarin Glazed Beets, p. 141

Okra Medley, p. 128

Hearty Twice-Baked Potatoes, p. 137

Side Dishes & Condiments

Scalloped Potatoes And Veggies, p. 133

When you need to round out a meal with delicious side dishes that complement your main course, turn to this chapter. You'll find tried-and-true classics plus some new favorites.

Orange-Nut Sweet Potatoes, p. 144

🎀🎀🎀
Okra Medley

(Pictured on page 126)

Nona Cheatham, McRae, Arkansas

My husband, Charles, came up with this recipe. Pair it with a crispy pan of hot corn bread and you have a wonderful, healthy meal.

> 1 medium onion, chopped
> 2 tablespoons butter
> 2 cups sliced fresh okra
> 3 to 4 medium tomatoes, peeled and chopped
> 2 cups fresh *or* frozen corn
> 1 teaspoon sugar
> 1 teaspoon salt
> 1/4 teaspoon pepper

In a large saucepan, saute onion in butter until tender. Add okra; cook and stir for 5 minutes. Stir in the remaining ingredients; bring to a boil. Reduce heat; cover and simmer for 10-15 minutes or until corn is tender. **Yield:** 4-6 servings.

🎀🎀🎀
Orange Candied Carrots

Lori Lockrey, West Hill, Ontario

My son always asks for these carrot coins at Thanksgiving. The orange flavor in the sweet, mild sauce really comes through. This pleasant side dish is a great way to dress up a meal of holiday leftovers.

> 1 pound carrots, cut into 1/2-inch slices
> 1/4 cup butter, softened, cubed
> 1/4 cup jellied cranberry sauce
> 1 orange peel strip (1 to 3 inches)
> 2 tablespoons brown sugar
> 1/2 teaspoon salt

1. Place 1 in. of water and carrots in a skillet; bring to a boil. Reduce heat; cover and simmer for 15-20 minutes or until crisp-tender.

2. Meanwhile, in a blender, combine the butter, cranberry sauce, orange peel, brown sugar and salt. Cover and process until blended. Drain carrots; drizzle with cranberry mixture. **Yield:** 3 servings.

★ ★ ★
Ham 'n' Cheese Mashed Potatoes

Debra Herlihy, Swedesboro, New Jersey

The way I dress up leftover ham and mashed potatoes is a sure-fire success in my house! Cheddar cheese and cream add richness to this casserole while garlic seasons it nicely. It's something my family looks forward to having on a regular basis.

　　2 **cups mashed potatoes**
3/4 **teaspoon garlic salt**
　　1 **cup diced fully cooked ham**
　　1 **cup (4 ounces) shredded cheddar cheese**
1/2 **cup heavy whipping cream, whipped**

1. In a bowl, combine the potatoes and garlic salt. Spread into a greased 1-1/2-qt. baking dish. Sprinkle with ham. Fold cheese into whipped cream; spoon over ham.

2. Bake, uncovered, at 450° for 15 minutes or until golden brown. **Yield:** 4-6 servings.

★ ★ ★
Homemade Cajun Seasoning

Onietta Loewer, Branch, Louisiana

We in Louisiana love seasoned foods. I use this in gravy, over meats and with salads. It makes an excellent gift for teachers. Many have asked for the recipe.

　　1 **carton (26 ounces) salt**
　　2 **containers (1 ounce *each*) cayenne pepper**
1/3 **cup pepper**
1/3 **cup chili powder**
　　3 **tablespoons garlic powder**

In a bowl, combine all ingredients. Store in an airtight container. Use to season pork, chicken, seafood, steaks or vegetables. **Yield:** about 3-1/2 cups.

🎀🎀🎀
Caramelized Onions

Melba Lowery, Rockwell, North Carolina

These golden onions have a delicate taste that complements green beans, peas and almost any type of meat. Try them over steaks, on burgers, with pork chops and more.

     4 large onions, thinly sliced
 1/4 cup vegetable oil
     3 tablespoons cider vinegar
     2 tablespoons brown sugar

In a large skillet, saute onions in oil over medium heat until tender, about 15 minutes. Stir in vinegar and brown sugar. Cook 10 minutes longer or until onions are golden. **Yield:** 4-6 servings.

🎀🎀🎀
Sweet Potato Bake

Pam Holloway, Marion, Louisiana

This is an easy dish to prepare and is a perfect addition to that special holiday meal. The topping is flavorful and gives a nice contrast of textures.

     7 large sweet potatoes (about 6 pounds),
        peeled and cubed
 1/4 cup butter
 1/2 cup orange marmalade
 1/4 cup orange juice
 1/4 cup packed brown sugar
     2 teaspoons salt
     1 teaspoon ground ginger
TOPPING:
    12 oatmeal cookies, crumbled
     6 tablespoons butter, softened

1. Place sweet potatoes in a Dutch oven and cover with water; bring to a boil. Reduce heat; cover and cook just until tender, about 15 minutes. Drain well.

2. Mash potatoes with butter. Add marmalade, orange juice, brown sugar, salt and ginger. Transfer to a greased 13-in. x 9-in. x 2-in. baking dish. Toss cookie crumbs with butter; sprinkle over the top.

3. Bake, uncovered, at 400° for 20 minutes or until browned. Let stand for 15 minutes before serving. **Yield:** 10-12 servings.

🎗🎗🎗
Southwestern Spuds

Penny Dykstra, Porterville, California

I came up with this attractive side dish when my best friend unexpectedly stayed for dinner. While my husband grilled pork chops, I perked up potatoes with tasty taco fixings. The results received rave reviews. This recipe is even quicker to fix with leftover baked potatoes.

> **3 medium potatoes**
> **Salt and pepper to taste**
> **1 cup (4 ounces) shredded cheddar cheese**
> **1 cup (4 ounces) shredded pepper Jack cheese**
> **3 green onions, chopped**
> **1 can (2-1/4 ounces) sliced ripe olives, drained**
> **Sour cream and salsa, optional**

1. Pierce potatoes; place on a microwave-safe plate. Microwave on high for 8-10 minutes or until almost tender. Cool slightly; peel and cut into 1/8-in. slices.

2. Arrange half of the potatoes in a greased microwave-safe 9-in. pie plate. Season with salt and pepper. Sprinkle with half of the cheeses. Repeat layers. Top with onions and olives.

3. Microwave, uncovered, for 10 minutes or until cheese is melted and potatoes are tender. Serve with sour cream and salsa if desired. **Yield:** 4-6 servings.

Editor's Note: This recipe was tested in an 850-watt microwave.

🎀🎀🎀 Candied Sweet Potatoes

Essie Nealey, Tabor City, North Carolina

My town is known as the Yam Capital of the United States. This is a trouble-free recipe that goes well with baked ham or roasted turkey.

    3 pounds sweet potatoes *or* yams
1/2 cup packed brown sugar
    1 teaspoon ground cinnamon
1/4 cup butter, cubed
1/4 cup corn syrup

1. Place sweet potatoes in a large kettle and cover with water; cover and boil gently for 30-45 minutes or until potatoes can be easily pierced with the tip of a sharp knife. When cool enough to handle, peel the potatoes and cut into wedges.

2. Place in an ungreased 11-in. x 7-in. x 2-in. baking dish. Sprinkle with brown sugar and cinnamon. Dot with butter; drizzle with corn syrup. Bake, uncovered, at 375° for 15-20 minutes or until bubbly, basting with sauce occasionally. **Yield:** 8-10 servings.

🎀🎀🎀 Loaded Mashed Potatoes

Dawn Reuter, Oxford, Wisconsin

Tired of the same old mashed potatoes, I whipped up this new family favorite. We can't get enough of them at our house. Often, I'll prepare this dish ahead and refrigerate it. Then I bake it just before serving.

    5 pounds potatoes, peeled and cubed
3/4 cup sour cream
1/2 cup milk
    3 tablespoons butter
Salt and pepper to taste
    3 cups (12 ounces) shredded cheddar cheese
        blend, *divided*
1/2 pound sliced bacon, cooked and crumbled
    3 green onions, sliced

1. Place potatoes in a Dutch oven and cover with water; bring to a boil. Reduce heat; cover and simmer until tender. Drain and place in a mixing bowl. Add sour cream, milk, butter, salt and pepper. Beat on medium-low speed until light and fluffy. Stir in 2 cups cheese, bacon and onions.

2. Transfer to a greased 3-qt. baking dish. Top with remaining cheese. Bake, uncovered, at 350° for 30 minutes or until heated through and cheese is melted. **Yield:** 14 servings.

🎀🎀🎀
Cranberry Stuffing Balls

Bernadine Dirmeyer, Harpster, Ohio

When you're looking for a different way to prepare stuffing, you'll find these balls tasty and easy to make. They're great served with pork roast and gravy.

    1 pound bulk pork sausage
  1/2 cup chopped celery
  1/4 cup chopped onion
    2 tablespoons minced fresh parsley
    1 package (7 ounces) herb-seasoned stuffing
      croutons
  3/4 cup fresh *or* frozen cranberries, halved
    2 eggs, beaten
    1 to 1-1/2 cups chicken broth

1. In a skillet, cook sausage, celery and onion over medium heat until sausage is no longer pink and vegetables are tender; drain. Place in a large bowl; add parsley, croutons, cranberries, eggs and enough broth to hold mixture together.

2. Shape into 8-10 balls. Place in a greased shallow baking dish. Bake, uncovered, at 325° for 30 minutes. **Yield:** 8-10 servings.

🎀🎀🎀
Scalloped Potatoes And Veggies

(Pictured on page 127)

Linda Renberger, Derby, Kansas

If you're like me, you're always searching for easy side dishes. This vegetable medley in a creamy cheese sauce couldn't be simpler.

    2 large potatoes, peeled and sliced
    1 cup sliced carrots
    1 small onion, sliced
  1/4 cup water
    1 cup frozen peas
    2 tablespoons all-purpose flour
1-1/2 teaspoons seasoned salt
  1/4 teaspoon ground mustard
  1/8 teaspoon pepper
    1 cup milk
  1/2 cup cubed process cheese (Velveeta)

1. In a 2-qt. microwave-safe dish, combine the potatoes, carrots, onion and water. Cover and microwave on high for 7 minutes. Add peas; cook 4 minutes longer or until vegetables are tender.

2. Meanwhile, in a 1-qt. microwave-safe dish, combine the flour, seasoned salt, mustard, pepper and milk until smooth. Microwave, uncovered, on high for 4-5 minutes or until thickened and bubbly, stirring occasionally. Stir in cheese until melted. Drain vegetables; add cheese sauce and toss. **Yield:** 7 servings.

Editor's Note: This recipe was tested in an 850-watt microwave.

🎀 🎀 🎀

Confetti Carrot Fritters

Peggy Camp, Twain, California

Crispy, sweet and savory, these delicate fritters are a fun twist on the traditional fruit-filled variety. They're yummy served with a mustard dipping sauce, but our kids enjoy them with a drizzle of warm maple syrup, too.

      6 cups water
2-1/2 cups finely chopped carrots
   1/4 cup all-purpose flour
   1/4 teaspoon salt
   1/4 teaspoon pepper
      2 eggs, *separated*
      3 tablespoons milk
      2 tablespoons finely chopped onion
      2 tablespoons minced fresh parsley
Vegetable oil for deep-fat frying
MUSTARD SAUCE:
      1 tablespoon minced fresh parsley

      1 tablespoon red wine vinegar
      1 tablespoon Dijon mustard
      1 teaspoon finely chopped green onion
   1/4 cup olive oil

1. In a saucepan, bring water to a boil; add carrots. Return to a boil; cover and cook for 2 minutes. Drain and immediately place the carrots in ice water; drain and pat dry.

2. In a bowl, combine the flour, salt and pepper. Combine egg yolks and milk; stir into the flour mixture until smooth. Stir in the onion, parsley and carrots. In a mixing bowl, beat egg whites until stiff peaks form; fold into batter.

3. In an electric skillet, heat 1/4 in. of oil to 375°. Drop batter by 1/3 cupfuls into oil. Fry until golden brown, about 2 minutes on each side.

4. For mustard sauce, combine the parsley, vinegar, mustard and green onion in a bowl. Slowly whisk in oil until blended. Serve with the fritters. **Yield:** 9 servings.

Dutch Potato Poultry Stuffing

Sarah Krout, Warrington, Pennsylvania

All of my ancestors were Pennsylvania Dutch. Add to that the fact my father was a potato farmer, and you see why we never had a holiday dinner without potato "filling" (Pennsylvania Dutch for stuffing)!

> 5 cups mashed potatoes (without added milk, butter or seasoning)
> 6 cups cubed crustless day-old white bread
> 2-1/2 cups chopped onion
> 1 cup chopped celery leaves
> 1 cup chopped fresh parsley
> 3 tablespoons butter, melted
> 1 teaspoon salt
> 3/4 teaspoon pepper
> 1 tablespoon all-purpose flour
> 3/4 cup egg substitute
> 1 cup milk

1. In a large bowl, combine potatoes, bread cubes, onion, celery leaves, parsley, butter, salt and pepper. In a small bowl, beat flour and egg substitute; gradually stir in milk. Pour into the potato mixture and mix well. (Add more milk if stuffing seems dry.)

2. Transfer to a greased 3-qt. baking dish. Cover and bake at 325° for 60 minutes. Uncover and bake 10 minutes longer or until lightly browned. **Yield:** about 10 cups (enough for one 12- to 14-pound turkey).

Zucchini Pancakes

Teressa Eastman, El Dorado, Kansas

In place of potato pancakes, try these cute rounds that are very simple to prepare with on-hand ingredients. Not only are they tasty, they're pretty, too. To eliminate some of the fat, I use a nonstick griddle coated with butter-flavored cooking spray.

> 1/3 cup biscuit/baking mix
> 1/4 cup grated Parmesan cheese
> 1/8 teaspoon pepper
> 2 eggs, lightly beaten
> 2 cups shredded zucchini
> 2 tablespoons butter

1. In a bowl, combine the biscuit mix, Parmesan cheese, pepper and eggs just until blended. Add the zucchini; mix well.

2. In a large skillet, melt butter. Drop batter by about 1/3 cupfuls into skillet; press lightly to flatten. Fry until golden brown, about 3 minutes on each side. **Yield:** 5 pancakes.

🎗🎗🎗
Spinach Parmesan Linguine

Mary Curran, Sandwich, Illinois

If you're looking for a tasty change from plain buttered noodles, serve this pleasing pasta toss as a streamlined side dish. Frozen spinach and Parmesan cheese add lively flavor to linguine.

- 1 package (16 ounces) linguine
- 1 cup chicken broth
- 1 small onion, chopped
- 2 garlic cloves, minced
- 1 package (10 ounces) frozen chopped spinach, thawed and well drained
- 1/3 cup milk
- 2 tablespoons cream cheese
- Salt and pepper to taste
- 1 cup (4 ounces) shredded Parmesan cheese
- 1/2 cup shredded mozzarella cheese

1. Cook linguine according to package directions. Meanwhile, in a saucepan over medium-high heat, bring broth to a boil. Add onion and garlic. Reduce heat; cook, uncovered, for 5 minutes. Stir in spinach; cook for 2 minutes.

2. Add the milk, cream cheese, salt and pepper; stir until cheese is melted. Drain linguine and place in a serving bowl. Add sauce and toss to coat. Sprinkle with Parmesan and mozzarella cheeses; toss to coat. **Yield:** 10 servings.

🎗🎗🎗
Rich 'n' Cheesy Macaroni

Gwen Miller, Rolling Hills, Alberta

This delicious dish puts a new twist on traditional macaroni and cheese. The three different cheese flavors blend together wonderfully. Plus, it's easy to prepare—I plan to make it often when my husband, Ken, and I start traveling.

- 2-1/2 cups uncooked elbow macaroni
- 6 tablespoons butter, *divided*
- 1/4 cup all-purpose flour
- 1 teaspoon salt
- 1 teaspoon sugar
- 2 cups milk
- 8 ounces process cheese (Velveeta), cubed
- 1-1/3 cups small-curd cottage cheese
- 2/3 cup sour cream
- 2 cups (8 ounces) shredded sharp cheddar cheese
- 1-1/2 cups soft bread crumbs

1. Cook macaroni according to package directions; drain. Place in a greased 2-1/2-qt. baking dish. In a saucepan, melt 4 tablespoons butter. Stir in flour, salt and sugar until smooth. Gradually stir in milk. Bring to a boil; cook and stir for 2 minutes or until thickened.

2. Reduce heat; stir in process cheese until melted. Stir in cottage cheese and sour cream. Pour over macaroni. Sprinkle with cheddar cheese.

3. Melt remaining butter and toss with bread crumbs; sprinkle over top. Bake, uncovered, at 350° for 30 minutes or until golden brown. **Yield:** 6-8 servings.

🎗🎗🎗
Hearty Twice-Baked Potatoes

(Pictured on page 126)

Rebecca Williams, Alapaha, Georgia

Everyone raves about these extra-special spuds that are perfect for meat-and-potato lovers. The nicely seasoned potatoes are a great accompaniment to grilled chicken but hearty enough to serve as a comforting meal on their own.

    8 large baking potatoes
  1/2 pound bulk pork sausage
  1/4 cup butter, softened
    2 cups (8 ounces) shredded cheddar cheese
1-1/2 cups diced fully cooked ham
    6 bacon strips, cooked and crumbled
    1 cup (8 ounces) sour cream
  1/2 cup Italian salad dressing
Salt and pepper to taste

1. Scrub and pierce potatoes. Bake at 400° for 40-60 minutes or microwave, uncovered, on high for 12-14 minutes or until tender. Meanwhile, in a skillet, cook the sausage over medium heat until no longer pink; drain.

2. When potatoes are cool enough to handle, cut in half lengthwise; scoop out pulp, leaving a 1/4-in. shell. In a large mixing bowl, mash the pulp with butter. Stir in the sausage, cheese, ham, bacon, sour cream, salad dressing, salt and pepper.

3. Spoon into potato shells. Place on two ungreased baking sheets. Bake at 400° for 30 minutes or until golden brown. **Yield:** 16 servings.

🎗🎗🎗
Creamy Vegetable Casserole

Tami Kratzer, West Jordan, Utah

Searching for a different way to prepare vegetables? Look no further. I have a fussy eater in my house who absolutely loves this medley. It can be assembled in a snap, leaving time to fix the main course, set the table or just sit back and relax.

    1 package (16 ounces) frozen broccoli, carrots
        and cauliflower
    1 can (10-3/4 ounces) condensed cream of
        mushroom soup, undiluted
    1 carton (8 ounces) spreadable garden
        vegetable cream cheese
  1/2 to 1 cup seasoned croutons

1. Prepare vegetables according to package directions; drain and place in a large bowl. Stir in soup and cream cheese.

2. Transfer to a greased 1-qt. baking dish. Sprinkle with croutons. Bake, uncovered, at 375° for 25 minutes or until bubbly. **Yield:** 6 servings.

🎀🎀🎀
Dilly Zucchini Casserole

Esther Kilborn, Bridgton, Maine

Whenever I take this time-saving side-dish casserole to a potluck, I seldom bring any home, and folks often ask for the recipe. If I have fresh dill, I'll substitute a couple tablespoons for the dill weed.

> 1 cup biscuit/baking mix
> 1/2 cup grated Parmesan cheese
> 1 tablespoon dill weed
> 1 teaspoon salt
> 1/8 teaspoon pepper
> 4 eggs, beaten
> 1/2 cup vegetable oil
> 3 cups chopped zucchini
> 1 large onion, chopped

1. In a bowl, combine biscuit mix, Parmesan cheese, dill, salt and pepper. Add eggs and oil; mix well. Stir in zucchini and onion until blended. Pour into a greased 1-1/2-qt. baking dish.

2. Bake, uncovered, at 375° for 25-30 minutes or until golden brown. **Yield:** 5 servings.

🎀🎀🎀
Oven-Roasted Carrots

Marlene Schott, Devine, Texas

My seven children and 15 grandchildren really look forward to carrots when they're prepared this flavorful way. As a cook at our local school, I served two generations of my brood, plus relatives and friends from all over our area.

> 2 pounds baby carrots
> 4 small onions, quartered
> 6 garlic cloves, peeled
> 2 tablespoons olive oil
> 2 teaspoons white wine vinegar
> 1 to 2 teaspoons dried thyme
> 1/2 teaspoon salt
> 1/8 teaspoon pepper

1. Place carrots, onions and garlic in two greased 15-in. x 10-in. x 1-in. baking pans. Drizzle with oil and vinegar. Sprinkle with thyme, salt and pepper; gently toss to coat.

2. Cover and bake at 450° for 20 minutes; stir. Bake, uncovered, for 10 minutes; stir again. Bake 10 minutes longer or until carrots are crisp-tender. **Yield:** 8 servings.

Molly's Mexicorn

Molly Mason, Denver, Colorado

I jazzed up a corn recipe with some spicy seasonings to create this offering for a Mexican potluck. Everyone liked it so much that now it's all I'm ever asked to bring. The bright mix of colors makes it attractive for most any occasion.

6 cups fresh *or* frozen corn
2 jars (4 ounces *each*) sliced pimientos, drained
1/3 cup sliced green onions
1 small green pepper, diced
2 tablespoons butter
1 tablespoon chili powder
1 tablespoon ground cumin
1/2 teaspoon salt

In a large saucepan, combine all of the ingredients. Cover and cook over medium heat for 10 minutes or until vegetables are tender. **Yield:** 8 servings.

★ ★ ★
Chunky Ketchup

Susan Stahr, Driftwood, Pennsylvania

I came up with this chunky, homemade ketchup to jazz up chopped steak sandwiches and hot sausage sandwiches for my family. I gave some to our friends, too, and they enjoyed it on hamburgers and stuffed peppers. It's fresh-tasting and delicious.

> 8 **cups chopped seeded peeled tomatoes**
> 2 **medium onions, chopped**
> 2 **medium green peppers, chopped**
> 2 **cups sugar**
> 2 **cans (6 ounces *each*) tomato paste**
> 2 **tablespoons salt**
> 1/2 **cup white vinegar**

1. In a large saucepan, combine the tomatoes, onions, green peppers, sugar, tomato paste and salt; bring to a boil. Reduce heat; simmer, uncovered, for 1-1/2 hours or until slightly thickened.

2. Stir in vinegar; heat through. Ladle hot mixture into hot jars, leaving 1/4-in. headspace. Adjust the caps. Process for 20 minutes in a boiling-water bath. **Yield:** 3-1/2 pints.

★ ★ ★
Creole Green Beans

Sue Kuhn, Dublin, Ohio

Even though our children are grown, my husband and I remain busy. So we rely on recipes that call for everyday ingredients. This peppery treatment really wakes up green beans. It makes enough that we have leftovers, which is helpful since our schedules sometimes keep us from eating together.

> 1 **package (16 ounces) frozen cut green beans**
> 5 **bacon strips, diced**
> 1 **medium onion, chopped**
> 1/2 **cup chopped green pepper**
> 2 **tablespoons all-purpose flour**
> 2 **tablespoons brown sugar**
> 1 **tablespoon Worcestershire sauce**
> 1 **teaspoon salt**
> 1/2 **teaspoon pepper**
> 1/2 **teaspoon ground mustard**
> 1 **can (14-1/2 ounces) diced tomatoes, undrained**

1. Cook beans according to package directions. Meanwhile, in a skillet, cook the bacon, onion and green pepper over medium heat until bacon is crisp and vegetables are tender. Remove with a slotted spoon.

2. Stir the flour, brown sugar, Worcestershire sauce, salt, pepper and mustard into the drippings until blended. Stir in tomatoes. Bring to a boil; cook and stir for 2 minutes or until thickened. Drain beans and add to skillet. Stir in bacon mixture. **Yield:** 6 servings.

Mandarin Glazed Beets

(Pictured on page 126)

Shirley Dehler, Columbus, Wisconsin

Mandarin oranges and a warm glaze transform canned beets into a super side dish. Lemon juice provides a bit of tartness. If your family doesn't like the tart flavor, I suggest adding a little more sugar.

- 1/4 **cup sugar**
- 2 **teaspoons cornstarch**
- 1/4 **cup lemon juice**
- 2 **tablespoons butter**
- 2 **cans (15 ounces *each*) sliced beets, drained**
- 1 **can (11 ounces) mandarin oranges, drained**

1. In a large saucepan, combine the sugar and cornstarch. Add lemon juice and butter. Bring to a boil; cook and stir for 2 minutes or until thickened.

2. Stir in beets; heat through. Gently stir in oranges; heat through. **Yield:** 4 servings.

Green Tomatoes Parmesan

Clara Mifflin, Creal Springs, Illinois

If you follow the recipe directions, you should end up with firm tomatoes. It's been a tried-and-true method for me. I started cooking as a teenager. My first meal was spaghetti, and it was so salty we couldn't eat it!

- 3 **medium green tomatoes, sliced 1/4 inch thick**

Salt
- 1/4 **cup cornmeal**
- 1/4 **cup grated Parmesan cheese**
- 2 **tablespoons all-purpose flour**
- 3/4 **teaspoon garlic salt**
- 1/2 **teaspoon dried oregano**
- 1/8 **teaspoon pepper**
- 1 **egg, beaten**
- 1/4 **cup vegetable oil**

1. Lightly sprinkle tomatoes with salt; drain on paper towels for 30-60 minutes. Meanwhile, combine the cornmeal, Parmesan, flour, garlic salt, oregano and pepper in a shallow plate. Dip each tomato slice into egg, then into cornmeal mixture.

2. In a medium skillet, heat oil over medium-high. Fry tomatoes, a few at a time, for 2 minutes per side or until golden brown. Drain on a paper towel-lined wire rack. Serve immediately. **Yield:** 4-6 servings.

🎖 🎖 🎖
Cheesy Zucchini Bake

Sue Stanton, Linville, North Carolina

Ever since a friend shared this classic casserole with me, I actually look forward to our annual bounty of zucchini. This cheesy veggie bake makes a pretty entree or brunch item. I keep the recipe handy—I know I'll get requests!

4-1/2 cups sliced zucchini
    2 to 3 tablespoons olive oil
Salt and pepper to taste
    1 large onion, chopped
    2 tablespoons minced garlic
    1 can (10-3/4 ounces) tomato puree
    1 can (6 ounces) tomato paste
    3 tablespoons sugar
    1 teaspoon Italian seasoning
    1 teaspoon dried basil

    2 cans (2-1/4 ounces *each*) sliced ripe olives, drained
    3 cups (12 ounces) shredded mozzarella cheese
    6 eggs, lightly beaten
1-1/2 cups grated Parmesan cheese

1. In a large skillet, saute zucchini in oil until tender. Sprinkle with salt and pepper; stir. Transfer to an ungreased 13-in. x 9-in. x 2-in. baking dish.

2. In the same skillet, saute onion until crisp-tender. Add garlic; saute 3 minutes longer. Stir in tomato puree, tomato paste, sugar, Italian seasoning and basil. Bring to a boil. Reduce heat; simmer, uncovered, for 10-15 minutes or until slightly thickened. Stir in olives. Pour over zucchini. Sprinkle with mozzarella.

3. Combine the eggs and Parmesan cheese; pour over zucchini. Bake, uncovered, at 375° for 25-30 minutes or until a knife inserted near the center comes out clean. Let the dish stand for 15 minutes before serving. **Yield:** 12-16 servings.

🎖🎖🎖
Maple Apple Rings

Alma Jacklin, New Durham, New Hampshire

I live in maple syrup country and got this recipe from a sugarhouse. These are wonderful served with baked beans.

- 3/4 cup all-purpose flour
- 1 egg, beaten
- 1/4 cup maple syrup
- 1/4 cup buttermilk
- 3 large apples, peeled, cored and cut into 1/4-inch rings
- Oil for deep-fat frying
- Confectioners' sugar

1. In a shallow bowl, combine the flour, egg, syrup and buttermilk. Dip apple rings on both sides into batter.

2. In an electric skillet or deep-fat fryer, heat 2 in. of oil to 375°. Fry apple rings, a few at a time, for 2 minutes or until golden brown. Drain on paper towels. Dust with confectioners' sugar. **Yield:** 4 servings.

🎖🎖🎖
Zesty Broccoli and Artichokes

Mildred Sherrer, Bay City, Texas

We grow a lot of broccoli in our garden, so I've experimented with different ways to prepare it. Fixed this way, it tastes very good plus it's good for you.

- 2 cups water
- 4 cups fresh broccoli florets
- 1 can (14 ounces) artichoke hearts, drained
- 2 garlic cloves, minced
- 1 tablespoon olive oil
- 1/4 teaspoon salt
- 1/4 teaspoon pepper
- 1/8 teaspoon hot pepper sauce
- 1 tablespoon lemon juice
- 2 tablespoons grated Parmesan cheese

1. In a saucepan, bring water to a boil. Add broccoli; cook, uncovered, for 2 minutes. Remove with a slotted spoon and set aside. Add artichokes to the water; cook for 2 minutes. Drain.

2. In a skillet, saute garlic in oil until tender. Add artichokes and saute for 2 minutes. Add broccoli, salt, pepper and hot pepper sauce; saute 3 minutes longer or until broccoli is tender. Remove from the heat; sprinkle with lemon juice and Parmesan cheese. **Yield:** 6 servings.

🎗🎗🎗
Artichokes Au Gratin

Marjorie Bowen, Colorado Springs, Colorado

This makes a great side dish for Thanksgiving, Christmas or any dinner. My niece served this at a family gathering and was kind enough to share the recipe.

>   2 **cans (14 ounces** *each*) **water-packed artichoke hearts, drained and quartered**
>   1 **garlic clove, minced**
> 1/4 **cup butter,** *divided*
>   2 **tablespoons all-purpose flour**
> 1/2 **teaspoon salt**
> 1/4 **teaspoon pepper**
> 1-1/2 **cups milk**
>   1 **egg, lightly beaten**
> 1/2 **cup shredded Swiss cheese,** *divided*
>   1 **tablespoon dry bread crumbs**
> 1/8 **teaspoon paprika**

1. In a skillet, saute the artichokes and garlic in 2 tablespoons butter until tender. Transfer to a greased 1-qt. baking dish.

2. In a saucepan, melt the remaining butter. Stir in flour, salt and pepper until smooth. Gradually add milk. Bring to a boil; cook and stir for 2 minutes or until thickened. Remove from the heat. Stir a small amount of hot mixture into egg; return all to pan, stirring constantly. Stir in 1/4 cup cheese until melted.

3. Pour over artichokes; sprinkle with remaining cheese. Combine crumbs and paprika; sprinkle over top. Bake, uncovered, at 400° for 20-25 minutes or until heated through. **Yield:** 4-6 servings.

🎗🎗🎗
Orange-Nut Sweet Potatoes

(Pictured on page 127)

Kathleen Wright, Richmond, Kentucky

When my siblings and I were young, my mom created this recipe in hopes that we would eat more vegetables. It worked! The citrus sauce went so well with the tender sweet potatoes that the dish quickly became a family favorite and is now a standard at our holiday table.

>   2 **pounds sweet potatoes, peeled and cubed**
> 2/3 **cup sugar**
> 4-1/2 **teaspoons cornstarch**
>   1 **teaspoon salt**
>   1 **cup orange juice**
>   2 **tablespoons butter**
> 1/2 **teaspoon grated orange peel**
> 1/4 **cup chopped walnuts**

1. Place the sweet potatoes in a large saucepan; cover with water. Bring to a boil. Reduce heat; cover and simmer for 6-8 minutes or until tender.

2. Meanwhile, in a small saucepan, combine the sugar, cornstarch and salt. Gradually stir in orange juice. Bring to a boil; cook and stir for 2 minutes or until thickened. Add butter and orange peel; stir until butter is melted.

3. Drain sweet potatoes; place in a serving dish. Add orange juice mixture and gently stir to coat. Sprinkle with walnuts. **Yield:** 6 servings.

♛ ♛ ♛
Maple Baked Beans

Brenda Tetreault, Newport Center, Vermont

I came up with this recipe in a pinch after running out of baked beans at our oldest daughter's birthday party. I dressed up canned beans with maple syrup and a few other ingredients to produce this sweet, saucy version that tastes like homemade. They're so easy to fix that I rarely make baked beans from scratch anymore.

    1 medium onion, chopped
    1 to 2 tablespoons vegetable oil
    3 cans (28 ounces *each*) baked beans
1-1/2 teaspoons ground mustard
    1 teaspoon garlic salt
  3/4 to 1 cup maple syrup

In a Dutch oven or large kettle, cook onion in oil until tender. Add the beans, mustard and garlic salt. Cook over medium heat until bubbly, stirring occasionally. Add maple syrup; heat through, stirring occasionally. **Yield:** 8-10 servings.

♛ ♛ ♛
Scalloped Carrots

Joyce Tornholm, New Market, Iowa

A cookbook my husband gave me as a wedding gift included this recipe—he remembers having the dish as a child at church dinners. Now I make it whenever I need a special vegetable side. It's rich and cheesy even after reheating.

    6 cups water
   12 medium carrots, sliced 1/4 inch thick
       (about 4 cups)
    1 medium onion, finely chopped
  1/2 cup butter, *divided*
  1/4 cup all-purpose flour
    1 teaspoon salt
  1/4 teaspoon ground mustard
  1/4 teaspoon celery salt
Dash pepper
    2 cups milk
    2 cups (8 ounces) shredded cheddar cheese
    3 slices whole wheat bread, cut into small cubes

1. In a saucepan, bring water to a boil; add carrots. Return to a boil; cover and cook for 4 minutes. Drain and immediately place the carrots in ice water; drain and pat dry.

2. In a saucepan, saute onion in 1/4 cup butter. Stir in the flour, salt, mustard, celery salt and pepper until blended. Gradually add milk. Bring to a boil; cook and stir for 2 minutes or until thickened.

3. In a greased 11-in. x 7-in. x 2-in. baking dish, layer half of the carrots, cheese and white sauce. Repeat layers. Melt remaining butter; toss with bread cubes. Sprinkle over the top. Bake, uncovered, at 350° for 35-40 minutes or until hot and bubbly. **Yield:** 4-6 servings.

Nut Swirl Bread, p. 152

Garlic Parmesan Breadsticks, p. 157

Muenster Bread, p. 164

Almond-Filled Butterhorns, p. 148

Breads & Rolls

Nothing draws the family to the kitchen like the aroma of fresh bread baking—except, of course, the announcement that you're ready to slice into a warm, tasty loaf.

Cranberry Eggnog Braid, p. 155

Southern Banana Nut Bread, p. 161

Buttermilk Pan Rolls

Patricia Young, Bella Vista, Arkansas

These wonderful rolls can be made very quickly. Hot, fresh rolls go well with just about any meal.

    2 packages (1/4 ounce *each*) active dry yeast
    1/4 cup warm water (110° to 115°)
1-1/2 cups warm buttermilk (110° to 115°)
    1/2 cup vegetable oil
    3 tablespoons sugar
4-1/2 cups all-purpose flour
    1 teaspoon baking soda
    1/2 teaspoon salt

1. In a large mixing bowl, dissolve yeast in warm water. Add the buttermilk, oil and sugar. Combine flour, baking soda and salt; add to yeast mixture and beat until smooth. Do not knead. Let stand for 10 minutes.

2. Turn dough onto a lightly floured surface; punch down. Shape into 24 balls and place in two greased 9-in. square baking pans. Cover and let rise in a warm place until doubled, about 30 minutes. Bake at 400° for 20 minutes or until golden brown. Remove to wire racks. **Yield:** 2 dozen.

Editor's Note: Warmed buttermilk will appear curdled.

🎀 🎀 🎀

Almond-Filled Butterhorns

(Pictured on page 146)

Lillian Tripke, Janesville, Wisconsin

These are very light and flavorful rolls. The filling gives them a fantastic taste.

3-1/4 teaspoons active dry yeast
    1 cup warm milk (110° to 115°)
    1/2 cup sugar, *divided*
    1 cup butter, softened
    4 cups all-purpose flour
    1/8 teaspoon salt
    4 eggs
FILLING:
    5 tablespoons butter, softened, *divided*
    1 cup sugar
    1 cup ground almonds
    1 egg, lightly beaten
    1 teaspoon almond extract
    1/2 teaspoon grated lemon peel

GLAZE:
    1 cup confectioners' sugar
    2 tablespoons milk
    1/4 teaspoon vanilla extract

1. In a bowl, dissolve yeast in milk. Add 1/4 cup sugar and butter; mix well. In a large mixing bowl, combine the flour, salt and remaining sugar. Add the eggs, one at a time, beating well after each addition. Add yeast mixture; beat until smooth. Cover and refrigerate overnight.

2. Punch dough down; divide into thirds. On a lightly floured surface, roll each portion into a 12-in. circle. Melt 3 tablespoons butter; brush 1 tablespoon over each circle. In a bowl, combine the sugar, almonds, egg, extract, lemon peel and remaining butter; mix well. Spread a third over each circle of dough.

3. Cut each into 12 wedges. Roll up wedges from the short end; place pointed side down 2 in. apart on greased baking sheets.

4. Cover and let rise in a warm place for 30 minutes or until doubled. Bake at 375° for 10-12 minutes or until lightly browned. Combine glaze ingredients; brush over warm rolls. **Yield:** 3 dozen.

✿✿✿ Chocolate Chip Pumpkin Bread

Lora Stanley, Bennington, Kansas

A touch of cinnamon helps blend the chocolate and pumpkin flavors you'll find in this tender bread. And since the recipe makes two loaves, you can send one to a bake sale and keep one at home for your family to enjoy.

    3 cups all-purpose flour
    2 teaspoons ground cinnamon
    1 teaspoon salt
    1 teaspoon baking soda
    4 eggs
    2 cups sugar
    2 cups canned pumpkin
1-1/4 cups vegetable oil
1-1/2 cups semisweet chocolate chips

1. In a large bowl, combine the flour, cinnamon, salt and baking soda. In another bowl, beat the eggs, sugar, pumpkin and oil. Stir into dry ingredients just until moistened. Fold in chocolate chips.

2. Pour into two greased 8-in. x 4-in. x 2-in. loaf pans. Bake at 350° for 60-70 minutes or until a toothpick inserted near the center comes out clean. Cool for 10 minutes before removing from pans to wire racks. **Yield:** 2 loaves.

✿✿✿ Apricot Scones

Linda Swanson, Riverside, Washington

Besides farming and raising cattle, our family has a home bakery that serves area restaurants and health food stores. We dry lots of local fruit for use in recipes, like these moist, golden scones that are so popular with our customers.

1-1/2 cups all-purpose flour
  1/2 cup quick-cooking oats
  1/4 cup sugar
2-1/2 teaspoons baking powder
  1/4 teaspoon salt
  1/3 cup cold butter, cubed
    2 eggs
  1/4 cup sour cream
    1 tablespoon milk
  3/4 cup finely chopped dried apricots
FILLING:
    3 tablespoons brown sugar
    1 tablespoon quick-cooking oats
    1 tablespoon butter, softened
Additional sugar

1. In a bowl, combine the first five ingredients; cut in butter until mixture resembles fine crumbs. In a small bowl, beat eggs; set aside 1 tablespoon for glaze. In another bowl, combine sour cream, milk and remaining beaten eggs; add apricots. Stir into crumb mixture until the dough clings together.

2. Turn onto a lightly floured surface; knead 12-15 times. Divide dough in half. Pat one portion into a 7-in. circle on a greased baking sheet.

3. Combine the brown sugar, oats and butter; sprinkle over dough. Roll out remaining dough into a 7-in. circle; place over filling. Brush with reserved egg; sprinkle with additional sugar.

4. Cut into wedges but do not separate. Bake at 400° for 15-20 minutes or until scones are golden brown. Cool slightly; cut again if necessary. Serve warm. **Yield:** 6 servings.

🎗🎗🎗
Funnel Cakes

Mary Faith Yoder, Unity, Wisconsin

These are much simpler to make than doughnuts but taste just as good. They have been a regular treat of ours since we came across them when we lived in the Ozarks.

> 2 eggs
> 1 cup milk
> 1 cup water
> 1/2 teaspoon vanilla extract
> 3 cups all-purpose flour
> 1/4 cup sugar
> 1 tablespoon baking powder
> 1/4 teaspoon salt

Oil for deep-fat frying
Confectioners' sugar

1. In a mixing bowl, beat eggs. Add milk, water and vanilla; mix well. Combine flour, sugar, baking powder and salt; beat into egg mixture until smooth.

2. In an electric skillet or deep-fat fryer, heat oil to 375°. Cover the bottom of a funnel spout with your finger; ladle 1/2 cup of batter into the funnel. Holding the funnel several inches above the skillet, release your finger and move the funnel in a spiral motion until all the batter is released (scraping with a rubber spatula if needed). Fry for 2 minutes on each side or until golden brown.

3. Drain on paper towels. Dust with confectioners' sugar and serve warm. **Yield:** 8 cakes.

Editor's Note: The batter can be poured from a liquid measuring cup instead of a funnel.

🎗🎗🎗
Lemon Tea Muffins

Terrie Cox, Honeyville, Utah

When it comes to baking, muffins are No. 1 to me. I bake a batch every day. These are great with your favorite tea.

> 2 eggs, *separated*
> 1/2 cup butter, softened
> 1/2 cup sugar
> 1 cup all-purpose flour
> 1 teaspoon baking powder
> 1/4 teaspoon salt
> 3 tablespoons lemon juice
> 1 teaspoon grated lemon peel

TOPPING:

> 1 tablespoon sugar
> 1/8 teaspoon ground cinnamon

Dash ground nutmeg

1. In a small mixing bowl, beat egg yolks until light and lemon-colored, about 3 minutes. In a large mixing bowl, cream butter and sugar. Fold in yolks.

2. Combine flour, baking powder and salt; add to the creamed mixture alternately with lemon juice and peel, stirring just until combined. Beat egg whites until stiff peaks form; fold into batter. Fill greased or paper-lined muffin cups two-thirds full. Combine topping ingredients; sprinkle over muffins.

3. Bake at 350° for 20-25 minutes or until a toothpick comes out clean. Cool in pan 10 minutes before removing to a wire rack. **Yield:** about 24 mini-muffins or 8 standard-size muffins.

🎀 🎀 🎀

Italian Cheese Twists

Marna Heitz, Farley, Iowa

My family loves breadsticks, and this recipe was an immediate success. The breadsticks look delicate and fancy, but they aren't tricky to make using prepared bread dough.

1 loaf (1 pound) frozen bread dough, thawed
1/4 cup butter, softened
1/4 teaspoon garlic powder
1/4 teaspoon *each* dried basil, oregano and marjoram
3/4 cup shredded mozzarella cheese
1 egg
1 tablespoon water
2 tablespoons sesame seeds *and/or* grated Parmesan cheese

1. On a lightly floured surface, roll dough into a 12-in. square. Combine butter and seasonings; spread over dough. Sprinkle with mozzarella cheese. Fold dough into thirds. Cut crosswise into 24 strips, 1/2 in. each. Twist each strip twice; pinch ends to seal. Place 2 in. apart on a greased baking sheet.

2. Cover and let rise in a warm place until almost doubled, about 30 minutes. In a small bowl, beat egg and water; brush over the twists. Sprinkle with sesame seeds and/or Parmesan cheese. Bake at 375° for 10-12 minutes or until light golden brown. **Yield:** 2 dozen.

★★★
Cheddar-Chili Bread Twists

Carol Whitfield, Mentmore, New Mexico

Green chilies are prolific here in New Mexico, so I'm always looking for ways to cook with them. These twists are often requested by my family.

1-1/4 cups buttermilk
   2 cups (8 ounces) shredded cheddar cheese
   2 tablespoons sugar
   1 package (1/4 ounce) active dry yeast

   1/4 cup warm water (110° to 115°)
   2 eggs
   1/2 teaspoon salt
5-1/4 to 5-3/4 cups all-purpose flour
TOPPING:
1-1/2 cups (6 ounces) shredded cheddar cheese
   1 can (4 ounces) chopped green chilies, drained
Grated Parmesan cheese

1. In a saucepan, heat the buttermilk and cheese over low heat, stirring until cheese is melted (mixture will appear curdled). Cool to 110°-115°. In a mixing bowl, dissolve sugar and yeast in warm water. Add buttermilk mixture, eggs, salt and 3 cups flour. Beat until smooth. Stir in enough remaining flour to form a soft dough.

2. Turn onto a floured surface; knead until smooth and elastic, about 6-8 minutes. Place in a greased bowl, turning once to grease top. Cover and let rise in a warm place until doubled, about 1 hour. Meanwhile, for topping, combine cheddar cheese and chilies; set aside.

3. Punch dough down; turn onto a lightly floured surface and divide in half. Roll each portion into an 18-in. x 12-in. rectangle. Spray one half with nonstick cooking spray. Top with cheese mixture and remaining dough.

4. Cut into twelve 1-1/2-in. strips. Cut each strip in half and twist. Place 1 in. apart on greased foil-lined baking sheets. Sprinkle with Parmesan cheese. Bake at 375° for 15-20 minutes or until lightly browned. Remove to wire racks. Serve warm. Refrigerate any leftovers. **Yield:** 2 dozen.

★★★
Nut Swirl Bread

(Pictured on page 146)

Darlene Simmons, Newfield, New Jersey

The best way that I can describe these is to say they taste like a celebration. Cooking from scratch like this is an easy way to cut a few corners in my food budget.

   2 packages (1/4 ounce *each*) active dry yeast
1/4 cup warm water (110° to 115°)
   2 cups warm milk (110° to 115°)
1/2 cup sugar
1/2 cup butter, softened
   2 eggs
   2 teaspoons salt
   7 to 7-1/2 cups all-purpose flour
FILLING:
   5 egg whites
   1 cup sugar
   5 cups finely chopped walnuts *or* pecans
     (about 1-1/2 pounds)

   1 tablespoon butter, melted
Additional melted butter
   1 egg, beaten

1. In a large mixing bowl, dissolve yeast in water. Add milk, sugar, butter, eggs, salt and 3-1/2 cups of flour; beat until smooth. Add enough remaining flour to form a soft dough. Turn onto a floured surface; knead until smooth and elastic, 6-8 minutes. Place in a greased bowl; turn once to grease top. Cover and let rise in a warm place until doubled, about 1 hour.

2. For filling, beat egg whites in a mixing bowl until foamy; gradually add sugar and beat well. Stir in nuts and butter; mix well. Punch dough down; divide into eight balls. Roll each into an 8-in. circle; brush with butter. Spread about 2/3 cup filling on each circle. Roll up tightly into loaves; seal ends. Place on greased baking sheets.

3. Cover and let rise until doubled, about 50 minutes. Brush with egg. Bake at 350° for 20-25 minutes or until golden brown. Cool on wire racks. **Yield:** 8 loaves.

🎗🎗🎗
No-Fry Doughnuts

Susie Baldwin, Columbia, Tennessee

We have four boys and these doughnuts never last long at our house. I like them because I don't have to clean up a greasy mess.

2 packages (1/4 ounce *each*) active dry yeast
1/4 cup warm water (110° to 115°)
1-1/2 cups warm milk (110° to 115°)
1/3 cup shortening
1/2 cup sugar
2 eggs
1 teaspoon salt
1 teaspoon ground nutmeg
1/4 teaspoon ground cinnamon
4-1/2 to 5 cups all-purpose flour
1/4 cup butter, melted
GLAZE:
1/2 cup butter
2 cups confectioners' sugar
5 teaspoons water
2 teaspoons vanilla extract

1. In a mixing bowl, dissolve yeast in water. Add milk and shortening; stir for 1 minute. Add sugar, eggs, salt, nutmeg, cinnamon and 2 cups flour; beat on low speed until smooth. Stir in enough remaining flour to form a soft dough (do not knead).

2. Cover and let rise in a warm place until doubled, about 1 hour. Punch dough down. Turn onto a floured surface; roll out to 1/2-in. thickness. Cut with a 2-3/4-in. doughnut cutter; place 2 in. apart on greased baking sheets. Brush with butter. Cover and let rise in a warm place until doubled, about 30 minutes. Bake at 350° for 20 minutes or until lightly browned.

3. Meanwhile, in a saucepan, melt butter; stir in sugar, water and vanilla. Stir over low heat until smooth (do not boil). Keep warm. Dip warm doughnuts, one at a time, into glaze and turn to coat. Drain on a wire rack. Serve immediately. **Yield:** 2 dozen.

🎗🎗🎗
Whole Wheat Pumpkin Nut Bread

Jean-Marie Hirsch, East Rochester, New York

Nicely spiced with cloves, cinnamon and pumpkin, this bread is a family favorite. Everyone who tastes a slice asks for the recipe. You can substitute raisins or chocolate chips for the walnuts.

1 cup whole wheat flour
1 cup sugar
2/3 cup all-purpose flour
1 teaspoon baking soda
1 teaspoon ground cinnamon
1/2 teaspoon baking powder
1/2 teaspoon salt
1/2 teaspoon ground cloves
1 cup canned pumpkin
1/2 cup egg substitute
1/3 cup water
1/4 cup canola oil
1/2 cup chopped walnuts

1. In a bowl, combine the first eight ingredients. In another bowl, combine the pumpkin, egg substitute, water and oil; mix well. Stir into dry ingredients just until moistened. Fold in walnuts.

2. Spoon into a 9-in. x 5-in. x 3-in. baking pan coated with nonstick cooking spray. Bake at 350° for 60-65 minutes or until a toothpick inserted near the center comes out clean. Cool for 15 minutes before removing from pan to a wire rack. **Yield:** 1 loaf (12 slices).

🎗 🎗 🎗
Orange Biscuits

Winifred Brown, Wilmette, Illinois

These biscuits are a special treat with a ham dinner, but they're also delicious just by themselves. They're often requested by my five children and seven grandchildren.

- 1/2 cup orange juice
- 3/4 cup sugar, *divided*
- 1/4 cup butter
- 2 teaspoons grated orange peel
- 2 cups all-purpose flour
- 1 tablespoon baking powder
- 1/2 teaspoon salt
- 1/4 cup shortening
- 3/4 cup milk

Melted butter
- 1/2 teaspoon ground cinnamon

1. In a saucepan, combine orange juice, 1/2 cup sugar, butter and orange peel. Cook and stir over medium heat for 2 minutes. Divide among 12 muffin cups; set aside.

2. In a large bowl, combine flour, baking powder and salt. Cut in shortening until mixture resembles coarse crumbs. With a fork, stir in milk until mixture forms a ball. On a lightly floured surface, knead the dough 1 minute. Roll into a 9-in. square, about 1/2 in. thick. Brush with melted butter.

3. Combine the cinnamon and remaining sugar; sprinkle over butter. Roll up. Cut into 12 slices, about 3/4 in. thick. Place slices, cut side down, over orange mixture in muffin cups. Bake at 450° for 12-16 minutes. Cool for 2-3 minutes; remove from pan. **Yield:** 1 dozen.

🎗🎗🎗
Cranberry Eggnog Braid

(Pictured on page 147)

Mary Lindow, Florence, Wisconsin

Whether at Thanksgiving, Christmas or New Year's, this is a good party bread. You can't beat it as a gift, either.

      3 to 3-1/2 cups all-purpose flour, *divided*
    1/4 cup sugar
    1/2 teaspoon salt
      1 package (1/4 ounce) active dry yeast
    1/2 teaspoon ground nutmeg
  1-1/4 cups eggnog
    1/4 cup butter
    1/2 cup dried cranberries
GLAZE:
      1 cup confectioners' sugar
      1 to 2 tablespoons eggnog
    1/4 teaspoon vanilla extract
Dash nutmeg

1. In a mixing bowl, combine 1-1/2 cups of flour, sugar, salt, yeast and nutmeg; set aside. In a saucepan, heat eggnog and butter to 120°-130° (the butter does not need to melt); add to flour mixture. Beat on low until moistened; beat on medium for 3 minutes. Stir in cranberries and enough remaining flour to make a soft dough. Turn onto a floured surface; knead until smooth and elastic, about 6-8 minutes. Place in a greased bowl, turning once to grease top.

2. Cover and let rise in a warm place until doubled, about 1 hour. Punch dough down; divide into thirds. Shape each third into a 16-in. rope. Braid ropes on a greased baking sheet; seal ends. Cover and let rise until nearly doubled, about 30 minutes.

3. Bake at 350° for 25-30 minutes or until golden. Immediately remove from pan to a wire rack to cool completely. Combine the first three glaze ingredients; drizzle over braid. Dust with nutmeg. **Yield:** 1 loaf.

Editor's Note: This recipe was tested with commercially prepared eggnog.

🎗🎗🎗
Candy Cane Rolls

Janice Peterson, Huron, South Dakota

Fun and lightly sweet, these festive rolls will delight children of all ages. Make them as part of a holiday brunch or an evening snack served with hot chocolate.

      1 package (1/4 ounce) active dry yeast
    1/4 cup warm water (110° to 115°)
    3/4 cup warm milk (110° to 115°)
    1/4 cup sugar
    1/4 cup shortening
      1 teaspoon salt
      1 egg, lightly beaten
  3-1/4 to 3-3/4 cups all-purpose flour
      1 cup red candied cherries, quartered
      1 cup confectioners' sugar
      1 tablespoon milk

1. In a large mixing bowl, dissolve yeast in warm water. Add warm milk, sugar, shortening, salt, egg and 2 cups flour; beat until smooth. Stir in cherries. Add enough of the remaining flour to form a soft dough.

2. Turn onto a floured board; knead until smooth and elastic, about 6-8 minutes. Place in a greased bowl, turning once to grease top. Cover and let rise in a warm place until doubled, about 1 hour. Punch dough down; let rest for 10 minutes. Divide in half.

3. Roll each half into a 12-in. x 7-in. rectangle. Cut twelve 1-in. strips from each rectangle. Twist each strip and place 2 in. apart on greased baking sheets, shaping one end like a cane. Cover and let rise until doubled, about 45 minutes.

4. Bake at 375° for 12-15 minutes or until golden brown. Cool completely. Combine confectioners' sugar and milk; frost rolls. **Yield:** 2 dozen.

★★★
Creole Corn Bread

Enid Hebert, Lafayette, Louisiana

This is an old favorite that I found in the bottom of my recipe drawer, and it really tastes wonderful.

 2 cups cooked rice
 1 cup yellow cornmeal
 1/2 cup chopped onion
 1 to 2 tablespoons seeded chopped jalapeno
   peppers
 1 teaspoon salt
 1/2 teaspoon baking soda
 2 eggs
 1 cup milk
 1/4 cup vegetable oil
 1 can (16-1/2 ounces) cream-style corn
 3 cups (12 ounces) shredded cheddar cheese
Additional cornmeal

1. In a large bowl, combine the rice, cornmeal, onion, peppers, salt and baking soda. In another bowl, beat eggs, milk and oil. Add corn; mix well. Stir into rice mixture until blended. Fold in cheese.

2. Sprinkle a well-greased 10-in. ovenproof skillet with cornmeal. Pour batter into skillet. Bake at 350° for 45-50 minutes or until a toothpick inserted near the center comes out clean. Cut into wedges and serve warm. **Yield:** 12 servings.

   Editor's Note: When cutting or seeding hot peppers, use rubber or plastic gloves to protect your hands. Avoid touching your face.

★★★
Pull-Apart Bacon Bread

Traci Collins, Cheyenne, Wyoming

I stumbled across this recipe while looking for something different to take to a brunch. Boy, am I glad I did! Everyone asked for the recipe and could not believe it only called for five ingredients. It's the perfect item to bake for an informal get-together.

 12 bacon strips, diced
 1 loaf (1 pound) frozen bread dough, thawed
 2 tablespoons olive oil, *divided*
 1 cup (4 ounces) shredded mozzarella cheese
 1 envelope (1 ounce) ranch salad dressing mix

1. In a skillet, cook bacon over medium heat for 5 minutes or until partially cooked; drain on paper towels. Roll out dough to 1/2-in. thickness; brush with 1 tablespoon of oil. Cut into 1-in. pieces; place in a large bowl. Add the bacon, cheese, dressing mix and remaining oil; toss to coat.

2. Arrange pieces in a 9-in. x 5-in. oval on a greased baking sheet, layering as needed. Cover and let rise in a warm place for 30 minutes or until doubled. Bake at 350° for 15 minutes. Cover with foil; bake 5-10 minutes longer or until golden brown. **Yield:** 1 loaf.

Garlic Parmesan Breadsticks

(Pictured on page 146)

Barbara Gross, Warden, Washington

I receive many compliments when I make these delicious breadsticks. I've passed the recipe on to a number of family members and friends.

1 tablespoon active dry yeast
1-1/2 cups warm water (110° to 115°)
2 tablespoons sugar
3/4 cup butter, melted, *divided*
1/2 teaspoon salt
4-1/2 cups all-purpose flour
Garlic salt
Grated Parmesan cheese
Marinara *or* spaghetti sauce, warmed, optional

1. In a mixing bowl, dissolve yeast in water. Add sugar; let stand for 5 minutes. Add 1/2 cup butter, salt and 2 cups flour; beat until smooth. Stir in enough remaining flour to form a soft dough.

2. Turn onto a floured surface; knead until smooth and elastic, about 6-8 minutes. Place in a greased bowl, turning once to grease top. Cover and let rise in a warm place until doubled, about 45 minutes.

3. Punch dough down. Turn onto a lightly floured surface; roll into a 24-in. x 10-in. rectangle. Cut dough in half lengthwise, then into 5-in. x 1-in. strips. Twist each strip and place 2 in. apart on greased baking sheets.

4. Brush strips with remaining butter; sprinkle with garlic salt and Parmesan cheese. Cover and let rise in a warm place until doubled, about 20 minutes.

5. Bake at 350° for 20 minutes or until golden brown. Remove from pans to wire racks. If desired, serve with warmed marinara or spaghetti sauce for dipping. **Yield:** 4 dozen.

Tropical Muffins

Sylvia Osborn, Clay Center, Kansas

I entered these muffins at our county fair and won the grand champion award for baked goods. They're so moist, they don't need butter.

1/4 cup butter, softened
1/2 cup sugar
1 egg
1 cup (8 ounces) sour cream
1-1/2 teaspoons rum extract
1-1/2 cups all-purpose flour
1 teaspoon baking powder
1/2 teaspoon baking soda
1/2 teaspoon salt
1 can (8 ounces) crushed pineapple, drained
1/2 cup flaked coconut
1/3 cup chopped pecans

1. In a mixing bowl, cream the butter and sugar. Add the egg, sour cream and extract; mix well. Combine the flour, baking powder, baking soda and salt; stir into the creamed mixture just until moistened. Fold in the pineapple, coconut and pecans.

2. Fill greased or paper-lined muffin cups two-thirds full. Bake at 375° for 22-25 minutes or until a toothpick comes out clean. Cool for 5 minutes removing from pan to a wire rack. **Yield:** about 1 dozen.

🎗🎗🎗
Swedish Rye Bread

Mary Ann Ross, Crown Point, Indiana

This recipe came from my mother, and it's long been a family favorite. You can make a meal of it with soup and a salad.

 1 package (1/4 ounce) active dry yeast
1-3/4 cups warm water (110° to 115°), *divided*
 1/4 cup packed brown sugar
 1/4 cup molasses
 2 tablespoons shortening
 2 teaspoons salt
2-1/2 cups rye flour
3-3/4 to 4-1/4 cups all-purpose flour
 2 tablespoons butter, melted

1. In a mixing bowl, dissolve yeast in 1/4 cup water. Add sugar, molasses, shortening, salt and remaining water; stir well. Add rye flour; beat until smooth. Add enough all-purpose flour to form a soft dough.

2. Turn onto a floured surface; knead until smooth and elastic, about 6-8 minutes. Place in a greased bowl, turning once to grease top. Cover and let rise in a warm place until doubled, about 1-1/2 hours. Punch dough down.

3. Shape into four round loaves. Place on greased baking sheets. Cover and let rise until doubled, about 45-60 minutes. Bake at 350° for 30-35 minutes or until golden brown. Brush with the melted butter. **Yield:** 4 loaves.

🎗🎗🎗
Whole Wheat Biscuits

Margie Thomason, Belvidere, Kansas

This quick and easy recipe adds a special touch to everyday meals. You'll get a lot of compliments when you serve these biscuits fresh from the oven.

1-1/2 cups all-purpose flour
 1/2 cup whole wheat flour
 2 tablespoons sugar
 1 tablespoon baking powder
 1/2 teaspoon cream of tartar
 1/4 teaspoon salt
 1/2 cup shortening
 1 egg
 1/2 cup milk
 1 tablespoon butter, melted

1. In a bowl, combine first six ingredients. Cut in shortening until mixture resembles coarse crumbs. Beat egg and milk; stir into dry ingredients until a ball forms.

2. Turn onto a floured surface, knead 5-6 times. Roll to 1/2-in. thickness; brush with butter. Cut with a 2-in. biscuit cutter. Place on an ungreased baking sheet. Bake at 450° for 10-12 minutes or until golden brown. **Yield:** about 1 dozen.

🎀 🎀 🎀

Strawberry Rhubarb Coffee Cake

Benita Thomas, Falcon, Colorado

We have a rhubarb patch, so I'm always looking for recipes featuring this "fruit." I've served this to people who say they don't like rhubarb, and they've always told me they enjoyed it.

- 2/3 **cup sugar**
- 1/3 **cup cornstarch**
- 2 **cups chopped rhubarb**
- 1 **package (10 ounces) frozen sweetened sliced strawberries, thawed**
- 2 **tablespoons lemon juice**

CAKE:
- 3 **cups all-purpose flour**
- 1 **cup sugar**
- 1 **teaspoon baking powder**
- 1 **teaspoon baking soda**
- 1 **cup cold butter**
- 2 **eggs**
- 1 **cup buttermilk**
- 1 **teaspoon vanilla extract**

TOPPING:
- 3/4 **cup sugar**
- 1/2 **cup all-purpose flour**
- 1/4 **cup cold butter**

1. In a saucepan, combine sugar and cornstarch; stir in rhubarb and strawberries. Bring to a boil over medium heat; cook for 2 minutes or until thickened. Remove from the heat; stir in lemon juice. Cool.

2. For cake, combine flour, sugar, baking powder and baking soda in a large bowl. Cut in butter until mixture resembles coarse crumbs. Beat the eggs, buttermilk and vanilla; stir into crumb mixture just until moistened. Spoon two-thirds of the batter into a greased 13-in. x 9-in. x 2-in. baking pan. Spoon cooled filling over batter. Top with remaining batter.

3. For topping, combine sugar and flour. Cut in butter until mixture resembles coarse crumbs; sprinkle over batter. Bake at 350° for 45-50 minutes or until golden brown. Cool on a wire rack. **Yield:** 12-15 servings.

🎀🎀🎀
Caramel-Pecan Sticky Buns

Judy Powell, Star, Idaho

My mother used to make delicious cinnamon rolls when I was a child. Later, she taught my sister and me to make them. I've since added the caramel and pecans.

  1 package (1/4 ounce) active dry yeast
3/4 cup warm water (110° to 115°)
3/4 cup warm milk (110° to 115°)
1/4 cup sugar
  3 tablespoons vegetable oil
  2 teaspoons salt
3-3/4 to 4-1/4 cups all-purpose flour
FILLING:
1/4 cup butter, softened
1/4 cup sugar
  3 teaspoons ground cinnamon
3/4 cup packed brown sugar
1/2 cup heavy whipping cream
  1 cup coarsely chopped pecans

1. In a mixing bowl, dissolve yeast in warm water. Add the milk, sugar, oil, salt and 1-1/4 cups flour. Beat on medium speed for 2-3 minutes or until smooth. Stir in enough remaining flour to form a soft dough. Turn onto a floured surface; knead until smooth and elastic, about 6-8 minutes. Place in a greased bowl, turning once to grease top. Cover and let rise in a warm place until doubled, about 1 hour.

2. Punch dough down. Turn onto a lightly floured surface. Roll into an 18-in. x 12-in. rectangle. Spread butter to within 1/2 in. of edges. Combine sugar and cinnamon; sprinkle over butter. Roll up jelly-roll style, starting with a long side; pinch seam to seal. Cut into 12 slices.

3. Combine brown sugar and cream; pour into a greased 13-in. x 9-in. x 2-in. baking pan. Sprinkle with pecans. Place rolls, cut side down, over pecans. Cover and let rise until doubled, about 1 hour.

4. Bake at 350° for 30-35 minutes or until well browned. Cool for 1 minute before inverting onto a serving platter. **Yield:** 1 dozen.

🎀🎀🎀
Jalapeno Bread

Mary Alice Watt, Upton, Wyoming

This bread is a big hit at our house. Its unusual texture makes it a conversation piece, so almost everybody tries it.

  2 loaves (1 pound each) frozen bread dough, thawed
  1 can (8-3/4 ounces) whole kernel corn, drained
  1 egg, beaten
  1 can (3-1/2 ounces) whole jalapenos, chopped
  2 tablespoons taco seasoning mix
  1 jar (2 ounces) sliced pimientos, drained
1-1/2 teaspoons vinegar

1. Cut bread dough into 1-in. pieces. Place all ingredients in a large bowl and toss to mix well. Spoon into two greased 8-in. x 4-in. x 2-in. loaf pans. Cover and let stand for 15 minutes.

2. Bake at 350° for 35-40 minutes. Cool in pan 10 minutes before removing to a wire rack. Serve warm if desired. **Yield:** 2 loaves.

  Editor's Note: Remove the seeds from the jalapenos before chopping for a milder bread.

🎀🎀🎀
Southern Banana Nut Bread

(Pictured on page 147)

Viva Forman, Tallahassee, Florida

I found this recipe in an old church recipe book. Pecans in the bread and topping make it unique.

- 1/2 cup butter-flavored shortening
- 1-1/2 cups sugar
- 2 eggs
- 1 cup mashed ripe bananas (about 2 medium)
- 1 teaspoon vanilla extract
- 2 cups self-rising flour
- 1/2 cup buttermilk
- 3/4 cup chopped pecans

TOPPING:
- 1/4 to 1/3 cup mashed ripe bananas
- 1-1/4 cups confectioners' sugar
- 1 teaspoon lemon juice

Additional chopped pecans

1. In a mixing bowl, cream shortening and sugar; beat in eggs. Blend in bananas and vanilla. Add flour alternately with buttermilk. Fold in pecans. Pour into two greased 8-in. x 4-in. x 2-in. loaf pans.

2. Bake at 350° for 45-55 minutes or until a toothpick inserted near the center comes out clean. Cool in pan for 10 minutes before removing to a wire rack; cool completely.

3. For topping, combine bananas, confectioners' sugar and lemon juice; spread over loaves. Sprinkle with pecans. **Yield:** 2 loaves.

Editor's Note: As a substitute for *each* cup of self-rising flour, place 1-1/2 teaspoons baking powder and 1/2 teaspoon salt in a measuring cup; add all-purpose flour to equal 1 cup.

🎀🎀🎀
Rosemary Orange Bread

Deidre Fallavollita, Vienna, Virginia

Of all the herbs, rosemary is my favorite. This bread goes great with a roast, chicken or pasta with red sauce.

- 1 package (1/4 ounce) active dry yeast
- 3/4 cup warm water (110° to 115°)
- 3/4 cup orange juice
- 2 tablespoons honey
- 1 tablespoon vegetable oil
- 1 tablespoon minced fresh rosemary *or* 1 teaspoon dried rosemary, crushed
- 2 teaspoons salt
- 1 teaspoon grated orange peel
- 3-3/4 to 4-1/2 cups all-purpose flour
- 1 egg white

Additional fresh rosemary and whole peppercorns, optional

1. In a mixing bowl, dissolve yeast in warm water. Add orange juice, honey, oil, rosemary, salt, orange peel and 2 cups flour; beat until smooth. Stir in enough remaining flour to form a soft dough.

2. Turn onto a floured surface; knead until smooth and elastic, about 6-8 minutes. Place in a greased bowl, turning once to grease top. Cover and let rise in a warm place until doubled, about 1 hour.

3. Punch dough down. Roll into a 15-in. x 10-in. rectangle. Starting at the short end, roll up jelly-roll style. Pinch edges to seal and shape into an oval. Place with seam side down on a greased baking sheet. Cover and let rise until nearly doubled, about 30 minutes.

4. Bake at 375° for 20 minutes. Whisk egg white; brush over loaf. Place small sprigs of rosemary and peppercorns on top if desired. Bake 25 minutes longer or until brown. Cool on a wire rack. **Yield:** 1 loaf.

🎀 🎀 🎀

Chocolate Chip Carrot Bread

Sharon Setzer, Philomath, Oregon

My family likes sweet breads, and this loaf incorporates many of their favorite ingredients. I'm a former newspaper food columnist, and coming up with flavorful recipes that are a little out-of-the-ordinary is a favorite pastime.

    3 cups all-purpose flour
    1 cup sugar
    1 cup packed brown sugar
    2 to 3 teaspoons ground cinnamon
    2 teaspoons baking powder
    1 teaspoon baking soda
    1 teaspoon salt
    1 teaspoon ground ginger
1/4 to 1/2 teaspoon ground cloves
    3 eggs
    3/4 cup orange juice
    3/4 cup vegetable oil
    1 teaspoon vanilla extract
    2 cups grated carrots
    1 cup (6 ounces) semisweet chocolate chips

1. In a large bowl, combine the first nine ingredients. In a small bowl, beat the eggs, orange juice, oil and vanilla. Stir into the dry ingredients just until moistened. Fold in the carrots and chocolate chips.

2. Transfer to two greased 8-in. x 4-in. x 2-in. loaf pans. Bake at 350° for 55-60 minutes or until a toothpick comes out clean. Cool for 10 minutes before removing from pans to wire racks. **Yield:** 2 loaves.

Freeze-and-Bake Rolls

Jayne Duce, Raymond, Alberta

Almost any occasion's right for these handy rolls—I keep them in the freezer for Sunday meals and for company.

2 packages (1/4 ounce *each*) active dry yeast
1-1/2 cups warm water (110° to 115°)
2 teaspoons plus 1/2 cup sugar, *divided*
1-1/2 cups warm milk (110° to 115°)
1/4 cup vegetable oil
4 teaspoons salt
7-1/2 to 8-1/2 cups all-purpose flour
Butter, melted

1. In a large mixing bowl, dissolve yeast in water. Add 2 teaspoons sugar; let stand for 5 minutes. Add milk, oil, salt and remaining sugar. Add enough flour to form a stiff dough. Turn out onto a floured surface; knead until smooth and elastic, about 6-8 minutes. Place in a greased bowl, turning once to grease top. Cover and let rise in a warm place until doubled, about 1-1/2 hours.

2. Punch dough down. Divide into four pieces. Cover three pieces with plastic wrap. Divide one piece into 12 balls. To form knots, roll each ball into a 10-in. rope; tie into a knot and pinch ends together. Repeat with remaining dough. Place rolls on greased baking sheets; brush with melted butter. Cover and let rise until doubled, about 20-30 minutes.

3. To serve immediately, bake at 375° for 15-18 minutes. To freeze for later use, partially bake at 300° for 15 minutes. Allow to cool; freeze. Reheat frozen rolls at 375° for 12-15 minutes or until browned. **Yield:** 4 dozen.

Nutty Rhubarb Muffins

Mary Kay Morris, Cokato, Minnesota

This is one of the ways I use the rhubarb that grows abundantly here. I've been asked many times for this recipe.

3/4 cup packed brown sugar
1/2 cup buttermilk
1/3 cup vegetable oil
1 egg, beaten
1 teaspoon vanilla extract
2 cups all-purpose flour
1/2 teaspoon baking soda
1/2 teaspoon salt
1 cup diced rhubarb
1/2 cup chopped nuts
TOPPING:
1/4 cup packed brown sugar
1/4 cup chopped nuts
1/2 teaspoon ground cinnamon

1. In a small mixing bowl, combine brown sugar, buttermilk, oil, egg and vanilla; mix well. Set aside. In a medium mixing bowl, combine flour, baking soda and salt. Add egg mixture; stir just until combined. Fold in rhubarb and nuts.

2. Spoon the batter into 12 greased muffin cups. Mix together topping ingredients; sprinkle over tops of muffins. Bake at 375° for 20 minutes or until a toothpick inserted at center comes out clean. **Yield:** 1 dozen.

Muenster Bread

(Pictured on page 146)

Melanie Mero, Ida, Michigan

The recipe makes a beautiful, round loaf. With a layer of cheese peeking out of every slice, it's definitely worth the effort.

> **2 packages (1/4 ounce *each*) active dry yeast**
> **1 cup warm milk (110° to 115°)**
> **1/2 cup butter, softened**
> **2 tablespoons sugar**
> **1 teaspoon salt**
> **3-1/4 to 3-3/4 cups all-purpose flour**
> **1 egg plus 1 egg yolk**
> **4 cups (1 pound) shredded Muenster cheese**
> **1 egg white, beaten**

1. In a large mixing bowl, dissolve yeast in milk. Add butter, sugar, salt and 2 cups flour; beat until smooth. Stir in enough remaining flour to form a soft dough. Turn onto a floured board; knead until smooth and elastic, about 6-8 minutes. Place in a greased bowl, turning once to grease top. Cover and let rise in a warm place until doubled, about 1 hour.

2. In a large bowl, beat egg and yolk; stir in cheese. Punch dough down; roll into a 16-in. circle. Place in a greased 9-in. round cake pan, letting dough drape over the edges.

3. Spoon the cheese mixture into center of dough. Gather dough up over filling in 1-1/2-in. pleats. Gently squeeze pleats together at top and twist to make a top knot. Allow to rise 10-15 minutes. Brush loaf with egg white. Bake at 375° for 45-50 minutes. Cool on a wire rack for 20 minutes. Serve warm. **Yield:** 1 loaf.

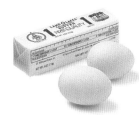

Golden Carrot Buns

Katharine Groine, Altona, Manitoba

These rolls have a nice flavor. Folks usually don't guess that carrots are one of the ingredients.

> **4 cups sliced carrots**
> **2 eggs, beaten**
> **1 cup warm water (110° to 115°), *divided***
> **2 packages (1/4 ounce *each*) active dry yeast**
> **3/4 cup vegetable oil**
> **1/2 cup sugar**
> **1 tablespoon molasses**
> **2 teaspoons salt**
> **8-1/2 to 9 cups all-purpose flour**

1. Place carrots in a saucepan and cover with water; cook until tender. Drain and place in a blender or food processor. Add eggs and 1/2 cup water; puree until smooth. In a large mixing bowl, dissolve yeast in remaining water. Add carrot mixture. Stir in oil, sugar, molasses, salt and 5 cups flour; beat until smooth. Add enough remaining flour to form a soft dough.

2. Turn onto a floured board; knead until smooth and elastic, about 6-8 minutes. Place in a greased bowl, turning once to grease top. Cover and let rise in a warm place until doubled, about 1 hour. Punch dough down.

3. Shape into 48 balls. Place 2 in. apart on greased baking sheets. Cover and let rise until almost doubled, about 1 hour. Bake at 350° for 18-20 minutes or until browned. **Yield:** 4 dozen.

✿✿✿ Peachy Sour Cream Coffee Cake

Alice Brandt, Marengo, Illinois

When I was a little girl, my grandma got up early every Saturday to make this coffee cake for our family breakfast.

    2 cups chopped pecans
1/3 cup packed brown sugar
    3 tablespoons sugar
    1 teaspoon ground cinnamon
CAKE:
1/2 cup butter-flavored shortening
    1 cup sugar
    2 eggs
    2 cups all-purpose flour
1/2 teaspoon baking powder
1/2 teaspoon baking soda
1/2 teaspoon salt
    1 cup (8 ounces) sour cream
    1 teaspoon vanilla extract
    2 cups sliced peeled fresh peaches

1. Combine first four ingredients; set aside. In a large mixing bowl, cream shortening and sugar until fluffy. Beat in eggs. Combine all dry ingredients; add alternately with the sour cream and vanilla to the creamed mixture. Beat until smooth.

2. Pour half the batter into a 9-in. springform pan. Sprinkle with 1 cup of the streusel. Top with remaining batter and 1/2 cup streusel.

3. Bake at 350° for 30 minutes. Arrange peaches over cake; sprinkle with remaining streusel. Bake 30-40 minutes longer or until a toothpick inserted into cake comes out clean. Cool cake 10 minutes before removing sides of pan. Serve warm or at room temperature. **Yield:** 12 servings.

✿✿✿ Apple Bran Muffins

Nancy Brown, Klamath Falls, Oregon

This recipe dates back to when our two girls were in preschool and it was my turn to bring a snack for the class.

    2 large Golden Delicious apples, peeled and
      chopped
1/2 cup butter
    3 cups All-Bran cereal
    1 cup boiling water
    2 cups buttermilk
    2 eggs, lightly beaten
2/3 cup sugar
    1 cup raisins
2-1/2 cups all-purpose flour
2-1/2 teaspoons baking soda
    2 teaspoons ground cinnamon
    1 teaspoon ground nutmeg
1/2 teaspoon ground cloves
1/2 teaspoon salt

1. In a skillet, saute apples in butter until tender, about 10 minutes. Combine cereal and water in a large bowl; stir in the buttermilk, eggs, sugar, raisins and apples with butter. Combine dry ingredients; stir into apple mixture just until moistened. Refrigerate in a tightly covered container for at least 24 hours (batter will be very thick).

2. Fill greased or paper-lined muffin cups three-fourths full. Bake at 400° for 20-25 minutes or until a toothpick comes out clean. Cool in pan 10 minutes before removing to a wire rack. **Yield:** about 24 muffins.

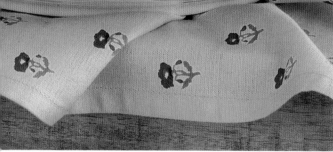

Chocolate Surprise Cookies, p. 173

Chocolate Chip Cheesecake Bars, p. 179

Swedish Butter Cookies, p. 174

Brownies, Bars & Cookies

If you've ever gotten caught with your hand in the cookie jar, you know the sweet reward is worth the risk. The bars, brownies and cookies in this chapter will have you thinking about baking—and eating—these magnificent morsels.

Cookie Dough Brownies p. 168

If you like cookies with a crunch, you'll love these golden treats. Crushed peanut brittle adds an unexpected kick to the vanilla chips and brown sugar that flavor the dough. It's hard to believe something this easy to make tastes so terrific.

- 1 cup butter, softened
- 3/4 cup packed brown sugar
- 1/4 cup sugar
- 2 eggs
- 1 teaspoon vanilla extract
- 2-1/4 cups all-purpose flour
- 1 package (3.4 ounces) instant vanilla pudding mix
- 1 teaspoon baking soda
- 1/4 teaspoon salt
- 1 package (10 to 12 ounces) vanilla *or* white chips
- 2 jars (3-1/4 ounces *each*) macadamia nuts, chopped
- 1/2 cup finely crushed peanut brittle

1. In a mixing bowl, cream butter and sugars until smooth. Add eggs, one at a time, beating well after each addition. Beat in vanilla. Combine the flour, dry pudding mix, baking soda and salt; gradually add to creamed mixture and mix well. Stir in chips, nuts and peanut brittle.

2. Drop by rounded tablespoonfuls 2 in. apart onto greased baking sheets. Bake at 375° for 10-12 minutes or until golden brown. Remove to wire racks to cool. **Yield:** 5-1/2 dozen.

🎀 🎀 🎀
Macadamia Chip Cookies

Dorothy Kollmeyer, Dupo, Illinois

🎀 🎀 🎀
Cookie Dough Brownies

(Pictured on page 167)

Wendy Bailey, Elida, Ohio

When I take these rich brownies to any get-together, I carry the recipe, too, because it always gets requested. Children of all ages love the tempting "cookie dough" filling. This special treat is typically the first to be gone from the buffet table—even before the entrees!

- 2 cups sugar
- 1-1/2 cups all-purpose flour
- 1/2 cup baking cocoa
- 1/2 teaspoon salt
- 1 cup vegetable oil
- 4 eggs
- 2 teaspoons vanilla extract
- 1/2 cup chopped walnuts, optional

FILLING:
- 1/2 cup butter, softened
- 1/2 cup packed brown sugar
- 1/4 cup sugar
- 2 tablespoons milk
- 1 teaspoon vanilla extract
- 1 cup all-purpose flour

GLAZE:
- 1 cup (6 ounces) semisweet chocolate chips
- 1 tablespoon shortening
- 3/4 cup chopped walnuts

1. In a mixing bowl, combine sugar, flour, cocoa and salt. Add oil, eggs and vanilla; beat at medium speed for 3 minutes. Stir in walnuts if desired. Pour into a greased 13-in. x 9-in. x 2-in. baking pan. Bake at 350° for 30 minutes or until brownies test done. Cool completely.

2. For filling, cream butter and sugars in a mixing bowl. Add milk and vanilla; mix well. Beat in flour. Spread over the brownies; chill until firm.

3. For glaze, melt chocolate chips and shortening in a saucepan, stirring until smooth. Spread over filling. Immediately sprinkle with nuts, pressing down slightly. **Yield:** 3 dozen.

🎗 🎗 🎗
S'more Sandwich Cookies

Abby Metzger, Larchwood, Iowa

Capture the taste of campfire s'mores in your kitchen. Graham cracker crumbs added to chocolate chip cookie dough bring out the flavor of the fireside favorite. Melting the cookies' marshmallow centers in the microwave makes them simple to assemble.

- 3/4 cup butter, softened
- 1/2 cup sugar
- 1/2 cup packed brown sugar
- 1 egg
- 2 tablespoons milk
- 1 teaspoon vanilla extract
- 1-1/4 cups all-purpose flour
- 1-1/4 cups graham cracker crumbs (about 20 squares)
- 1/2 teaspoon baking soda
- 1/4 teaspoon salt
- 1/8 teaspoon ground cinnamon
- 2 cups (12 ounces) semisweet chocolate chips
- 24 to 28 large marshmallows

1. In a mixing bowl, cream butter and sugars. Beat in egg, milk and vanilla. Combine the flour, graham cracker crumbs, baking soda, salt and cinnamon; gradually add to creamed mixture. Stir in chocolate chips.

2. Drop by tablespoonfuls 2 in. apart onto ungreased baking sheets. Bake at 375° for 8-10 minutes or until golden brown. Remove to wire racks to cool.

3. Place four cookies bottom side up on a microwave-safe plate; top each with a marshmallow. Microwave, uncovered, on high for 16-20 seconds or until marshmallows begin to puff (do not overcook). Top each with another cookie. Repeat. **Yield:** about 2 dozen.

Editor's Note: This recipe was tested in an 850-watt microwave.

🎗 🎗 🎗
Strawberry Jam Bars

Karen Mead, Pittsburgh, Pennsylvania

I bake for a group of seniors every week, and this is one of the goodies they request most. I always keep the ingredients on hand for last-minute baking emergencies. Give these bars your own twist by replacing the strawberry jam with the fruit jam of your choice.

- 1/2 cup butter, softened
- 1/2 cup packed brown sugar
- 1 egg
- 1 package (18-1/4 ounces) white cake mix
- 1 cup finely crushed cornflakes
- 1 cup strawberry jam or preserves

1. In a mixing bowl, cream butter and brown sugar until smooth. Add egg; mix well. Gradually add dry cake mix and cornflakes. Set aside 1-1/2 cups for topping. Press remaining dough into a greased 13-in. x 9-in. x 2-in. baking pan.

2. Carefully spread jam over crust. Sprinkle with reserved dough; gently press down. Bake at 350° for 30 minutes or until golden brown. Cool completely on a wire rack. Cut into bars. **Yield:** 2 dozen.

★★★
Vanilla Chip Maple Cookies

Debra Hogenson, Brewster, Minnesota

Since my husband farms, I try to have simple meals and snacks available, as I never know when he will come in from the fields. These cookies have a distinct maple flavor and stay moist and soft, although they're never in my cookie jar for long!

    1 cup shortening
1/2 cup butter, softened
    2 cups packed brown sugar
    2 eggs
    1 teaspoon vanilla extract
    1 teaspoon maple flavoring
    3 cups all-purpose flour
    2 teaspoons baking soda
    2 cups vanilla *or* white chips
1/2 cup chopped pecans
FROSTING:
1/4 cup butter, softened
    4 cups confectioners' sugar
    1 teaspoon maple flavoring
    4 to 6 tablespoons milk
3-1/2 cups pecan halves

1. In a mixing bowl, cream the shortening, butter and brown sugar. Add eggs, one at a time, beating well after each addition. Beat in vanilla and maple flavoring. Combine the flour and baking soda; gradually add to creamed mixture. Stir in vanilla chips and pecans.

2. Drop by rounded tablespoonfuls 2 in. apart onto ungreased baking sheets. Bake at 350° for 8-10 minutes or until golden brown. Cool for 2 minutes before removing to wire racks.

3. In a mixing bowl, cream butter and confectioners' sugar. Beat in maple flavoring and enough milk to achieve spreading consistency. Frost cooled cookies. Top each with a pecan half. **Yield:** about 7 dozen.

If you like your sweets with a cup of coffee, this recipe is for you! These no-nut brownies combine a mild coffee flavor with the richness of semisweet chocolate chips. They're a quick and easy dessert or anytime treat at our house.

    1 tablespoon instant coffee granules
    2 teaspoons boiling water
    1 cup (6 ounces) semisweet chocolate chips
1/4 cup butter, softened
1/2 cup sugar
    2 eggs
1/2 cup all-purpose flour
1/4 teaspoon ground cinnamon

1. In a small bowl, dissolve coffee in water; set aside. In a microwave-safe bowl or saucepan over low heat, melt chocolate chips. In a small mixing bowl, cream butter and sugar. Beat in eggs, melted chocolate and coffee mixture. Combine flour and cinnamon; add to the creamed mixture and mix well.

2. Pour into a greased 8-in. square baking pan. Bake at 350° for 25-30 minutes or until a toothpick inserted near the center comes out clean. Cool on a wire rack. Cut into squares. **Yield:** 16 bars.

★★★
Cappuccino Cake Brownies

Mary Houchin, Swansea, Illinois

★ ★ ★
Two-Tone Fudge Brownies

Rebecca Kays, Klamath Falls, Oregon

These moist, fudgy brownies have a scrumptious topping that tastes just like chocolate chip cookie dough! Everyone loves these brownies…and they make enough to feed a crowd.

1 cup (6 ounces) semisweet chocolate chips
1/2 cup butter, softened
1 cup sugar
3 eggs
1 teaspoon vanilla extract
1-1/4 cups all-purpose flour
1/4 teaspoon baking soda
3/4 cup chopped walnuts
COOKIE DOUGH LAYER:
1/2 cup butter, softened
1/2 cup packed brown sugar
1/4 cup sugar
3 tablespoons milk
1 teaspoon vanilla extract
1 cup all-purpose flour
1 cup (6 ounces) semisweet chocolate chips

1. In a microwave-safe bowl, melt chocolate chips. Cool slightly. In a mixing bowl, cream butter and sugar. Add eggs and vanilla; mix well. Stir in melted chocolate. Combine flour and baking soda; add to batter. Stir in walnuts.

2. Spread into a greased 13-in. x 9-in. x 2-in. baking pan. Bake at 350° for 16-22 minutes or until a toothpick inserted near the center comes out clean. Cool on a wire rack.

3. In a mixing bowl, cream butter and sugars. Beat in milk and vanilla. Gradually add flour. Stir in chocolate chips. Drop by tablespoonfuls over cooled brownies; carefully spread over top. Cut into squares. Store in the refrigerator. **Yield:** 4 dozen.

Editor's Note: Cookie dough layer is not baked and does not contain eggs.

★ ★ ★
Chocolate Meringues
Nancy Grace, San Diego, California

These cookies are great for fancy occasions but easy enough to make as a snack. My grandma was an avid baker, known in her neighborhood as the "cookie lady." With 18 nieces and nephews, I'm carrying on her tradition.

   1 cup (6 ounces) semisweet chocolate chips
   2 egg whites
1/4 teaspoon cream of tartar
1/8 teaspoon salt
1/2 cup sugar
1/2 teaspoon white vinegar
1/2 teaspoon vanilla *or* almond extract
1/2 cup flaked coconut
1/4 cup chopped almonds

1. In a microwave or heavy saucepan, melt chocolate chips and stir until smooth; set aside. In a mixing bowl, beat egg whites, cream of tartar and salt until soft peaks form. Add sugar, 1 tablespoon at a time, beating until stiff peaks form, about 5 minutes. Beat in vinegar and vanilla. Fold in melted chocolate until combined; fold in coconut and almonds.

2. Drop by tablespoonfuls 2 in. apart onto lightly greased baking sheets. Bake at 350° for 10-11 minutes or until firm. Remove to wire racks to cool. Store in an airtight container. **Yield:** about 2-1/2 dozen.

★ ★ ★
Apple Walnut Squares
Jennifer Dzubinski, San Antonio, Texas

If you need a homespun snack or bake sale treat that can be assembled in a hurry, try these moist, nutty bars. The squares are sweet, flavorful and loaded with chopped apple and nuts.

1/2 cup butter, softened
   1 cup sugar
   1 egg
   1 cup all-purpose flour
1/2 teaspoon baking powder
1/2 teaspoon baking soda
1/2 teaspoon ground cinnamon
   1 medium tart apple, peeled and chopped
3/4 cup chopped walnuts

1. In a mixing bowl, cream butter and sugar. Add the egg. Combine flour, baking powder, baking soda and cinnamon; gradually add to the creamed mixture, beating just until combined. Stir in apple and walnuts.

2. Pour into a greased 8-in. square baking dish. Bake at 350° for 35-40 minutes or until a toothpick inserted near the center comes out clean. Cool on a wire rack. **Yield:** 16 servings.

Peanut Butter Swirl Brownies

Linda Craig, Hay River, Northwest Territories

Peanut butter and chocolate are always a delicious duo, but they're extra-special paired in this tempting treat.

1/2 cup butter, softened
2/3 cup sugar
1/2 cup packed brown sugar
2 eggs
2 tablespoons milk
3/4 cup all-purpose flour
1/2 teaspoon baking powder
1/4 teaspoon salt
1/4 cup creamy peanut butter
1/3 cup peanut butter chips
1/3 cup baking cocoa
1/2 cup semisweet chocolate chips

1. In a mixing bowl, cream butter and sugars. Add eggs and milk; mix well. Combine flour, baking powder and salt; add to creamed mixture and mix well. Divide batter in half. To one portion, add peanut butter and peanut butter chips; mix well. To the other portion, add the cocoa and chocolate chips; mix well.

2. In a greased 9-in. square baking pan, spoon chocolate batter in eight mounds in a checkerboard pattern. Spoon seven mounds of peanut butter batter between the chocolate batter. Cut through batters with a knife to swirl.

3. Bake at 350° for 25-30 minutes or until a toothpick inserted near the center comes out clean. Cool on a wire rack. **Yield:** 3 dozen.

Chocolate Surprise Cookies

(Pictured on page 166)

Grace Crary, West Linn, Oregon

It's fun watching folks' faces when they bite into the middle of these pretty cookies. The surprise is a burst of peanut butter.

3/4 cup peanut butter
3/4 cup confectioners' sugar
CHOCOLATE DOUGH:
1/2 cup butter, softened
1/4 cup peanut butter
1/2 cup sugar
1/2 cup packed brown sugar
1 egg white
1 teaspoon vanilla extract
1-1/2 cups all-purpose flour
1/2 cup baking cocoa
1/2 teaspoon baking soda
ICING:
2 tablespoons shortening
1 cup confectioners' sugar
1/4 teaspoon vanilla extract
1 to 2 tablespoons milk

1. In a mixing bowl, cream peanut butter and confectioners' sugar until smooth. Roll into thirty 3/4-in. balls. Cover and refrigerate for 30 minutes. Meanwhile, in a mixing bowl, cream butter, peanut butter and sugars. Beat in egg white and vanilla. Combine flour, cocoa and baking soda; gradually add to creamed mixture. Roll into thirty 1-1/2-in. balls.

2. Using floured hands, flatten chocolate balls and shape one around each peanut butter ball, sealing edges. Place 2 in. apart on greased baking sheets. Flatten with a glass dipped in sugar. Bake at 375° for 7-9 minutes or until cookies are set and tops are cracked. Cool for 1 minute before removing to wire racks.

3. For icing, in a small mixing bowl, cream shortening and confectioners' sugar. Beat in vanilla and enough milk to reach spreading consistency. Spoon into a resealable plastic bag or pastry bag; cut a small hole in corner of bag. Pipe icing over cookies in a zigzag pattern. **Yield:** 2-1/2 dozen.

Editor's Note: Reduced-fat or generic brands of peanut butter are not recommended for this recipe.

🎀🎀🎀
Swedish Butter Cookies

(Pictured on page 166)

Sue Soderlund, Elgin, Illinois

It's impossible to eat just one of these treats. Naturally, they're a favorite with my Swedish husband and children— but anyone with a sweet tooth will appreciate them. My recipe is "well-traveled" among our friends and neighbors.

- 1 cup butter, softened
- 1 cup sugar
- 2 teaspoons maple syrup
- 2 cups all-purpose flour
- 1 teaspoon baking soda
  Confectioners' sugar

1. In a mixing bowl, cream butter and sugar. Add syrup; mix well. Combine flour and baking soda; gradually add to creamed mixture. Divide dough into eight portions. Roll each portion into a 9-in. log.

2. Place 3 in. apart on ungreased baking sheets. Bake at 300° for 25 minutes or until lightly browned. Cut into 1-in. slices. Remove to wire racks to cool. Dust with confectioners' sugar. **Yield:** about 6 dozen.

🎀🎀🎀
Frosted Peanut Butter Fingers

Leah Gallington, Corona, California

I first learned about these quick crowd-pleasers from a next-door neighbor when I sniffed the delightful aroma of a batch baking. Topped with extra peanut butter and chocolate frosting, the chewy bars became a family favorite that day when she brought us a plateful and shared the recipe.

- 1 cup butter, softened
- 1-1/2 cups packed brown sugar
- 1 cup sugar
- 2-1/2 cups creamy peanut butter, *divided*
- 1 egg
- 1-1/2 teaspoons vanilla extract
- 2-1/2 cups quick-cooking oats
- 2 cups all-purpose flour
- 1 teaspoon baking soda
- 1/2 teaspoon salt
  CHOCOLATE FROSTING:
- 6 tablespoons butter, softened
- 4 cups confectioners' sugar
- 1/2 cup baking cocoa
- 1 teaspoon vanilla extract
- 6 to 8 tablespoons milk

1. In a mixing bowl, cream butter and sugars. Add 1 cup peanut butter, egg and vanilla; mix well. Combine oats, flour, baking soda and salt; add to the creamed mixture. Spread into a greased 15-in. x 10-in. x 1-in. baking pan.

2. Bake at 350° for 13-17 minutes or until golden brown. Cool slightly on a wire rack, about 12 minutes. Spread with remaining peanut butter. Cool completely.

3. In a mixing bowl, combine the butter, confectioners' sugar, cocoa, vanilla and enough milk to achieve spreading consistency. Spoon over peanut butter layer, then spread. Cut into bars. **Yield:** about 3 dozen.

Editor's Note: Reduced-fat or generic brands of peanut butter are not recommended for this recipe.

🎖🎖🎖
Peanut Mallow Bars

Claudia Ruiss, Massapequa, New York

Searching for the perfect combination of salty and sweet sensations? Well, look no further! Salted peanuts and rich caramel topping join marshmallow creme and brown sugar in these irresistible chewy bars. You won't be able to stop at just one!

> 1 cup chopped salted peanuts
> 3/4 cup all-purpose flour
> 3/4 cup quick-cooking oats
> 2/3 cup packed brown sugar
> 1/2 teaspoon salt
> 1/2 teaspoon baking soda
> 1 egg, lightly beaten
> 1/3 cup cold butter

TOPPING:

> 1 jar (7 ounces) marshmallow creme
> 2/3 cup caramel ice cream topping
> 1-3/4 cups salted peanuts

1. In a bowl, combine the first six ingredients; stir in the egg. Cut in butter until crumbly. Press into a greased 13-in. x 9-in. x 2-in. baking pan. Bake at 350° for 8-10 minutes or until lightly browned.

2. Spoon marshmallow creme over hot crust; carefully spread evenly. Drizzle with the caramel topping; sprinkle with peanuts. Bake for 15-20 minutes or until lightly browned. Cool on a wire rack. Cut into bars. **Yield:** 3 dozen.

🎖🎖🎖
Toffee Malted Cookies

Sharon Timpe, Mequon, Wisconsin

As much as I delight in sharing these goodies, my family considers them "keepers." It's a wonder I ever get them out the door to take to meetings! With their buttery, melt-in-your-mouth texture, they're always popular.

> 1 cup butter, softened
> 1/2 cup sugar
> 1/2 cup packed brown sugar
> 2 eggs
> 1 package (3.4 ounces) instant vanilla pudding mix
> 1 teaspoon vanilla extract
> 2-1/4 cups all-purpose flour
> 1 cup quick-cooking oats
> 1 teaspoon baking soda
> 1/2 teaspoon salt
> 1 cup malted milk balls, chopped
> 3/4 cup English toffee bits *or* almond brickle chips

1. In a mixing bowl, cream the butter and sugars. Add eggs, one at a time, beating well after each addition. Add pudding mix and vanilla.

2. Combine the flour, oats, baking soda and salt; add to creamed mixture. Fold in the malted milk balls and

the toffee bits (dough will be stiff).

3. Drop by rounded teaspoonfuls 2 in. apart onto ungreased baking sheets. Bake at 350° for 12-15 minutes or until golden brown. Cool for 2 minutes before removing to wire racks. **Yield:** about 6 dozen.

Raspberry Almond Bars

Mimi Priesman, Pace, Florida

A co-worker's mother gave me this gem of a recipe a few years back. I can never decide what's more appealing—the attractive look of the bars or their incredible aroma while they're baking! Everyone who tries these asks for the recipe.

1/2 cup butter
  1 package (10 to 12 ounces) vanilla *or* white chips, *divided*
  2 eggs
1/2 cup sugar
  1 teaspoon almond extract
  1 cup all-purpose flour
1/2 teaspoon salt

1/2 cup seedless raspberry jam
1/4 cup sliced almonds

1. In a saucepan, melt butter. Remove from the heat; add 1 cup chips (do not stir). In a small mixing bowl, beat eggs until foamy; gradually add sugar. Stir in chip mixture and almond extract. Combine flour and salt; add to egg mixture just until combined. Spread half of the batter into a greased 9-in. square baking pan. Bake at 325° for 15-20 minutes or until golden brown.

2. In a small saucepan over low heat, melt jam; spread over warm crust. Stir remaining chips into remaining batter; drop by teaspoonfuls over the jam layer. Sprinkle with almonds. Bake 30-35 minutes longer or until a toothpick inserted near the center comes out clean. Cool on a wire rack. Cut into bars. **Yield:** 2 dozen.

Blond Toffee Brownies

Mary Williams, Lancaster, California

Whenever my co-worker brought these brownies to company bake sales, they sold in minutes. After getting the recipe from her, I was happy to discover how quickly they could be thrown together. I was even more excited when my family said that the thin, chewy bars are the best they've ever tasted.

1/2 cup butter, softened
1 cup sugar
1/2 cup packed brown sugar
2 eggs
1 teaspoon vanilla extract
1-1/2 cups all-purpose flour
2 teaspoons baking powder
1/4 teaspoon salt
1 cup English toffee bits *or almond brickle chips*

1. In a mixing bowl, cream butter and sugars. Add eggs, one at a time, beating well after each addition. Beat in

vanilla. Combine the flour, baking powder and salt; gradually add to creamed mixture. Stir in toffee bits.

2. Spread evenly into a greased 13-in. x 9-in. x 2-in. baking pan. Bake at 350° for 35-40 minutes or until a toothpick inserted near the center comes out clean. Cool on a wire rack. Cut into bars. **Yield:** 1-1/2 dozen.

Sour Cream Chocolate Cookies

Tina Sawchuk, Ardmore, Alberta

These soft, chocolaty cookies can be easily altered to make several different varieties—I've added everything from mints to macadamia nuts to them.

1/2 cup butter, softened
3/4 cup sugar
1/2 cup packed brown sugar
1 egg
1/2 cup sour cream
1 teaspoon vanilla extract
1-3/4 cups all-purpose flour
1/2 cup baking cocoa
1 teaspoon baking powder
1/2 teaspoon baking soda
1/4 teaspoon salt
1 cup (6 ounces) semisweet chocolate chips
1/2 cup vanilla *or white chips*

1. In a mixing bowl, cream butter and sugars. Beat in egg, sour cream and vanilla. Combine dry ingredients; gradually add to the creamed mixture. Stir in chips.

2. Drop by rounded tablespoonfuls 2 in. apart onto greased baking sheets. Bake at 350° for 12-15 minutes or until set. Cool for 2 minutes before removing to wire racks to cool completely. **Yield:** about 3 dozen.

🎗️ 🎗️ 🎗️
Cherry Chewbilees

Debbi Smith, Crossett, Arkansas

This is a good dish to carry to potlucks and parties. It's a hit at home, too—my husband rates it as one of his favorite desserts.

CRUST:
1-1/4 cups all-purpose flour
  1/2 cup packed brown sugar
  1/2 cup butter-flavored shortening
    1 cup chopped walnuts, *divided*
  1/2 cup flaked coconut
FILLING:
    2 packages (8 ounces *each*) cream cheese, softened
  2/3 cup sugar
    2 eggs
    2 teaspoons vanilla extract
    2 cans (21 ounces *each*) cherry pie filling

1. In a bowl, combine flour and brown sugar; cut in shortening until fine crumbs form. Stir in 1/2 cup nuts and coconut. Reserve 1/2 cup crumb mixture for topping. Press remaining mixture into the bottom of a greased 13-in. x 9-in. x 2-in. baking pan.

2. Bake at 350° for 12-15 minutes or until lightly browned. Meanwhile, for filling, beat cream cheese, sugar, eggs and vanilla in a mixing bowl until smooth. Spread over the hot crust. Bake 15 minutes.

3. Spread pie filling on top. Combine remaining nuts and reserved crumbs; sprinkle over cherries. Bake 15 minutes more. Cool. Refrigerate until serving. **Yield:** 20 servings.

🎗️ 🎗️ 🎗️
Five-Star Brownies

Pam Buerki Rogers, Victoria, Kansas

There's a bit of my state's history behind these brownies' name and shape. In 1990, when I entered them at our state fair, Kansas was celebrating the 100th birthday of a famous native son…Dwight Eisenhower. In fact, that occasion was the theme of the fair. So I renamed my brownies, in honor of the rank he'd achieved as a general and cut them out with a star cookie cutter. They ended up winning a blue ribbon!

    3 eggs
    2 cups sugar
1-1/2 teaspoons vanilla extract
  1/2 cup butter, melted
  1/4 cup shortening, melted
1-1/2 cups all-purpose flour
  3/4 cup baking cocoa
1-1/4 teaspoons salt
    1 cup chopped nuts, optional

1. In a mixing bowl, beat eggs, sugar and vanilla until well mixed. Add butter and shortening. Combine flour, cocoa and salt; stir into egg mixture and mix well. Add nuts if desired.

2. Line a 13-in. x 9-in. x 2-in. baking pan with foil and grease the foil; pour batter into pan. Bake at 350° for 30 minutes or until a toothpick comes out with moist crumbs. Cool in pan.

3. Turn brownies out of pan onto a cookie sheet; remove foil. Place a wire rack over brownies; turn over and remove cookie sheet. Cut with a star cutter or into bars. **Yield:** about 3 dozen.

🎀🎀🎀
Chocolate Chip Cheesecake Bars

(Pictured on page 166)

Jane Nolt, Narvon, Pennsylvania

I received this recipe from a co-worker who made these heavenly bars for a potluck. Since they combine two great flavors—chocolate chip cookies and cheesecake—in one bite, they were a hit with our three grown children.

- 3/4 cup shortening
- 3/4 cup sugar
- 1/3 cup packed brown sugar
- 1 egg
- 1-1/2 teaspoons vanilla extract
- 1-1/2 cups all-purpose flour
- 1 teaspoon salt
- 3/4 teaspoon baking soda
- 1-1/2 cups miniature chocolate chips
- 3/4 cup chopped pecans

FILLING:
- 2 packages (8 ounces *each*) cream cheese, softened
- 3/4 cup sugar
- 2 eggs
- 1 teaspoon vanilla extract

1. In a mixing bowl, cream shortening and sugars. Beat in egg and vanilla. Combine the flour, salt and baking soda; add to the creamed mixture and mix well. Fold in the chocolate chips and pecans. Set aside a third of the dough for topping. Press remaining dough into a greased 13-in. x 9-in. x 2-in. baking pan. Bake at 350° for 8 minutes.

2. Meanwhile, in a small mixing bowl, beat cream cheese and sugar until smooth. Add eggs and vanilla; mix well. Spoon over crust. Drop teaspoonfuls of reserved dough over filling.

3. Bake at 350° for 35-40 minutes or until golden brown. Cool on a wire rack. Cover and store in the refrigerator. **Yield:** 3 dozen.

🎀🎀🎀
Butter Fudge Fingers

Peggy Mangus, Worland, Wyoming

These scrumptious brownies get dressed up with a delicious browned butter frosting. The combination is delightfully different and assures that they vanish fast around the house or at a party.

- 2/3 cup butter
- 4 squares (1 ounce *each*) unsweetened chocolate
- 4 eggs
- 1 teaspoon salt
- 2 cups sugar
- 1-1/2 cups all-purpose flour
- 1 teaspoon baking powder
- 1 cup chopped pecans

BROWNED BUTTER FROSTING:
- 1/2 cup butter
- 1/3 cup heavy whipping cream
- 2 teaspoons vanilla extract
- 4 cups confectioners' sugar

GLAZE:
- 1 square (1 ounce) unsweetened chocolate
- 1 tablespoon butter

1. In a microwave or double boiler, melt butter and chocolate; cool for 10 minutes. In a mixing bowl, beat eggs and salt until foamy. Gradually add sugar; mix well. Stir in chocolate mixture. Combine flour and baking

powder; gradually add to chocolate mixture. Stir in pecans. Pour into a greased 15-in. x 10-in. x 1-in. baking pan. Bake at 350° for 20-25 minutes or until a toothpick inserted near the center comes out clean. Cool.

2. For frosting, heat butter in a saucepan over medium heat until golden brown, about 7 minutes. Remove from the heat; add cream and vanilla. Beat in sugar until smooth and thick. Frost bars. For glaze, melt the chocolate and butter in a microwave or double boiler; cool slightly. Drizzle over bars. **Yield:** about 5 dozen.

❧❧❧
Raspberry Citrus Bars

Ruby Nelson, Mountain Home, Arkansas

This recipe was an instant hit with my family when I first made it. The combination of raspberries, lemon juice and orange peel gives it a unique taste.

      1 cup butter, softened
    3/4 cup confectioners' sugar
  2-1/4 cups all-purpose flour, *divided*
      4 eggs
  1-1/2 cups sugar
    1/3 cup lemon juice
      2 tablespoons grated orange peel
      1 teaspoon baking powder
  1-1/2 cups unsweetened raspberries

1. In a mixing bowl, cream butter and confectioners' sugar. Add 2 cups flour; beat until combined. Press mixture into a greased 13-in. x 9-in. x 2-in. baking pan. Bake at 350° for 20 minutes or until lightly browned.

2. Meanwhile, in a mixing bowl, beat the eggs, sugar, lemon juice and orange peel. Add the baking powder and remaining flour; mix well. Sprinkle raspberries over the crust. Pour filling over the berries.

3. Bake for 30-35 minutes or until lightly browned and filling is set. Cool on a wire rack. Store in the refrigerator. **Yield:** 12-15 servings.

❧❧❧
Cinnamon Snaps

Cathy Cain, Carmel, California

Since I'm a longtime cinnamon fan, I decided to give traditional gingersnaps a different twist. My husband and son agree I spiced them up just right.

    3/4 cup shortening
      1 cup packed brown sugar
      1 egg
    1/4 cup molasses
  2-1/4 cups all-purpose flour
      2 teaspoons baking soda
      2 teaspoons ground cinnamon
    1/2 teaspoon salt
Additional sugar

1. In a mixing bowl, cream shortening and brown sugar. Add egg and molasses. Combine the flour, baking soda, cinnamon and salt; gradually add to creamed mixture. Roll into 1-in. balls, then roll in additional sugar.

2. Place 2 in. apart on ungreased baking sheets. Bake at 350° for 10-12 minutes or until cookies are set and tops are cracked. Remove to wire racks to cool. **Yield:** 4-1/2 dozen.

Ginger Bars

Deborah Haake, Minnetonka, Minnesota

We always had dessert when we visited my grandparents' farm, and this was one of our favorites. During harvesttime, my brothers and sisters and I would take this or another dessert out to the field for the workers.

1 cup shortening
1 cup sugar
2 eggs
1 cup water
1/2 cup molasses
2-1/2 cups all-purpose flour

1 teaspoon baking soda
1 teaspoon ground cinnamon
1/2 teaspoon ground cloves
1/2 teaspoon ground ginger
1/2 teaspoon salt
Confectioners' sugar, optional

1. In a mixing bowl, cream shortening and sugar. Add eggs; beat well. Beat in water and molasses. Combine flour, baking soda, cinnamon, cloves, ginger and salt; add to molasses mixture and mix well. Spread into a greased 15-in. x 10-in. x 1-in. baking pan.

2. Bake at 350° for 20-22 minutes or until a toothpick comes out clean. Cool. Dust with confectioners' sugar if desired. **Yield:** 16-20 servings.

🏅🏅🏅

White Chocolate Oatmeal Cookies

Edith Pluhar, Cohagen, Montana

My sons and grandsons manage our ranch, and they always seem to have one hand in the cookie jar—especially when I bake these crunchy morsels! Away from the kitchen, I enjoy my large garden and our fast-growing family.

- 1 cup butter, softened
- 1/2 cup sugar
- 1/2 cup packed brown sugar
- 1 egg
- 3 teaspoons vanilla extract
- 1 teaspoon coconut extract
- 6 squares (1 ounce *each*) white baking
  chocolate, melted

- 1-1/4 cups all-purpose flour
- 1 teaspoon salt
- 1 teaspoon baking soda
- 1-1/2 cups quick-cooking oats
- 1 cup flaked coconut, toasted

Additional sugar

1. In a mixing bowl, cream the butter and sugars. Add the egg and extracts; mix well. Stir in the melted chocolate. Combine the flour, salt and baking soda; gradually add to creamed mixture. Stir in the oats and the coconut.

2. Drop by tablespoonfuls 3 in. apart onto ungreased baking sheets. Flatten with a glass dipped in sugar. Bake at 350° for 9-11 minutes or until golden brown. Cool for 1 minute before removing to wire racks. **Yield:** about 5 dozen.

🎀🎀🎀
Butterscotch Cashew Bars

Lori Berg, Wentzville, Missouri

I knew these nutty bars were a success when I took them on our annual family vacation. My husband couldn't stop eating them…and my sister-in-law, who is a great cook, asked for the recipe. It makes a big batch, but they go quickly!

    1 cup plus 2 tablespoons butter, softened
  3/4 cup plus 2 tablespoons packed brown sugar
2-1/2 cups all-purpose flour
1-3/4 teaspoons salt
TOPPING:
    1 package (10 to 11 ounces) butterscotch chips
  1/2 cup plus 2 tablespoons light corn syrup
    3 tablespoons butter
    2 teaspoons water
2-1/2 cups salted cashew halves

1. In a mixing bowl, cream the butter and brown sugar. Combine flour and salt; add to creamed mixture just until combined. Press into a greased 15-in. x 10-in. x 1-in. baking pan. Bake at 350° for 10-12 minutes or until lightly browned.

2. Meanwhile, combine butterscotch chips, corn syrup, butter and water in a saucepan. Cook and stir over medium heat until chips and butter are melted. Spread over crust. Sprinkle with cashews; press down lightly.

3. Bake for 11-13 minutes or until topping is bubbly and lightly browned. Cool on a wire rack. Cut into bars. **Yield:** 3-1/2 dozen.

🎀🎀🎀
Honey Chip Granola Bars

RosAnna Troyer, Millersburg, Ohio

I first tried these not-too-sweet bars at my mother-in-law's house. A marshmallow, honey and peanut butter mixture is delicious over crunchy cereal, oats and nuts. Be sure to let the bars cool before pressing the mini chips on top or they'll melt.

  1/4 cup butter
  1/4 cup vegetable oil
1-1/2 pounds miniature marshmallows
  1/4 cup honey
  1/4 cup peanut butter
    5 cups old-fashioned oats
4-1/2 cups crisp rice cereal
    1 cup graham cracker crumbs (about 16 squares)
    1 cup flaked coconut
    1 cup crushed peanuts
  1/2 cup miniature chocolate chips

1. In a large saucepan, combine the butter, oil and marshmallows. Cook and stir over low heat until mixture is melted and smooth. Remove from the heat; stir in honey and peanut butter. Combine the oats, cereal, cracker crumbs, coconut and peanuts. Add to the marshmallow mixture; mix well.

2. Press into a greased 15-in. x 10-in. x 1-in. pan. Cool for 10-15 minutes. Sprinkle with chips and gently press into top. Cool completely. Cut into bars. **Yield:** about 4 dozen.

   Editor's Note: Reduced-fat or generic brands of peanut butter are not recommended for this recipe.

1/2 cup butter
1-1/2 cups sugar
4-2/3 cups (28 ounces) semisweet chocolate chips, *divided*
3 tablespoons hot water
4 *eggs*
5 teaspoons vanilla extract
1-1/2 cups all-purpose flour
1/2 teaspoon baking soda
1/2 teaspoon salt
2 cups coarsely chopped macadamia nuts *or* pecans, *divided*

1. In a saucepan over medium heat, melt butter and sugar. Remove from the heat; stir in 2 cups chocolate chips until melted. Pour into a mixing bowl; beat in water. Add eggs, one at a time, beating well after each addition. Add vanilla. Combine flour, baking soda and salt; beat into the chocolate mixture until smooth. Stir in 2 cups of chocolate chips and 1 cup of nuts.

2. Pour into a greased 13-in. x 9-in. x 2-in. baking pan. Sprinkle with remaining chips and nuts. Bake at 325° for 55 minutes or until the center is set (do not overbake). **Yield:** about 3-1/2 dozen.

🏵 🏵 🏵
Super Brownies

Bernice Muilenburg, Molalla, Oregon

Even though he's not a chocolate fan, my husband likes these brownies. I fix them quite often for family and company and potlucks.

🏵 🏵 🏵
Rhubarb Custard Bars

Shari Roach, South Milwaukee, Wisconsin

Once I tried these rich, gooey bars, I had to have the recipe so I could make them for my family and friends. The shortbread-like crust and rhubarb and custard layers inspire people to find rhubarb they can use to fix a batch for themselves.

2 cups all-purpose flour
1/4 cup sugar
1 cup cold butter
FILLING:
2 cups sugar
7 tablespoons all-purpose flour
1 cup heavy whipping cream
3 eggs, beaten
5 cups finely chopped fresh *or* frozen rhubarb, thawed and drained
TOPPING:
2 packages (3 ounces *each*) cream cheese, softened
1/2 cup sugar
1/2 teaspoon vanilla extract
1 cup heavy whipping cream, whipped

1. In a bowl, combine the flour and sugar; cut in butter until the mixture resembles coarse crumbs. Press into a greased 13-in. x 9-in. x 2-in. baking pan. Bake at

350° for 10 minutes. Meanwhile, for filling, combine sugar and flour in a bowl. Whisk in cream and eggs. Stir in the rhubarb. Pour over crust.

2. Bake at 350° for 40-45 minutes or until custard is set. Cool. For topping, beat cream cheese, sugar and vanilla until smooth; fold in whipped cream. Spread over top. Cover and chill. Cut into bars. Store in the refrigerator. **Yield:** 3 dozen.

🎖 🎖 🎖

Fruit-Filled Spritz Cookies

Ingeborg Keith, Newark, Delaware

From the first time I baked these cookies, they've been a lip-smacking success. Old-fashioned and attractive, they make a perfect holiday pastry.

1-1/2 cups chopped dates
   1 cup water
  1/2 cup sugar
   2 teaspoons orange juice
   2 teaspoons grated orange peel
   1 cup maraschino cherries, chopped
  1/2 cup flaked coconut
  1/2 cup ground nuts
DOUGH:
   1 cup butter, softened
   1 cup sugar
  1/2 cup packed brown sugar
   3 eggs
  1/2 teaspoon almond extract
  1/2 teaspoon vanilla extract
   4 cups all-purpose flour
  1/2 teaspoon baking soda
  1/2 teaspoon salt
Confectioners' sugar

1. In a saucepan, combine the first five ingredients; bring to a boil, stirring constantly. Reduce heat; cook and stir for 8 minutes or until thickened. Cool completely. Stir in cherries, coconut and nuts; set aside.

2. In a mixing bowl, cream butter and sugars. Beat in eggs and extracts. Combine the flour, baking soda and salt; gradually add to creamed mixture.

3. Using a cookie press fitted with a bar disk, press a 12-in.-long strip of dough onto an ungreased baking sheet. Spread fruit filling over dough. Press another strip over filling. Cut into 1-in. pieces (there is no need to separate the pieces). Repeat with remaining dough and filling.

4. Bake at 375° for 12-15 minutes or until edges are golden. Recut into pieces if necessary. Remove to wire racks to cool. Dust with confectioners' sugar. **Yield:** about 7-1/2 dozen.

Peaches 'n' Cream Pie, p. 201

Hot Fudge Sundae Cake, p. 193

Toffee-Mocha Cream Torte, p. 196

Cakes & Pies

When an occasion calls for a down-home dessert, nothing beats a slice of freshly made pie or cake. In this chapter you'll find dozens of choices to please your family.

Strawberry Lover's Pie, p. 205

Peanut Butter Lover's Cake, p. 188

🎀 🎀 🎀
Pumpkin Pound Cake

Jean Volk, Jacksonville, Florida

This recipe for nicely spiced pumpkin pound cake is one I've come to rely on. It's impossible to resist a slice topped with the sweet walnut sauce.

1-1/2 cups butter, softened
2-3/4 cups sugar
   6 eggs
   1 teaspoon vanilla extract
   3 cups all-purpose flour

3/4 teaspoon ground cinnamon
1/2 teaspoon baking powder
1/2 teaspoon salt
1/2 teaspoon ground ginger
1/4 teaspoon ground cloves
   1 cup canned pumpkin
WALNUT SAUCE:
   1 cup packed brown sugar
1/2 cup heavy whipping cream
1/4 cup corn syrup
   2 tablespoons butter
1/2 cup chopped walnuts
1/2 teaspoon vanilla extract

1. In a mixing bowl, cream butter and sugar. Add eggs, one at a time, beating well after each addition. Stir in vanilla. Combine the dry ingredients; add to creamed mixture alternately with pumpkin, beating just until combined. Pour into two greased and floured 9-in. x 5-in. x 3-in. loaf pans.

2. Bake at 350° for 65-70 minutes or until a toothpick inserted near the center comes out clean. Cool for 10 minutes before removing from pans to wire racks to cool completely.

3. For sauce, combine brown sugar, cream, corn syrup and butter in a saucepan. Bring to a boil over medium heat, stirring constantly. Reduce heat; cook and stir 5 minutes longer. Remove from the heat; stir in walnuts and vanilla. Serve warm over the cake. **Yield:** 16 servings (1-2/3 cups sauce).

🎀 🎀 🎀
Peanut Butter Lover's Cake

(Pictured on page 187)

Teresa Mozingo, Camden, South Carolina

My family thrives on peanut butter, so they just love it when I make this recipe.

   3 eggs
1-2/3 cups sugar, *divided*
1-1/2 cups milk, *divided*
   3 squares (1 ounce *each*) unsweetened chocolate, finely chopped
1/2 cup shortening
   1 teaspoon vanilla extract
   2 cups cake flour
   1 teaspoon baking soda
1/2 teaspoon salt
PEANUT BUTTER FROSTING:
   2 packages (8 ounces *each*) cream cheese, softened
   1 can (14 ounces) sweetened condensed milk
1-1/2 cups peanut butter
1/4 cup salted peanuts, chopped

   3 milk chocolate candy bars (1.55 ounces *each*), broken into squares

1. In a saucepan, whisk 1 egg until blended. Stir in 2/3 cup sugar, 1/2 cup milk and chocolate. Cook and stir over medium heat until chocolate is melted and mixture just comes to a boil. Remove from the heat; cool to room temperature.

2. In a mixing bowl, cream shortening and remaining sugar. Add remaining eggs, one at a time, beating well after each. Beat in vanilla. Combine the flour, baking soda and salt; add to creamed mixture alternately with remaining milk. Add chocolate mixture; mix well.

3. Pour into three greased and floured 9-in. round baking pans. Bake at 325° for 25-30 minutes or until a toothpick comes out clean. Cool for 10 minutes before removing from pans to wire racks.

4. For frosting, in a mixing bowl, beat cream cheese until light and fluffy. Gradually add milk and peanut butter, beating well after each addition. Spread between layers and over top and sides of cooled cake. Sprinkle with peanuts. Garnish with candy bars. Store in the refrigerator. **Yield:** 12-14 servings.

🎀🎀🎀
Sweet Apple Pie

Irene Evenson, Minto, North Dakota

By pairing apples and candy, I came up with this creation—a kind of toffee apple in a pie crust!

Pastry for double-crust pie (9 inches)
- 3/4 cup sugar
- 1/4 cup all-purpose flour
- 1/2 teaspoon ground cinnamon
- 1/2 teaspoon ground nutmeg
Dash salt
- 6 cups thinly sliced peeled tart apples (about 6 medium)
- 1 cup English toffee bits *or* almond brickle chips
- 2 tablespoons butter
Heavy whipping cream, optional

1. Line a 9-in. pie plate with bottom pastry; trim pastry even with edge of plate. In a large bowl, combine the sugar, flour, cinnamon, nutmeg and salt; add apples and toss to coat. Stir in toffee bits. Pour into crust. Dot with butter.

2. Roll out remaining pastry to fit top of pie; make decorative cutouts in the pastry. Place pastry over filling. Trim, seal and flute edges. Top with cutouts; brush top pastry with cream if desired. Cover edges loosely with foil.

3. Bake at 425° for 30 minutes. Remove foil; bake 10-15 minutes longer or until crust is golden brown and filling is bubbly. Cool on a wire rack. Store in the refrigerator. **Yield:** 6-8 servings.

🎀🎀🎀
Praline Ice Cream Cake

Joan Hallford, North Richland Hills, Texas

Melted ice cream is a key ingredient in this delectable golden cake. My family loves the pecan praline flavor.

- 1 cup packed brown sugar
- 1/2 cup sour cream
- 2 tablespoons plus 1/2 cup butter, *divided*
- 2 teaspoons cornstarch
- 1 teaspoon vanilla extract, *divided*
- 2 cups vanilla ice cream, softened
- 2 eggs
- 1-1/2 cups all-purpose flour
- 1 cup graham cracker crumbs (about 16 squares)
- 2/3 cup sugar
- 2-1/2 teaspoons baking powder
- 1/2 teaspoon salt
- 1/2 cup chopped pecans, toasted
Whipped cream, optional

1. In a heavy saucepan, combine the brown sugar, sour cream, 2 tablespoons butter and cornstarch. Cook and stir over medium heat until mixture comes to a boil. Remove from the heat. Stir in 1/2 teaspoon of vanilla; set aside.

2. Melt the remaining butter; place in a mixing bowl. Add ice cream; stir to blend. Add eggs, one at a time, beating well after each addition; stir in the remaining vanilla. Combine the flour, cracker crumbs, sugar, baking powder and salt; gradually add to ice cream mixture until combined. Pour into a greased 13-in. x 9-in. x 2-in. baking pan. Drizzle with half of the praline sauce.

3. Bake at 350° for 25-30 minutes or until a toothpick inserted near the center comes out clean. Cool on a wire rack. Add pecans to remaining sauce; spoon over warm cake (sauce will not cover the entire cake top). Cool in pan. Serve with whipped cream if desired. **Yield:** 15 servings.

🎗🎗🎗
Fluffy Strawberry Meringue Pie

Roxanna Shoffstall, Lakeview, Ohio

The combination of the cool, creamy berry filling and the delightfully different meringue crust guarantees you'll hear, "Pass the pie, please," all around the table.

- 3 **egg whites**
- 1/4 **teaspoon cream of tartar**
- 1 **cup sugar**
- 1/2 **cup crushed saltines (about 12 crackers)**
- 1/2 **cup chopped pecans**
- 1 **teaspoon vanilla extract**
- 2 **pints fresh strawberries,** *divided*
- 4 **cups miniature marshmallows**
- 1 **carton (8 ounces) frozen whipped topping, thawed**

Red food coloring, optional

1. In a mixing bowl, beat egg whites and cream of tartar on medium speed until soft peaks form. Gradually beat in sugar, 1 tablespoon at a time, on high until stiff glossy peaks form and sugar is dissolved. Fold in the crackers, pecans and vanilla.

2. Spread onto the bottom and up the sides of a greased 10-in. deep-dish pie plate. Bake at 350° for 25-30 minutes or until meringue is lightly browned. Cool on a wire rack.

3. Set aside one strawberry for garnish. Slice half of the strawberries; set aside. In a bowl, mash the remaining strawberries; drain juice, reserving 1/2 cup. In a saucepan, combine marshmallows and reserved juice. Cook and stir over low heat until marshmallows are melted. Refrigerate until partially set.

4. Fold the sliced and mashed strawberries and whipped topping into marshmallow mixture. Add food coloring if desired. Spoon into meringue shell. Garnish with the reserved strawberry. Refrigerate for 3 hours or until set. Refrigerate leftovers. **Yield:** 8-10 servings.

🎗🎗🎗
Moist Chocolate Cake

Christa Hageman, Telford, Pennsylvania

You don't have to spend a lot of time to serve an elegant and delicious dessert. You can quickly mix up the batter in one bowl, bake your cake and serve a crowd.

- 2 **cups sugar**
- 1-3/4 **cups all-purpose flour**
- 3/4 **cup baking cocoa**
- 2 **teaspoons baking soda**
- 1 **teaspoon baking powder**
- 1 **teaspoon salt**
- 2 **eggs**
- 1 **cup strong brewed coffee**
- 1 **cup buttermilk**
- 1/2 **cup vegetable oil**
- 1 **teaspoon vanilla extract**
- 1 **tablespoon confectioners' sugar**

1. In a large mixing bowl, combine first six ingredients. Add eggs, coffee, buttermilk, oil and vanilla; beat on medium speed for 2 minutes (batter will be thin). Pour into a greased and floured 10-in. fluted tube pan.

2. Bake at 350° for 45-50 minutes or until a toothpick comes out clean. Cool for 10 minutes before removing from pan to a wire rack to cool completely. Dust with confectioners' sugar. **Yield:** 12 servings.

Sponge Cake with Blueberry Topping

Frances Cooley, Coos Bay, Oregon

This recipe puts the blueberries grown in our area to good use. It's a great summertime treat.

    6 eggs, *separated*
1-1/2 cups sugar
   3/4 cup orange juice
1-1/2 cups all-purpose flour
1-1/2 teaspoons baking powder
   1/4 teaspoon cream of tartar
BLUEBERRY TOPPING:
   1/2 cup sugar
     2 teaspoons cornstarch
     1 tablespoon grated orange peel
   1/2 cup orange juice
     2 cups fresh *or* frozen blueberries
SOUR CREAM TOPPING:
     2 cups (16 ounces) sour cream
     1 tablespoon confectioners' sugar

     1 **teaspoon vanilla extract**
Shredded orange peel, optional

1. In a large mixing bowl, beat egg yolks for 4-5 minutes or until thickened and light yellow. Gradually add sugar, beating for 1-2 minutes or until sugar is dissolved. Add orange juice; beat for 2-3 minutes or until mixture slightly thickens. Combine flour and baking powder; gradually add to yolk mixture and mix well.

2. In a small mixing bowl, beat egg whites and cream of tartar until stiff peaks form. Fold into egg yolk mixture until well blended. Pour into an ungreased 10-in. tube pan. Bake at 325° for 50-55 minutes or until cake springs back when lightly touched. Immediately invert pan to cool.

3. For blueberry topping, combine sugar, cornstarch and orange peel in a saucepan. Stir in orange juice until smooth. Bring to a boil; cook and stir for 2 minutes or until thickened. Remove from the heat. Stir in blueberries.

4. In a bowl, combine the sour cream, confectioners' sugar and vanilla. Remove cooled cake from pan; cut into slices. Serve with warm blueberry topping and the sour cream topping. Garnish with orange peel if desired.
Yield: 12-16 servings.

3/4 cup sugar
    2 tablespoons quick-cooking tapioca
    4 cups sliced fresh apricots (about 16)
    1 tablespoon lemon juice
Pastry for single-crust pie (9 inches)
TOPPING:
    2/3 cup all-purpose flour
    1/2 cup sugar
    1/2 cup chopped pecans, toasted
    1/4 cup butter, melted

1. In a bowl, combine sugar and tapioca; mix well. Add apricots and lemon juice; toss to coat. Let stand for 15 minutes. Line a 9-in. pie plate with pastry. Trim pastry to 1/2 in. beyond edge of plate; flute edges. Pour filling into crust.

2. In a small bowl, combine flour, sugar and pecans. Stir in butter. Sprinkle over filling. Cover edges loosely with foil. Bake at 350° for 15 minutes. Remove foil; bake 25-30 minutes longer or until crust is golden brown and filling is bubbly. Cool on a wire rack. Store in the refrigerator. **Yield:** 6-8 servings.

🎀 🎀 🎀
Dutch Apricot Pie

Joanne Hutmacher, Lemoore, California

I freeze several bagfuls of apricots when they are in season, thinking of this pie all the while.

🎀 🎀 🎀
Upside-Down German Chocolate Cake

Mrs. Harold Sanders, Glouster, Ohio

This simple recipe yields a delectable German chocolate cake that folks will "flip over!"

    1/2 cup packed brown sugar
    1/4 cup butter
    2/3 cup pecan halves
    2/3 cup flaked coconut
    1/4 cup evaporated milk
CAKE:
    1/3 cup butter, softened
    1 cup sugar
    1 package (4 ounces) German sweet chocolate, melted
    2 eggs
    1 teaspoon vanilla extract
1-1/2 cups all-purpose flour
    1/2 teaspoon baking soda
    1/2 teaspoon baking powder
    1/2 teaspoon salt
    3/4 cup buttermilk
Whipped topping, optional

1. In a saucepan over low heat, cook and stir brown sugar and butter until sugar is dissolved and butter is melted. Spread into a greased 9-in. square baking pan. Sprinkle with pecans and coconut. Drizzle with evaporated milk; set aside. In a mixing bowl, cream butter and sugar. Beat in the chocolate, eggs and vanilla. Combine the dry ingredients; add to the creamed mixture alternately with buttermilk. Pour over topping in pan.

2. Bake at 350° for 40-45 minutes or until a toothpick inserted near the center comes out clean. Cool for 5 minutes before inverting onto a serving plate. Serve with whipped topping if desired. **Yield:** 9 servings.

Butternut Squash Layer Cake

Deanna Richter, Fenton, Iowa

The recipe for this lovely cake with its yummy, old-fashioned frosting has been in our family for as long as I can remember.

  1/2 cup butter, softened
     1 cup sugar
     1 cup packed brown sugar
     2 eggs
     1 cup mashed cooked butternut squash
     1 teaspoon maple flavoring
     3 cups cake flour
     4 teaspoons baking powder
  1/4 teaspoon baking soda
  1/2 cup milk
     1 cup chopped walnuts
BROWN SUGAR FROSTING:
1-1/2 cups packed brown sugar
     3 egg whites
     6 tablespoons water
  1/4 teaspoon cream of tartar
  1/8 teaspoon salt
     1 teaspoon vanilla extract

1. In a mixing bowl, cream butter and sugars. Add eggs, one at a time, beating well after each addition. Add squash and maple flavoring; mix well. Combine flour, baking powder and baking soda; add to creamed mixture alternately with milk. Stir in walnuts. Pour into two greased and floured 9-in. round baking pans.

2. Bake at 350° for 25-30 minutes or until a toothpick inserted near the center comes out clean. Cool 10 minutes before removing from pans to wire racks.

3. For frosting, combine the brown sugar, egg whites, water, cream of tartar and salt in a heavy saucepan. With a portable mixer, beat on low speed for 1 minute. Continue beating over low heat until a thermometer reads 160°, about 8-10 minutes.

4. Pour frosting into a large mixing bowl; add vanilla. Beat on high speed until stiff peaks form, about 3 minutes. Spread between layers and over top and sides of cake. Refrigerate. **Yield:** 10-12 servings.

   Editor's Note: A stand mixer is recommended for beating the frosting after it reaches 160°.

Hot Fudge Sundae Cake

(Pictured on page 186)

Hildy Adams, Alma, Michigan

My husband is a real chocolate lover, so I'm always on the lookout for great dessert recipes like this one, which I found years ago. Who can resist the combination of chocolate cake, ice cream and hot fudge sauce? It gets rave reviews whenever I serve it.

     1 package (11-1/2 ounces) milk chocolate chips
  1/3 cup butter
     4 eggs, *separated*
  1/3 cup all-purpose flour
  1/3 cup sugar
  1/2 cup slivered almonds, toasted
HOT FUDGE SAUCE:
  1/2 cup sugar
  1/2 cup baking cocoa
  1/2 cup heavy whipping cream
  1/2 cup semisweet chocolate chips
  1/4 cup butter
     1 teaspoon vanilla extract
Vanilla ice cream

1. In a heavy saucepan, melt milk chocolate chips and butter over low heat. Cool slightly. Whisk in egg yolks. Add flour just until combined. In a small mixing bowl, beat egg whites until foamy. Gradually add sugar, beating until stiff peaks form. Fold into chocolate mixture until blended. Fold in almonds.

2. Pour into a greased 10-in. pie plate or quiche dish. Bake at 350° for 25-30 minutes or until a toothpick comes out clean. Cool on a wire rack.

3. For sauce, combine sugar, cocoa and cream in a saucepan until smooth. Add semisweet chips and butter. Cook and stir over low heat until chips and butter are melted and mixture is smooth. Remove from the heat; stir in vanilla.

4. Cut cake into wedges; top with ice cream. Drizzle with warm sauce. **Yield:** 12 servings.

🎗🎗🎗

Lemon Meringue Cake

Julie Courie, Macomb, Michigan

This cake tastes just like lemon meringue pie! Fresh lemon fla-vor shines through in the custard filling between the layers.

>   1 package (18-1/4 ounces) lemon *or* yellow
>   cake mix
>   3 eggs
>   1 cup water
>   1/3 cup vegetable oil
> FILLING:
>   1 cup sugar
>   3 tablespoons cornstarch
>   1/4 teaspoon salt
>   1/2 cup water
>   1/4 cup lemon juice
>   4 egg yolks, beaten
>   4 teaspoons butter
>   1 teaspoon grated lemon peel
> MERINGUE:
>   4 egg whites
>   1/4 teaspoon cream of tartar
>   3/4 cup sugar

1. In a mixing bowl, combine cake mix, eggs, water and oil. Beat on low until moistened. Beat on high for 2 minutes or until blended. Pour into two greased and floured 9-in. round baking pans. Bake at 350° for 25-30 minutes or until a toothpick comes out clean. Cool for 10 minutes; remove from pans to wire racks.

2. For filling, combine sugar, cornstarch and salt in a saucepan. Stir in water and juice until smooth. Bring to a boil over medium heat; cook and stir 1-2 minutes or until thickened. Remove from heat. Stir a small amount of hot filling into egg yolks; return all to pan, stirring constantly. Bring to a gentle boil; cook and stir for 2 minutes. Remove from heat; stir in butter and lemon peel. Cool completely.

3. For meringue, in a mixing bowl, beat egg whites and cream of tartar until foamy. Gradually beat in sugar on high until stiff peaks form. To assemble, split each cake into two layers. Place bottom layer on an ovenproof serving plate; spread with a third of the filling.

4. Repeat layers twice. Top with fourth cake layer. Spread meringue over top and sides. Bake at 350° for 10-15 minutes or until meringue is lightly browned. Serve or refrigerate. **Yield:** 12-14 servings.

🎀🎀🎀
Chocolate Chip Pound Cake

Michele Strunks, Brookville, Ohio

My mom has been making this cake for over 30 years. Dotted with chips and topped with a chocolate glaze, it is absolutely divine.

- 1 cup butter, softened
- 2 cups sugar
- 4 eggs
- 1 teaspoon vanilla extract
- 4 cups all-purpose flour
- 4 teaspoons baking powder
- 1 teaspoon baking soda
- 2 cups (16 ounces) sour cream
- 2 cups (12 ounces) semisweet chocolate chips

GLAZE:
- 1/4 cup semisweet chocolate chips
- 2 tablespoons butter
- 1-1/4 cups confectioners' sugar
- 3 tablespoons milk
- 1/2 teaspoon vanilla extract

1. In a mixing bowl, cream butter and sugar. Add the eggs, one at a time, beating well after each addition. Beat in vanilla. Combine the flour, baking powder and baking soda; add to creamed mixture alternately with sour cream. Fold in chocolate chips.

2. Pour into a greased and floured 10-in. fluted tube pan. Bake at 350° for 60-65 minutes or until a toothpick inserted near the center comes out clean. Cool for 10 minutes before removing from pan to a wire rack to cool completely.

3. For glaze, in a saucepan over low heat, melt chocolate chips and butter. Remove from the heat; whisk in confectioners' sugar, milk and vanilla until smooth. Working quickly, drizzle over cooled cake. **Yield:** 12-14 servings.

🎀🎀🎀
Raspberry Meringue Pie

Karen Rempel Arthur, Wainfleet, Ontario

Whether my husband and I host a backyard barbecue or a formal dinner, we love treating guests to this raspberry pie.

- 1/3 cup plus 1/4 cup sugar, *divided*
- 3 tablespoons cornstarch
- 1-1/2 cups milk
- 4 eggs, *separated*
- 1 teaspoon butter
- 1/4 teaspoon almond extract
- 1 graham cracker crust (10 inches)
- 1-1/8 teaspoons unflavored gelatin
- 2 tablespoons plus 1/4 teaspoon cold water, *divided*
- 1 can (21 ounces) raspberry pie filling
- 3/4 teaspoon cream of tartar

1. In a saucepan, combine 1/3 cup sugar and cornstarch. Stir in milk until smooth. Cook and stir over medium heat until thickened and bubbly. Reduce heat; cook and stir 2 minutes longer. Remove from the heat. Stir a small amount of mixture into egg yolks. Return all to the pan, stirring constantly. Bring to a gentle boil; cook and stir 2 minutes longer. Remove from heat; stir in butter and extract. Pour hot filling into crust.

2. Sprinkle gelatin over 2 tablespoons cold water; let stand for 2 minutes. In a saucepan, bring raspberry filling and gelatin mixture to a boil. Reduce heat; simmer, uncovered, for 5 minutes.

3. Meanwhile, in a mixing bowl, beat egg whites and cream of tartar on medium speed until soft peaks form. Beat in remaining water. Gradually beat in remaining sugar on high until stiff glossy peaks form and sugar is dissolved.

4. Pour hot filling over custard. Spread meringue evenly over hot filling, sealing edges to crust. Bake at 325° for 15-18 minutes or until meringue is golden. Cool on a wire rack for 1 hour. Refrigerate for at least 3 hours before serving. Refrigerate leftovers. **Yield:** 8-10 servings.

✦✦✦
Gingerbread with Lemon Sauce

Kristen Oak, Pocatello, Idaho

I asked my mother-in-law for this recipe once I learned that this spice cake topped with tangy sauce is my husband's favorite.

   1 **cup shortening**
   1 **cup sugar**
   1 **cup light molasses**
   2 **eggs**
   3 **cups all-purpose flour**
1-1/2 **teaspoons salt**
1-1/2 **teaspoons baking soda**
   1 **teaspoon ground ginger**
   1 **teaspoon ground cinnamon**
   1 **cup hot water**
LEMON SAUCE:
 1/2 **cup sugar**
   2 **teaspoons cornstarch**
Dash salt
Dash nutmeg
   1 **cup water**
   2 **egg yolks, beaten**
   2 **tablespoons butter**
   2 **tablespoons lemon juice**
 1/2 **teaspoon grated lemon peel**

1. In a mixing bowl, combine the first four ingredients; mix well. Combine the dry ingredients; add to molasses mixture alternately with hot water. Pour into a greased 13-in. x 9-in. x 2-in. baking pan. Bake at 350° for 35-40 minutes or until a toothpick inserted near the center comes out clean. Cool on a wire rack.

2. Meanwhile, in a saucepan, combine the first five sauce ingredients until smooth. Bring to a boil: cook and stir for 1-2 minutes or until thickened. Remove from the heat. Stir a small amount of hot mixture into egg yolks. Return all to pan, stirring constantly. Cook and stir for 2 minutes or until a thermometer reads 160°.

3. Remove from the heat; stir in butter, lemon juice and peel. Serve with warm cake. Refrigerate leftover sauce. **Yield:** 16-20 servings.

✦✦✦
Toffee-Mocha Cream Torte

(Pictured on page 186)

Lynn Rogers, Richfield, North Carolina

When you really want to impress someone, this scrumptious torte is just the thing to make! Instant coffee granules give the moist chocolate cake a mild mocha flavor.

   1 **cup butter, softened**
   2 **cups sugar**
   2 **eggs**
1-1/2 **teaspoons vanilla extract**
2-2/3 **cups all-purpose flour**
 3/4 **cup baking cocoa**
   2 **teaspoons baking soda**
 1/4 **teaspoon salt**
   1 **cup buttermilk**
   2 **teaspoons instant coffee granules**
   1 **cup boiling water**
TOPPING:
 1/2 **teaspoon instant coffee granules**
   1 **teaspoon hot water**
   2 **cups heavy whipping cream**
   3 **tablespoons light brown sugar**
   6 **Heath candy bars (1.4 ounces *each*), crushed, *divided***

1. In a mixing bowl, cream butter and sugar. Beat in eggs and vanilla. Combine the flour, cocoa, baking soda and salt; add to creamed mixture alternately with buttermilk. Dissolve coffee in water; add to batter. Beat for 2 minutes. Pour into three greased and floured 9-in. round baking pans.

2. Bake at 350° for 16-20 minutes or until a toothpick inserted near the center comes out clean. Cool for 10 minutes before removing from pans to wire racks to cool completely.

3. For topping, dissolve coffee in water in a mixing bowl; cool. Add cream and brown sugar. Beat until stiff peaks form. Place bottom cake layer on a serving plate; top with 1-1/3 cups of topping. Sprinkle with 1/2 cup of crushed candy bars. Repeat layers twice. Store in the refrigerator. **Yield:** 12-14 servings.

🎀🎀🎀
No-Bake Cheesecake Pie

Geneva Mayer, Olney, Illinois

I came up with this creamy white chocolate cheesecake after remembering one evening that I needed to bring a treat to the office the next day. It was a tremendous hit.

- 1 cup vanilla *or* white chips
- 2 packages (8 ounces *each*) cream cheese, cubed
- 1 carton (8 ounces) frozen whipped topping, thawed
- 1 graham cracker crust (9 inches)
- 1/3 cup English toffee bits *or* almond brickle chips

1. In a heavy saucepan, melt chips over medium-low heat; stir until smooth. Remove from the heat; stir in cream cheese until smooth. Fold in whipped topping.

2. Pour into the crust. Cover and refrigerate overnight or until set. Just before serving, sprinkle with toffee bits. **Yield:** 6-8 servings.

🎀🎀🎀
Maple Nut Cake

Emma Magielda, Amsterdam, New York

Our state is famous for its maple syrup. I like using maple syrup in desserts because it lends a distinct flavor.

- 1/2 cup butter, softened
- 1/2 cup sugar
- 1 cup maple syrup
- 2 eggs
- 2-1/4 cups cake flour
- 3 teaspoons baking powder
- 1 teaspoon salt
- 1/2 cup milk
- 1/2 cup chopped nuts

FROSTING:
- 1 cup sugar
- 1/2 cup maple syrup
- 2 egg whites
- 1 teaspoon corn syrup
- 1/8 teaspoon salt
- 1/4 teaspoon cream of tartar

1. In a bowl, cream the butter, sugar, syrup and eggs. Combine flour, baking powder and salt; add to the creamed mixture alternately with milk. Fold in nuts. Pour into two greased and floured 8-in. baking pans.

2. Bake at 350° for 20-25 minutes or until a toothpick inserted near the center comes out clean. Cool for 10 minutes before removing from pans to wire racks to cool completely.

3. In a heavy saucepan or double boiler, combine the frosting ingredients. With a portable mixer, beat on low speed for 1 minute. Continue beating over low heat until frosting reaches 160°, about 8-10 minutes. Pour into a large mixing bowl. Beat on high until stiff peaks form, about 7 minutes. Frost between layers and over top and sides of cake. **Yield:** 12-14 servings.

🎗🎗🎗 Mississippi Mud Cake

Tammi Simpson, Greensburg, Kentucky

Make this tempting cake, and you'll satisfy kids of all ages! A fudgy brownie-like base is topped with marshmallow creme and a nutty frosting.

- 1 cup butter, softened
- 2 cups sugar
- 4 eggs
- 1-1/2 cups self-rising flour
- 1/2 cup baking cocoa
- 1 cup chopped pecans
- 1 jar (7 ounces) marshmallow creme

FROSTING:
- 1/2 cup butter, softened
- 3-3/4 cups confectioners' sugar
- 3 tablespoons baking cocoa
- 1 tablespoon vanilla extract
- 4 to 5 tablespoons milk
- 1 cup chopped pecans

1. In a mixing bowl, cream butter and sugar. Add eggs, one at a time, beating well after each addition. Combine flour and cocoa; gradually add to creamed mixture. Fold in the pecans. Transfer to a greased 13-in. x 9-in. x 2-in. baking pan. Bake at 350° for 35-40 minutes or until a toothpick inserted near the center comes out clean. Cool for 3 minutes (cake will fall in the center). Spoon the marshmallow creme over cake; carefully spread to cover top. Cool completely.

2. For frosting, in a mixing bowl, cream butter. Beat in confectioners' sugar, cocoa, vanilla and enough milk to achieve frosting consistency. Fold in pecans. Spread over marshmallow creme layer. Store in the refrigerator. **Yield:** 16-20 servings.

Editor's Note: As a substitute for *each* 1/2 cup of self-rising flour, place 3/4 teaspoon baking powder and 1/4 teaspoon salt in a 1/2-cup measuring cup. Add all-purpose flour to measure 1/2 cup.

🎗🎗🎗 Cherry Blueberry Pie

Betty Williams, Scotts, Michigan

I came up with this pie recipe that combines cherries and blueberries. It's especially good served warm with ice cream.

- Pastry for a double-crust pie (9 inches)
- 2 cups pitted sweet cherries
- 2 cups fresh blueberries
- 3/4 cup sugar
- 1/4 cup all-purpose flour
- 1/8 teaspoon ground nutmeg
- 1 tablespoon butter

Additional sugar

1. Line a 9-in. pie plate with bottom crust; trim pastry even with edge. Set aside. In a bowl, gently combine cherries and blueberries. Combine the sugar, flour and nutmeg; stir into fruit. Let stand for 10 minutes. Pour into crust; dot with butter. Roll out remaining pastry; make a lattice crust. Seal and flute edges. Sprinkle with sugar. Cover edges of pastry loosely with foil.

2. Bake at 425° for 15 minutes. Reduce heat to 350°; bake 30-35 minutes longer or until pastry is golden brown and filling is bubbly. Cool on a wire rack. **Yield:** 6-8 servings.

🏵 🏵 🏵
Apricot Hazelnut Torte

Enid Stoehr, Emsdale, Ontario

My husband, Gerry, and I love it when our children and grandchildren visit. One cake that gets oohs and aahs from the family every time is this luscious torte. It's as light as a feather and tastes heavenly.

      1 **cup ground hazelnuts**
  3/4 **cup all-purpose flour**
      2 **teaspoons baking powder**
  1/2 **teaspoon salt**
      4 **eggs,** *separated*
      2 **tablespoons water**
      1 **teaspoon vanilla extract**
      1 **cup sugar,** *divided*
      2 **cups heavy whipping cream**
  1/4 **cup confectioners' sugar**
  2/3 **cup pureed canned apricots**
  1/2 **cup apricot jam,** *warmed*
Whipped cream, sliced apricots and whole *or* **chopped hazelnuts, optional**

1. In a bowl, combine hazelnuts, flour, baking powder and salt; set aside. In a mixing bowl, beat the egg yolks, water and vanilla until lemon-colored. Gradually add 3/4 cup sugar; set aside. In another mixing bowl, beat egg whites until soft peaks form. Add remaining sugar, 1 tablespoon at a time, beating until stiff peaks form. Fold a fourth of the dry ingredients into egg yolk mixture. Repeat three times. Fold in egg white mixture.

2. Line two greased 9-in. round baking pans with waxed paper; grease the paper. Spread batter evenly into pans. Bake at 350° for 20-25 minutes or until cake springs back when lightly touched. Cool for 10 minutes before removing from pans to wire racks to cool completely.

3. In a mixing bowl, beat cream and confectioners' sugar until stiff peaks form. Fold in apricots. Split each cake into two layers. Spread filling between layers and over sides of torte. Spread jam over top. Garnish with whipped cream, apricots and hazelnuts if desired. Store in the refrigerator. **Yield:** 12-14 servings.

❦❦❦ Very Lemony Meringue Pie

Betty Bradley, Sebring, Florida

As a winter resident of Florida, I have access to juicy, tree-fresh lemons. They're at their zesty best in this mouthwatering family pie recipe.

1-1/4 cups sugar
  1/3 cup cornstarch
    1 cup cold water
    3 egg yolks
    1 cup lemon juice
    3 tablespoons butter
    1 pastry shell (9 inches), baked
MERINGUE:
    1 tablespoon cornstarch
  1/3 cup cold water
    3 egg whites
    1 teaspoon vanilla extract
Dash salt
    6 tablespoons sugar

1. In a saucepan, combine sugar and cornstarch. Stir in water until smooth. Cook and stir over medium heat until thickened and bubbly. Reduce heat; cook and stir 2 minutes longer. Remove from the heat.

2. Stir a small amount of hot filling into egg yolks. Return all to the pan, stirring constantly. Bring to a gentle boil; cook and stir 2 minutes longer. Remove from the heat. Add lemon juice and butter; stir until butter is melted and mixture is blended. Pour hot filling into pastry shell.

3. In a saucepan, combine cornstarch and water until smooth. Cook and stir over medium-low heat until mixture is thickened, about 2 minutes. Remove from the heat. In a mixing bowl, beat egg whites, vanilla and salt until foamy. Gradually beat in sugar, 1 tablespoon at a time, on medium speed until soft peaks form and sugar is dissolved. Gradually beat in cornstarch mixture, 1 tablespoon at a time, on high until stiff peaks form.

4. Spread evenly over hot filling, sealing edges to crust. Bake at 325° for 18-20 minutes or until meringue is golden. Cool on a wire rack for 1 hour. Refrigerate pie for at least 3 hours before serving. Refrigerate leftovers. **Yield:** 6-8 servings.

❦❦❦ Harvest Snack Cake

Hilary Carroll, Dearborn, Michigan

This tasty treat was my first successful attempt at baking light. The ginger, cinnamon and nutmeg give it a familiar spice cake flavor, and raisins and shredded carrots help keep it moist.

    2 cups whole wheat flour
1-1/4 cups packed brown sugar
    2 teaspoons baking soda
  3/4 teaspoon ground cinnamon
  1/2 teaspoon ground nutmeg
  1/8 to 1/4 teaspoon ground ginger
    2 eggs
  1/2 cup unsweetened applesauce
    1 teaspoon vanilla extract
1-1/2 cups shredded carrots
    1 cup raisins

1. In a bowl, combine the flour, brown sugar, baking soda, cinnamon, nutmeg and ginger. Combine the eggs, applesauce and vanilla; stir into dry ingredients just until moistened. Fold in the carrots and raisins (batter will be thick).

2. Spread evenly in a 13-in. x 9-in. x 2-in. baking pan coated with nonstick cooking spray. Bake at 350° for 30-35 minutes or until a toothpick inserted near the center comes out clean. Cool on a wire rack. **Yield:** 15 servings.

Peaches 'n' Cream Pie

(Pictured on page 186)

Tamrah Tso, Flagstaff, Arizona

In summer, my aunt and uncle provide me with tree-fresh fruit from their peach orchard. My husband gets so excited when they have a bumper crop because he knows this dessert will be on our menu often.

Pastry for double-crust pie (9 inches)
     1 cup sugar
 1/4 cup all-purpose flour
     1 tablespoon quick-cooking tapioca
Dash salt
     1 cup heavy whipping cream, *divided*
 1/4 teaspoon vanilla extract

4 cups sliced fresh *or* frozen peaches, thawed
Additional sugar

1. Line a 9-in. pie plate with bottom pastry; trim pastry even with edge of plate. In a bowl, combine the sugar, flour, tapioca and salt; mix well. Set aside 2 tablespoons cream. Combine remaining cream with vanilla; add to the sugar mixture. Add peaches; toss to coat. Let stand for 15 minutes.

2. Pour peach mixture into crust. Roll out the remaining pastry; make a lattice top crust. Seal and flute edges. Brush with reserved cream; sprinkle with additional sugar.

3. Cover edges loosely with foil. Bake at 400° for 50-55 minutes or until golden brown and bubbly. Cool on a wire rack. Store pie in the refrigerator. **Yield:** 6-8 servings.

Sour Cream Chocolate Cake

Patsy Foster, Marion, Arkansas

This luscious chocolate layer cake gets wonderful moistness from sour cream. Its irresistible topping and marvelous, from-scratch goodness make it a classic!

     4 squares (1 ounce *each*) unsweetened
        chocolate, melted and cooled
     1 cup water
 3/4 cup sour cream
 1/4 cup shortening
     1 teaspoon vanilla extract
     2 eggs, beaten
     2 cups all-purpose flour
     2 cups sugar
 1-1/4 teaspoons baking soda
     1 teaspoon salt
 1/2 teaspoon baking powder
FROSTING:
 1/2 cup butter, softened
     6 squares (1 ounce *each*) unsweetened
        chocolate, melted and cooled
     6 cups confectioners' sugar
 1/2 cup sour cream
     6 tablespoons milk
     2 teaspoons vanilla extract
 1/8 teaspoon salt

1. In a mixing bowl, combine the first six ingredients; mix well. Combine the dry ingredients; gradually add to chocolate mixture. Beat on low speed just until moistened. Beat on high for 3 minutes.

2. Pour into two greased and floured 9-in. round baking pans. Bake at 350° for 30 minutes or until a toothpick inserted near the center comes out clean. Cool for 10 minutes before removing from pans to wire racks to cool completely.

3. In a mixing bowl, combine frosting ingredients. Beat until smooth and creamy. Spread over cake. Store in the refrigerator. **Yield:** 12-16 servings.

🎗 🎗 🎗
Surprise Carrot Cake

Lisa Bowen, Little Britain, Ontario

A cousin gave me this recipe. It's a wonderful potluck pleaser with its "surprise" cream cheese center. My husband and our two young children love it, too! It's a great way to use up the overabundance of carrots from my garden.

> 3 **eggs**
> 1-3/4 **cups sugar**
> 3 **cups shredded carrots**
> 1 **cup vegetable oil**
> 2 **cups all-purpose flour**
> 2 **teaspoons baking soda**
> 2 **teaspoons ground cinnamon**
> 1 **teaspoon salt**
> 1/2 **cup chopped pecans**

FILLING:
> 1 **package (8 ounces) cream cheese, softened**
> 1/4 **cup sugar**
> 1 **egg**

FROSTING:
> 1 **package (8 ounces) cream cheese, softened**
> 1/4 **cup butter, softened**
> 2 **teaspoons vanilla extract**
> 4 **cups confectioners' sugar**

1. In a mixing bowl, beat eggs and sugar. Add carrots and oil; beat until blended. Combine the flour, baking soda, cinnamon and salt. Add to carrot mixture; mix well. Stir in pecans. Pour 3 cups batter into a greased and floured 10-in. fluted tube pan.

2. In a mixing bowl, beat cream cheese and sugar. Add egg; mix well. Spoon over batter. Top with remaining batter.

3. Bake at 350° for 55-60 minutes or until a toothpick inserted near the center comes out clean. Cool for 10 minutes before removing from pan to a wire rack to cool completely.

4. For frosting, in a small mixing bowl, beat the cream cheese, butter and vanilla until smooth. Gradually add confectioners' sugar. Frost cake. Store in the refrigerator. **Yield:** 12-16 servings.

🎗🎗🎗 Caramel Apple Cupcakes

Diane Halferty, Corpus Christi, Texas

Bring these extra-special cupcakes to your next bake sale and watch how quickly they disappear—if your family doesn't gobble them up first! Kids will go for the fun appearance and tasty toppings while adults will appreciate the moist, spiced cake underneath.

- 1 package (18-1/4 ounces) spice or carrot cake mix
- 2 cups chopped peeled tart apples
- 20 caramels
- 3 tablespoons milk
- 1 cup finely chopped pecans, toasted
- 12 Popsicle sticks

1. Prepare cake batter according to package directions; fold in apples. Fill 12 greased or paper-lined jumbo muffin cups three-fourths full.

2. Bake at 350° for 20 minutes or until a toothpick comes out clean. Cool for 10 minutes before removing from pans to wire racks to cool completely.

3. In a saucepan, cook the caramels and milk over low heat until smooth. Spread over cupcakes. Sprinkle with pecans. Insert a wooden stick into the center of each cupcake. **Yield:** 1 dozen.

🎗🎗🎗 Upside-Down Raspberry Cake

Joy Beck, Cincinnati, Ohio

This delicious cake is great for any occasion. I've received many compliments from family and friends.

- 1-1/2 cups fresh or frozen unsweetened raspberries, divided
- 1 cup butter, softened
- 1 cup sugar
- 3 eggs
- 2 teaspoons lemon juice
- 1 teaspoon vanilla extract
- 2 cups all-purpose flour
- 1-1/2 teaspoons baking powder
- 1/2 teaspoon salt
- 2/3 cup milk
- Confectioners' sugar

1. Line the bottom and sides of a 9-in. square baking pan with foil; coat with nonstick cooking spray. Place 1/2 cup raspberries in pan; set aside. In a mixing bowl, cream butter and sugar. Add eggs, lemon juice and vanilla; mix well. Combine flour, baking powder and salt; add to creamed mixture alternately with milk.

2. Fold in the remaining raspberries. Carefully spoon over berries in pan. Bake at 350° for 40–45 minutes or until a toothpick inserted near the center comes out clean. Cool for 10 minutes. Invert cake onto a serving platter; carefully remove foil. Cool completely. Dust with confectioners' sugar. **Yield:** 9 servings.

Editor's Note: If using frozen raspberries, do not thaw before adding to batter.

⚜ ⚜ ⚜
Carrot Cupcakes

Doreen Kelly, Roslyn, Pennsylvania

I often "hide" nutritional foods inside sweet treats. The carrots add wonderful moistness to these cupcakes, which have a rich cream cheese frosting. Now we can have our cake and eat our vegetables, too!

      4 eggs
      2 cups sugar
      1 cup vegetable oil
      2 cups all-purpose flour
      2 teaspoons ground cinnamon
      1 teaspoon baking soda
      1 teaspoon baking powder
      1 teaspoon ground allspice
  1/2 teaspoon salt
      3 cups grated carrots
CHUNKY FROSTING:
      1 package (8 ounces) cream cheese, softened
  1/4 cup butter, softened
      2 cups confectioners' sugar
  1/2 cup flaked coconut
  1/2 cup chopped pecans
  1/2 cup chopped raisins

1. In a mixing bowl, beat eggs, sugar and oil. Combine the next six ingredients; gradually add to egg mixture. Stir in carrots. Fill greased or paper-lined muffin cups two-thirds full. Bake at 325° for 20-25 minutes or until a toothpick comes out clean. Cool for 5 minutes before removing from pans to wire racks.

2. For frosting, in a mixing bowl, beat cream cheese and butter until combined. Gradually beat in confectioners' sugar. Stir in coconut, pecans and raisins. Frost cupcakes. Store in the refrigerator. **Yield:** 2 dozen.

⚜ ⚜ ⚜
Cream Cheese Sheet Cake

Gaye Mann, Washington, North Carolina

This buttery sheet cake with its fudgy chocolate glaze is a real crowd-pleaser. It's not uncommon to see folks going back for second and even third slices.

      1 cup plus 2 tablespoons butter, softened
      2 packages (3 ounces *each*) cream cheese, softened
  2-1/4 cups sugar
      6 eggs
  3/4 teaspoon vanilla extract
  2-1/4 cups cake flour
FROSTING:
      1 cup sugar
  1/3 cup evaporated milk
  1/2 cup butter
  1/2 cup semisweet chocolate chips

1. In a mixing bowl, cream butter, cream cheese and sugar. Add eggs, one at a time, beating well after each addition. Beat in vanilla. Add flour; mix well. Pour into a greased 15-in. x 10-in. x 1-in. baking pan. Bake at 325° for 30-35 minutes or until a toothpick inserted near the center comes out clean. Cool completely.

2. For frosting, combine sugar and milk in a saucepan; bring to a boil over medium heat. Cover and cook for 3 minutes (do not stir). Stir in butter and chocolate chips until melted. Cool slightly. Stir; spread over cake. **Yield:** 24-30 servings.

🎗🎗🎗 Strawberry Lover's Pie

(Pictured on page 187 and on cover)

Lauretha Rowe, Scranton, Kansas

The second question people ask when I serve them this pie is, "What's your recipe?" It comes right after their first question— "May I have another slice?"

> 3 squares (1 ounce *each*) semisweet chocolate, *divided*
> 1 tablespoon butter
> 1 pastry shell (9 inches), baked
> 2 packages (3 ounces *each*) cream cheese, softened
> 1/2 cup sour cream
> 3 tablespoons sugar
> 1/2 teaspoon vanilla extract
> 3 to 4 cups fresh strawberries, hulled

1/3 cup strawberry jam, melted

1. In a saucepan, melt 2 ounces chocolate and butter over low heat, stirring constantly; spread or brush over the bottom and up the sides of pastry shell. Chill.

2. Meanwhile, in a mixing bowl, beat cream cheese, sour cream, sugar and vanilla until smooth. Spread over chocolate layer; cover and chill for 2 hours.

3. Arrange strawberries, tip end up, atop the filling. Brush jam over strawberries. Melt the remaining chocolate and drizzle over all. **Yield:** 6-8 servings.

🎗🎗🎗 Glazed Pineapple Pie

Joyce Dubois, Wolsey, South Dakota

Just for fun, I enter my favorite pie recipes in area contests and fairs. This one is a guaranteed winner. It's so pretty with a golden crust and drizzles of glaze. Plus, the coconut adds a tropical accent to the tangy pineapple inside.

> 1 can (20 ounces) crushed pineapple
> Pastry for double-crust pie (9 inches)
> 3/4 cup flaked coconut
> 1 cup sugar
> 1/4 cup all-purpose flour
> 1/4 teaspoon salt
> 1 tablespoon lemon juice
> 1 tablespoon butter, melted
> GLAZE:
> 1/2 cup confectioners' sugar
> 1/4 teaspoon rum *or* vanilla extract

1. Drain pineapple, reserving 2 tablespoons juice (discard remaining juice or refrigerate for another use); set pineapple aside. Line a 9-in. pie plate with bottom pastry; trim pastry even with edge of plate. Sprinkle with coconut.

2. In a bowl, combine the sugar, flour, salt, lemon juice, butter and pineapple. Spread over coconut. Roll out remaining pastry to fit top of pie; place over filling. Trim, seal and flute edges. Cut slits in pastry. Add decorative cutouts if desired.

3. Cover edges loosely with foil. Bake at 400° for 30 minutes. Remove foil; bake 5-10 minutes longer or until crust is golden brown and filling is bubbly.

4. In a bowl, combine confectioners' sugar, extract and enough of the reserved pineapple juice to achieve glaze consistency. Drizzle over warm pie. Cool on a wire rack. Store in the refrigerator. **Yield:** 6-8 servings.

🎀🎀🎀
Apple Blackberry Pie

Dorian Lucas, Corning, California

After a blackberry-picking trip, my husband and I decided to include a few in an apple pie we were making. It was the best we'd ever tasted! We live near the mountains with our two children. Ingredients for fruit pies grow all around us.

- 2 cups all-purpose flour
- 1 teaspoon sugar
- 1 teaspoon salt
- 1 teaspoon ground cinnamon
- 2/3 cup cold butter
- 4 to 6 tablespoons cold water

FILLING:

- 5 cups thinly sliced peeled tart apples (about 6 medium)
- 1 cup fresh blackberries
- 1/2 cup packed brown sugar
- 4-1/2 teaspoons cornstarch
- 1 teaspoon ground cinnamon
- 1 teaspoon ground nutmeg

1. In a bowl, combine the flour, sugar, salt and cinnamon; cut in butter until crumbly. Gradually add water, tossing with a fork until dough forms a ball. Divide dough in half. Roll out one portion to fit a 9-in. pie plate; place pastry in plate and trim even with edge.

2. In a bowl, combine apples and blackberries. Combine the brown sugar, cornstarch, cinnamon and nutmeg; add to fruit mixture and toss to coat. Pour into crust. Roll out remaining pastry to fit top of pie; place over filling. Trim, seal and flute edges. Cut slits in pastry. Add decorative cutouts if desired. Cover edges loosely with foil.

3. Bake at 450° for 10 minutes. Reduce heat to 350°; remove foil. Bake 40-50 minutes longer or until lightly browned and filling is bubbly. Cool on a wire rack. Store in the refrigerator. **Yield:** 6-8 servings.

🎀🎀🎀
Maple-Mocha Brownie Torte

Amy Flory, Cleveland, Georgia

This impressive-looking dessert is at the top of my list of speedy standbys. It's simple to make because it starts with a boxed brownie mix. Then the nutty brownie layers are dressed up with a fluffy frosting that has a rich creamy texture and irresistible maple taste.

- 1 package brownie mix (13-inch x 9-inch pan size)
- 1/2 cup chopped walnuts
- 2 cups heavy whipping cream
- 2 teaspoons instant coffee granules
- 1/2 cup packed brown sugar
- 1-1/2 teaspoons maple flavoring
- 1 teaspoon vanilla extract

Chocolate curls *or* additional walnuts, optional

1. Prepare batter for brownie mix according to package directions for cake-like brownies. Stir in walnuts. Pour into two greased 9-in. round baking pans. Bake at 350° for 20-22 minutes or until a toothpick inserted 2 in. from the edge comes out clean. Cool for 10 minutes before removing from pans to wire racks to cool completely.

2. In a bowl, beat cream and coffee granules until stiff peaks form. Gradually beat in brown sugar, maple flavoring and vanilla. Spread 1-1/2 cups over one brownie layer; top with second layer. Spread remaining cream mixture over top and sides of torte. Garnish with chocolate curls or walnuts if desired. Store in the refrigerator. **Yield:** 12 servings.

🎗🎗🎗
Strawberry Nut Roll

Judy Hayes, Peosta, Iowa

The oldest of seven children, I did a lot of cooking and baking while I was growing up. Desserts like this refreshing rolled shortcake are my favorite. The nutty cake, creamy filling and fresh strawberries make pretty swirled slices.

    6 eggs, *separated*
    3/4 cup sugar, *divided*
    1 cup ground walnuts, toasted
    1/4 cup dry bread crumbs
    1/4 cup all-purpose flour
    1/8 teaspoon salt
Confectioners' sugar
FILLING:
    1 pint fresh strawberries
    1 cup heavy whipping cream
    2 tablespoons sugar
    1 teaspoon vanilla extract
Confectioners' sugar

1. In a mixing bowl, beat egg whites until soft peaks form. Gradually add 1/4 cup sugar, beating until stiff peaks form. Set aside. In another mixing bowl, beat egg yolks and remaining sugar until thick and lemon-colored. Combine walnuts, bread crumbs, flour and salt; add to yolk mixture. Mix well. Fold in egg white mixture. Line a greased 15-in. x 10-in. x 1-in. baking pan with waxed paper; grease the paper. Spread batter evenly into pan.

2. Bake at 375° for 15 minutes or until cake springs back when lightly touched. Cool for 5 minutes. Invert cake onto a kitchen towel dusted with confectioners' sugar. Gently peel off waxed paper. Roll up cake in the towel jelly-roll style, starting with a short side. Cool on a wire rack.

3. Slice six large strawberries in half; set aside for garnish. Thinly slice remaining berries; set aside. In a mixing bowl, beat cream until soft peaks form. Gradually add sugar and vanilla, beating until stiff peaks form.

4. Unroll cake; spread with filling to within 1/2 in. of edges. Top with sliced berries. Roll up again. Place, seam side down, on serving platter. Chill until serving. Dust with confectioners' sugar. Garnish with reserved strawberries. Refrigerate leftovers. **Yield:** 12 servings.

Three-Chip English Toffee, p. 214

Deluxe Chip Cheesecake, p. 222

Strawberry Shortcake Cups, p. 219

Just Desserts

When you want something special and different, turn to this chapter. You'll find delicious cheesecakes, yummy candies, homemade ice cream, silky custard, melt-in-your-mouth mousse and more!

Double Chocolate Fudge, p. 210

Banana Bread Pudding, p. 226

🎖🎖🎖
Apple Turnovers
With Custard

Leora Muellerleile, Turtle Lake, Wisconsin

When I was writing my own cookbook, I knew I had to include this recipe. With the flaky turnovers and rich sauce, it outshines every other apple recipe I make!

CUSTARD:
  - 1/3 cup sugar
  - 2 tablespoons cornstarch
  - 2 cups milk *or* half-and-half cream
  - 3 egg yolks, lightly beaten
  - 1 tablespoon vanilla extract

TURNOVERS:
  - 4 medium baking apples, peeled and cut into 1/4-inch slices
  - 1 tablespoon lemon juice
  - 2 tablespoons butter, diced
  - 1/3 cup sugar
  - 3/4 teaspoon ground cinnamon
  - 1 tablespoon cornstarch

Pastry for double-crust pie
Milk

1. Combine sugar and cornstarch in a saucepan. Stir in milk until smooth. Cook and stir over medium-high heat until thickened and bubbly. Reduce heat; cook and stir for 2 minutes. Remove from heat; stir 1 cup into yolks. Return all to pan. Bring to a gentle boil; cook and stir for 2 minutes. Remove from heat; stir in vanilla. Cool slightly.

2. Cover surface of custard with waxed paper; chill. Place apples in a bowl; sprinkle with lemon juice. Add butter. Combine sugar, cinnamon and cornstarch; mix with apples and set aside.

3. Divide pastry into eight portions; roll each into a 5-in. square. Spoon filling off-center on each. Brush edges with milk. Fold over to form a triangle; seal. Crimp with tines of fork. Make steam vents in top. Place on greased baking sheets. Chill 15 minutes. Brush with milk. Bake at 400° for 35 minutes. Serve warm with the custard. **Yield:** 8 servings.

🎖🎖🎖
Double Chocolate Fudge

(Pictured on page 209)

Marilyn Jordan, Hoosick Falls, New York

If you love chocolate, here's a recipe that's sure to please. This rich treat is a favorite of our family all year long, and especially around the holidays.

1-1/2 teaspoons plus 2 tablespoons butter, *divided*
4-1/2 cups sugar
  - 1 can (12 ounces) evaporated milk
Pinch salt
  - 1 jar (7 ounces) marshmallow creme
  - 2 cups (12 ounces) semisweet chocolate chips
  - 3 packages (4 ounces *each*) German sweet chocolate, broken into pieces
  - 2 cups chopped walnuts, optional

1. Line a 15-in. x 10-in. x 1-in. baking pan with foil. Grease the foil with 1-1/2 teaspoons butter; set aside. In a large saucepan, combine the sugar, milk, salt and remaining butter. Cook and stir over medium heat until sugar is dissolved. Bring to a rapid boil; boil for 5 minutes, stirring constantly.

2. Remove from the heat; stir in marshmallow creme until melted. Stir in chips and German sweet chocolate until melted. Add nuts if desired; mix well.

3. Pour into prepared pan. Refrigerate overnight or until firm. Using foil, remove fudge from pan; carefully peel off foil. Cut into 1-in. squares. Store in the refrigerator. **Yield:** 5 pounds.

Oat-Fashioned Strawberry Dessert

Linda Forrest, Belleville, Ontario

Thanks to this dessert, our house is a popular place in summertime. I make it for family get-togethers, picnics and potlucks. It's a treat on a breakfast or brunch buffet, too.

4 cups sliced fresh strawberries
1-1/4 cups whole wheat flour
1-1/4 cups quick-cooking oats
2/3 cup packed brown sugar
1/4 teaspoon baking soda
1/8 teaspoon salt
2/3 cup cold butter
2 tablespoons sugar
1/4 to 1/2 teaspoon ground cinnamon

1. Drain strawberries on paper towels; set aside. In a large bowl, combine the flour, oats, brown sugar, baking soda and salt. Cut in butter until mixture resembles coarse crumbs. Reserve 1-1/2 cups for topping. Pat the remaining crumb mixture into a greased 9-in. square baking pan.

2. In a bowl, combine sugar and cinnamon; stir in

strawberries. Spoon over the prepared crust. Sprinkle with the reserved crumb mixture. Bake at 350° for 35-40 minutes or until golden brown. Serve warm. **Yield:** 9 servings.

Praline Sundae Topping

Valerie Cook, Hubbard, Iowa

Necessity can be the mother of recipes, too! I came up with this one as a way of using up the extra evaporated milk I had from making fudge.

1/4 cup butter
1-1/4 cups packed brown sugar
16 large marshmallows
2 tablespoons light corn syrup
Dash salt
1 cup evaporated milk
1/2 cup chopped pecans, toasted
1 teaspoon vanilla extract
Ice cream

1. Melt butter in a saucepan. Add brown sugar, marshmallows, corn syrup and salt. Cook and stir over low heat until marshmallows are melted and mixture comes to a boil. Boil for 1 minute.

2. Remove from the heat; cool for 5 minutes. Stir in evaporated milk, pecans and vanilla; mix well. Serve warm or cold over ice cream. Store in the refrigerator. **Yield:** 2-1/2 cups.

🎗🎗🎗
Strawberry Ice

Kim Hammond, Watsonville, California

When we pick strawberries at a local farm, this is what many of the berries are used for. It's a great summertime treat.

5 cups fresh *or* frozen unsweetened strawberries
2/3 cup sugar
2/3 cup water
1/4 cup lemon juice

1. Place the strawberries in a blender or food processor; cover and process until smooth. In a saucepan, heat sugar and water until sugar is dissolved; pour into blender. Add lemon juice; cover and process until combined.

2. Pour into a shallow freezer container; cover and freeze for 4-6 hours or until almost frozen. Just before serving, whip mixture in a blender or food processor. **Yield:** 6 servings.

🎗🎗🎗
Pecan Delights

Linda Jonsson, Marion, Ohio

A relative visiting from Oklahoma brought these and the recipe with her. Who can resist rich, chewy caramel over crunchy pe-

cans drizzled with sweet chocolate? These candies have become a holiday favorite to both make and eat!

2-1/4 cups packed brown sugar
1 cup butter
1 cup light corn syrup
1/8 teaspoon salt
1 can (14 ounces) sweetened condensed milk
1 teaspoon vanilla extract
1-1/2 pounds whole pecans
1 cup (6 ounces) semisweet chocolate chips
1 cup (6 ounces) milk chocolate chips
2 tablespoons shortening

1. In a large saucepan, combine the first four ingredients. Cook over medium heat until all sugar is dissolved. Gradually add milk and mix well. Continue cooking until candy thermometer reads 248° (firm-ball stage).

2. Remove from the heat; stir in vanilla until blended. Fold in the pecans. Drop by tablespoonfuls onto a greased or parchment lined cookie sheet. Chill until firm. Loosen from paper.

3. Melt chocolate chips and shortening in a microwave-safe bowl or double boiler. Drizzle over each cluster. Cool. **Yield:** about 4 dozen.

Editor's Note: It is recommended to test your candy thermometer before each use by bringing water to a boil; the thermometer should read 212°. Adjust your recipe temperature up or down based on your test.

🎗 🎗 🎗
Lemon Whirligigs With Raspberries

Vicki Ayres, Wappingers Falls, New York

Golden whirligigs with a tart lemon flavor float on a ruby raspberry sauce in this delectable dessert. I love serving it for guests. My children also like it made with blackberries.

2/3 cup sugar
  2 tablespoons cornstarch
1/4 teaspoon ground cinnamon
1/8 teaspoon ground nutmeg
1/8 teaspoon salt
  1 cup water
  3 cups fresh raspberries
WHIRLIGIGS:
  1 cup all-purpose flour
  2 teaspoons baking powder
1/2 teaspoon salt
  3 tablespoons shortening
  1 egg, lightly beaten
  2 tablespoons half-and-half cream
1/4 cup sugar
  2 tablespoons butter, melted
  1 teaspoon grated lemon peel
Heavy whipping cream and additional raspberries, optional

1. In a saucepan, combine sugar, cornstarch, cinnamon, nutmeg and salt. Gradually add water; bring to a boil. Reduce heat to medium; cook and stir until the sauce thickens, about 5 minutes. Place berries in an ungreased 1-1/2-qt. shallow baking dish; pour hot sauce over top. Bake at 400° for 10 minutes; remove from the oven and set aside.

2. For whirligigs, combine dry ingredients in a bowl; cut in shortening until crumbly. Combine egg and cream; stir into dry ingredients to form a stiff dough. Shape into a ball; place on a lightly floured surface. Roll into a 12-in. x 6-in. rectangle. Combine sugar, butter and lemon peel; spread over dough. Roll up jelly roll style, starting at a long side.

3. Cut into 10 slices; pat each slice slightly to flatten. Place on top of berry mixture. Bake at 400° for 15 minutes or until whirligigs are golden. Garnish servings with cream and raspberries if desired. **Yield:** 10 servings.

Rich Chocolate Pudding

Verna Hainer, Aurora, Colorado

Creamy, smooth and fudgy, this dessert is a true chocolate indulgence. With just four ingredients, it might be the easiest from-scratch pudding you'll ever make. But it's so delicious and elegant-looking, your guests will think you spent hours stirring it up.

> 2 cups (12 ounces) semisweet chocolate chips
> 1/3 cup confectioners' sugar
> 1 cup milk
> 1/4 cup butter
> **Whipped topping and miniature semisweet chocolate chips, optional**

1. Place chocolate chips and confectioners' sugar in a blender; cover and process until the chips are coarsely chopped. In a saucepan over medium heat, bring milk and butter to a boil. Add to blender; cover and process until chips are melted and mixture is smooth.

2. Pour into six individual serving dishes. Refrigerate. Garnish with whipped topping and miniature chips if desired. **Yield:** 6 servings.

★ ★ ★

Three-Chip English Toffee

(Pictured on page 208)

Lana Petfield, Richmond, Virginia

With its melt-in-your-mouth texture and scrumptiously rich flavor, this is the ultimate toffee! Drizzled on top are three different kinds of melted chips, plus a sprinkling of walnuts. Packaged in colorful tins, these pretty pieces make great gifts.

> 1/2 teaspoon plus 2 cups butter, *divided*
> 2 cups sugar
> 1 cup slivered almonds
> 1 cup milk chocolate chips
> 1 cup chopped walnuts
> 1/2 cup semisweet chocolate chips
> 1/2 cup vanilla *or* white chips
> 1-1/2 teaspoons shortening

1. Butter a 15-in. x 10-in. x 1-in. baking pan with 1/2 teaspoon butter. In a heavy saucepan over medium-low heat, bring sugar and remaining butter to a boil, stirring constantly. Cover and cook for 2-3 minutes.

2. Uncover; add almonds. Cook and stir with a clean spoon until a candy thermometer reads 300° (hard-crack stage) and mixture is golden brown. Pour into prepared pan (do not scrape sides of saucepan). Surface will be buttery. Cool for 1-2 minutes. Sprinkle with milk chocolate chips. Let stand for 1-2 minutes; spread chocolate over the top. Sprinkle with walnuts; press down gently with the back of a spoon. Chill for 10 minutes.

3. In a microwave or heavy saucepan, melt semisweet chips; stir until smooth. Drizzle over walnuts. Refrigerate for 10 minutes. Melt vanilla chips and shortening; stir until smooth. Drizzle over walnuts. Cover and refrigerate for 1-2 hours. Break into pieces. **Yield:** about 2-1/2 pounds.

Editor's Note: It is recommended to test your candy thermometer before each use by bringing water to a boil; the thermometer should read 212°. Adjust your recipe temperature up or down based on your test. If toffee separates during cooking, add 1/2 cup hot water and stir vigorously. Bring back up to 300° and proceed as recipe directs.

Mint Chip Ice Cream

Farrah McGuire, Springdale, Washington

Homemade ice cream is a regular treat for our family. This version is very creamy with a mild mint flavor that goes well with the mini chocolate chips.

1-3/4 cups milk
  3/4 cup sugar
Pinch salt
    3 eggs, lightly beaten
1-3/4 cups heavy whipping cream
    1 teaspoon vanilla extract
  1/4 teaspoon peppermint extract
    4 drops green food coloring, optional
  1/2 cup miniature semisweet chocolate chips

1. In a small saucepan, heat the milk to 175°; stir in the sugar and salt until dissolved. Whisk in a small amount of the hot mixture to the eggs. Return all to the pan, whisking constantly. Cook and stir over low heat until mixture reaches at least 160° and coats the back of a metal spoon. Remove from the heat.

2. Cool quickly by placing pan in a bowl of ice water; stir for 2 minutes. Stir in whipping cream, extracts and food coloring if desired. Press plastic wrap onto surface of the custard. Refrigerate for several hours or overnight.

3. Stir in the chocolate chips. Fill ice cream freezer cylinder two-thirds full; freeze according to the manufacturer's directions. Refrigerate remaining mixture until ready to freeze. **Yield:** 1-1/2 quarts.

Frosty Chocolate Mousse

Myra Innes, Auburn, Kansas

This is a wonderful dessert that whips up fast. It's very smooth and silky and is a perfect complement to any meal.

1-1/2 cups heavy whipping cream
  1/2 cup sugar
  1/2 cup sifted baking cocoa
  1/2 teaspoon rum extract
  1/2 teaspoon vanilla extract

In a mixing bowl, combine all ingredients. Beat until mixture mounds softly. Spoon into dessert dishes. Freeze for at least 2 hours before serving. **Yield:** 4 servings.

🎗🎗🎗 Caramel Custard

Linda McBride, Austin, Texas

My husband and I have enjoyed this simple dessert many times, especially after a Tex-Mex meal. In fact, I've made it so often I don't even look at the recipe.

1-1/2 cups sugar, *divided*
     6 eggs
     2 teaspoons vanilla extract
     3 cups milk

1. In a heavy saucepan over low heat, cook and stir 3/4 cup sugar until melted and golden. Pour into eight 6-oz. custard cups, tilting to coat bottom of cup; let stand for 10 minutes. In a large bowl, beat eggs, vanilla, milk and remaining sugar until combined but not foamy. Pour over caramelized sugar.

2. Place the cups in two 8-in. square baking pans. Pour boiling water in pans to a depth of 1 in. Bake at 350° for 40-45 minutes or until a knife inserted near center comes out clean. Remove from pans to cool on wire racks. To unmold, run a knife around rim of cup and invert onto dessert plate. Serve warm or chilled. **Yield:** 8 servings.

🎗🎗🎗 Chocolate Souffle

Carol Ice, Burlingham, New York

This recipe came from my Aunt Clara, whose cooking was a blend of her country and rural French roots.

     2 squares (1 ounce *each***) unsweetened chocolate**
1/4 cup butter
     5 tablespoons all-purpose flour
1/3 cup plus 1 teaspoon sugar, *divided*
1/4 teaspoon salt
     1 cup milk
     3 eggs, *separated*
     1 teaspoon vanilla extract
1/4 teaspoon almond extract
SAUCE:
     1 cup heavy whipping cream
1/4 cup confectioners' sugar
1/4 teaspoon vanilla extract
Baking cocoa *or* **ground cinnamon, optional**

1. In the top of a double boiler over simmering water, melt chocolate and butter. In a bowl, combine flour, 1/3 cup sugar and salt. Add milk; stir into the melted chocolate. Cook and stir until thickened, about 7 minutes.

2. In a small bowl, beat egg yolks; add a small amount of hot mixture. Return all to pan. Remove from the heat; add extracts. In a small mixing bowl, beat egg whites and remaining sugar until stiff peaks form. Fold into chocolate mixture.

3. Grease the bottom of a 1-1/2-qt. baking dish; add chocolate mixture. Place dish in a larger pan; add 1 in. of hot water to pan. Bake at 325° for 1 hour or until a knife inserted near the center comes out clean.

4. Combine the first three sauce ingredients in a small mixing bowl; beat until soft peaks form. Serve souffle warm with a dollop of sauce. Sprinkle with cocoa or cinnamon if desired. **Yield:** 4-6 servings.

🎀 🎀 🎀

Rhubarb Cheesecake Dessert

Joyce Krumwiede, Mankato, Minnesota

After moving to our current home, we were thrilled to discover a huge rhubarb patch. Since I love to bake, I began searching for rhubarb recipes. Each spring, my family looks forward to these sensational squares.

   1 cup all-purpose flour
1/2 cup packed brown sugar
1/4 teaspoon salt
1/4 cup cold butter
1/2 cup chopped walnuts
   1 teaspoon vanilla extract
FILLING:
   2 packages (8 ounces *each*) cream cheese, softened
3/4 cup sugar
   3 eggs
   1 teaspoon vanilla extract
TOPPING:
   3 cups chopped fresh *or* frozen rhubarb, thawed and drained

   1 cup sugar
1/4 cup water
   1 tablespoon cornstarch
1/4 teaspoon ground cinnamon
   3 to 4 drops red food coloring, optional

1. In a bowl, combine flour, brown sugar and salt; cut in butter until mixture resembles coarse crumbs. Stir in walnuts and vanilla. Press into a greased 13-in. x 9-in. x 2-in. baking dish. Bake at 375° for 10 minutes. Cool slightly.

2. In a mixing bowl, beat cream cheese and sugar until light and fluffy. Add eggs and vanilla; mix well. Pour over the crust. Bake for 20-25 minutes or until center is set and edges are light brown. Cool.

3. In a saucepan, combine the rhubarb, sugar, water, cornstarch and cinnamon; bring to a boil over medium heat. Cook, stirring constantly, until mixture thickens, about 5 minutes. Stir in food coloring if desired. Remove from the heat; cool. Pour over filling. Cover and refrigerate for at least 1 hour. **Yield:** 12-15 servings.

✿✿✿
Macadamia Almond Brittle

Cheryl Miller, Fort Collins, Colorado

This is a nuttier version of a basic brittle recipe. I added macadamia nuts—my favorite—and the brittle turned out tastier than ever.

  1 cup sugar
1/2 cup light corn syrup
3/4 cup coarsely chopped macadamia nuts
3/4 cup coarsely chopped almonds
  1 tablespoon butter
  2 teaspoons vanilla extract
  1 teaspoon baking soda

1. Combine sugar and corn syrup in a 1-1/2-qt. microwave-safe bowl. Microwave on high for 5 minutes. Stir in nuts. Microwave on high for 4-5 minutes or until a candy thermometer reads 300° (hard-crack stage). Quickly stir in butter, vanilla and baking soda until mixture is light and foamy.

2. When bubbles subside, pour onto a greased cookie sheet, spreading as thinly as possible with a metal spatula. Cool completely; break into pieces. Store in an airtight container with waxed paper between layers. **Yield:** about 1 pound.

Editor's Note: This recipe was tested using a 700-watt microwave. It is recommended to test your candy thermometer before each use by bringing water to a boil; the thermometer should read 212°. Adjust your recipe temperature up or down based on your test.

✿✿✿
Old-Fashioned Rice Custard

Shirley Leister, West Chester, Pennsylvania

I don't remember where or how I found this dessert. When I took it to a family reunion many years ago, however, a great-uncle was sure I'd used my great-grandmother's recipe! I like to have it warm for dinner. Then, the next morning, I'll enjoy the cold leftovers for my breakfast.

1/2 cup uncooked long-grain rice
  4 cups milk, *divided*
1/4 cup butter
  3 eggs
3/4 cup sugar
  1 teaspoon vanilla extract
1/4 teaspoon salt
1/2 teaspoon ground nutmeg

1. In the top of a double boiler, combine rice and 2 cups milk. Cook, stirring occasionally, over boiling water until rice is tender and most of the water has evaporated, about 45 minutes. Stir in butter.

2. In a mixing bowl, beat eggs; blend in sugar, vanilla, salt and remaining milk. Stir into the hot rice mixture. Pour into a lightly greased 2-qt. casserole and top with nutmeg. Bake at 350° for 50 minutes or until firm. **Yield:** 6-8 servings.

🎀🎀🎀 Strawberry Shortcake Cups

(Pictured on page 208)

Althea Heers, Jewell, Iowa

Back when store-bought shortcake was an unheard-of thing, my grandmother passed this recipe down to my mother. Mother later shared it with me, and I've since given it to my daughter.

    1 quart fresh strawberries
    4 tablespoons sugar, *divided*
1-1/2 cups all-purpose flour
    1 tablespoon baking powder
  1/2 teaspoon salt
  1/4 cup cold butter
    1 egg
  1/2 cup milk
Whipped cream

1. Mash or slice the strawberries; place in a bowl. Add 2 tablespoons sugar and set aside. In another bowl, combine flour, baking powder, salt and remaining sugar; cut in butter until crumbly. In a small bowl, beat egg and milk; stir into flour mixture just until moistened.

2. Fill eight greased muffin cups two-thirds full. Bake at 425° for 12 minutes or until golden. Remove from the pan to cool on a wire rack.

3. Just before serving, split shortcakes in half horizontally. Spoon berries and whipped cream between layers and over the top. **Yield:** 8 servings.

🎀🎀🎀 Lemony Apple Dumplings

Kristy Deloach, Baker, Louisiana

The first time I made this recipe, I was serving guests who had two little daughters. The girls weren't sure about eating a dessert that looked so different. But after just one bite, they proclaimed the treat "yummy" and cleaned their plates.

1-1/2 cups all-purpose flour
1-1/4 teaspoons salt, *divided*
  1/3 cup shortening
    4 to 5 tablespoons cold milk
  1/2 cup packed brown sugar
    3 tablespoons butter, softened
  1/2 teaspoon ground cinnamon
    4 medium baking apples, peeled and cored
    1 egg white, beaten

LEMON SAUCE:
  1/2 cup sugar
    4 teaspoons cornstarch
    1 cup water
    3 tablespoons butter
    4 teaspoons lemon juice
    2 teaspoons grated lemon peel
  1/8 teaspoon salt

1. Combine flour and 1 teaspoon salt. Cut in shortening until crumbly. Stir in milk until pastry forms a ball; set aside. Stir brown sugar, butter, cinnamon and remaining salt to form a paste. Divide and press into center of each apple; pat any extra filling on outside of apples.

2. On a floured surface, roll pastry into a 14-in. square. Cut into four 7-in. squares. Place one apple in center of each square. Brush edges of pastry with egg white. Fold up corners to center; pinch to seal. Place in a greased 9-in. square baking dish. Bake at 375° for 35-40 minutes or until golden brown.

3. Meanwhile, combine sugar and cornstarch in a saucepan. Stir in water. Bring to a boil; boil 2 minutes. Remove from heat; stir in remaining ingredients until smooth. Serve warm over warm dumplings. **Yield:** 4 servings.

🎀🎀🎀
Pumpkin Crunch Parfaits

Lorraine Darocha, Berkshire, Massachusetts

Here's a fun dessert that your youngsters can help make. It's a great treat for Halloween or Thanksgiving.

    3/4 cup cold milk
      1 package (3.4 ounces) instant vanilla pudding
        mix
      2 cups whipped topping
      1 cup canned pumpkin
    1/2 teaspoon pumpkin pie spice
      1 cup chopped pecans
 1-1/2 cups crushed gingersnaps (about 32 cookies)
Additional whipped topping

1. In a mixing bowl, beat milk and pudding mix on low speed for 2 minutes. Stir in whipped topping, pumpkin and pumpkin pie spice; mix well. Fold in pecans.

2. Spoon half of the mixture into parfait glasses; top with half of the gingersnap crumbs. Repeat layers. Top with additional whipped topping. **Yield:** 6 servings.

🎀🎀🎀
Mocha Fondue

Gloria Jarrett, Loveland, Ohio

People have such fun dipping pieces of cake and fruit into this heavenly melted chocolate mixture. It's an exquisite treat to serve at wedding and baby showers or for another special gathering. I've found it to be a welcome part of any buffet.

      3 cups (18 ounces) milk chocolate chips
    1/2 cup heavy whipping cream
      1 tablespoon instant coffee granules
      2 tablespoons hot water
      1 teaspoon vanilla extract
    1/8 teaspoon ground cinnamon
      1 pound cake (16 ounces), cut into 1-inch cubes
Strawberries, kiwi or other fresh fruit

In a heavy saucepan, melt chocolate with cream over low heat, stirring constantly. Dissolve coffee in water; add to chocolate mixture with vanilla and cinnamon. Mix well. Serve warm, using cake pieces and fruit for dipping. **Yield:** 2 cups.

🎗️🎗️🎗️
Apple Strudel Cheesecake

Janice White, Encampment, Wyoming

Our cheesecake-loving children inspired this recipe I adapted from several others. It was a hit with them because the apples make it less rich and heavy.

CRUST:
- 1 cup all-purpose flour
- 1/3 cup sugar
- 1 egg yolk
- 1/4 teaspoon vanilla extract
- 1/3 cup cold butter

FILLING:
- 4 cups sliced peeled tart apples
- 2 packages (8 ounces *each*) cream cheese, softened
- 3/4 cup sugar, *divided*
- 2 eggs
- 1 teaspoon vanilla extract
- 1 teaspoon ground cinnamon
- 1/4 cup chopped walnuts

1. In a bowl, combine flour and sugar. In a small bowl, combine egg yolk and vanilla; add to dry ingredients. Cut in the butter until crumbly. Press onto the bottom of an ungreased 9-in. springform pan. Bake at 400° for 10-12 minutes. Cool.

2. Place apples in an ungreased 13-in. x 9-in. x 2-in. baking dish. Cover and bake at 350° for 20 minutes or until tender; drain and cool. Meanwhile, in a large bowl, combine cream cheese, 1/2 cup sugar, eggs and vanilla; mix until light and fluffy. Pour over crust.

3. Toss baked apples with cinnamon and remaining sugar. Arrange apples over cream cheese layer; drizzle with any remaining cinnamon mixture. Sprinkle with nuts.

4. Bake at 375° for 15 minutes. Reduce heat to 350°; bake 45-50 minutes longer or until set. Cool to room temperature. Refrigerate for at least 4 hours. Use a sharp knife to cut. Store in the refrigerator. **Yield:** 12 servings.

Deluxe Chip Cheesecake

(Pictured on page 208)

Kari Gollup, Madison, Wisconsin

My husband and I love cheesecake. Once, when we were asked to make a dessert for a "traveling basket" for our church, we prepared this luscious layered treat. It looked so good, we could not bear to give it away. We ended up contributing another sweet treat instead!

1-1/2 cups vanilla wafer crumbs
1/2 cup confectioners' sugar
1/4 cup baking cocoa
1/3 cup butter, melted
FILLING:
   3 packages (8 ounces *each*) cream cheese, softened
3/4 cup sugar
1/3 cup sour cream
   3 tablespoons all-purpose flour
   1 teaspoon vanilla extract
1/4 teaspoon salt
   3 eggs
   1 cup butterscotch chips, melted
   1 cup semisweet chocolate chips, melted
   1 cup vanilla *or* white chips, melted
TOPPING:
   1 tablespoon *each* butterscotch, semisweet and vanilla *or* white chips
1-1/2 teaspoons shortening, *divided*

1. In a bowl, combine wafer crumbs, confectioners' sugar, cocoa and butter. Press onto the bottom and 1-1/2 in. up the sides of a greased 9-in. springform pan. Bake crust at 350° for 7-9 minutes or until set. Cool on a wire rack.

2. In a mixing bowl, beat cream cheese and sugar until smooth. Add sour cream, flour, vanilla and salt; mix well. Add eggs; beat on low speed just until combined. Remove 1-1/2 cups batter to a bowl; stir in butterscotch chips. Pour over crust. Add chocolate chips to another 1-1/2 cups batter; carefully spoon over butterscotch layer. Stir vanilla chips into remaining batter; spoon over chocolate layer.

3. Bake at 350° for 55-60 minutes or until center is almost set. Cool on a wire rack for 10 minutes. Carefully run a knife around edge of pan to loosen. Cool for 1 hour.

4. For topping, place each flavor of chips and 1/2 teaspoon shortening in three small microwave-safe bowls. Microwave on high for 25 seconds; stir. Heat in 10- to 20-second intervals, stirring until smooth. Drizzle over cheesecake. Chill for at least 3 hours. Remove sides of pan. Refrigerate leftovers. **Yield:** 12-14 servings.

Easy Rhubarb Dessert

Mildred Mesick, Richmond, New York

This is a very tasty and attractive dessert. It's great served warm with ice cream.

   4 cups sliced fresh *or* frozen rhubarb
   1 package (3 ounces) raspberry gelatin
1/3 cup sugar
   1 package (18-1/4 ounces) yellow *or* white cake mix
   1 cup water
1/3 cup butter, melted
Ice cream, optional

Place rhubarb in a greased 13-in. x 9-in. x 2-in. baking dish. Sprinkle with the gelatin, sugar and cake mix. Pour water evenly over dry ingredients; drizzle with butter. Bake at 350° for 1 hour or until rhubarb is tender. Serve with ice cream if desired. **Yield:** 16-20 servings.

Blueberry Angel Dessert

Carol Johnson, Tyler, Texas

Make the most of angel food cake, pie filling and whipped topping by creating this light, impressive dessert that doesn't keep you in the kitchen for hours. It's the perfect way to end a summer meal. I frequently get requests for the recipe.

- 1 package (8 ounces) cream cheese, softened
- 1 cup confectioners' sugar
- 1 carton (8 ounces) frozen whipped topping, thawed
- 1 prepared angel food cake (14 ounces), cut into 1-inch cubes
- 2 cans (21 ounces *each*) blueberry pie filling

In a large mixing bowl, beat the cream cheese and sugar; fold in whipped topping and cake cubes. Spread evenly into an ungreased 13-in. x 9-in. x 2-in. dish; top with pie filling. Cover and refrigerate for at least 2 hours before cutting into squares. **Yield:** 12-15 servings.

Colorado Peach Cobbler

Clara Hinman, Flagler, Colorado

My husband and I live on our ranch/wheat farm. I've served this dessert for family, hired help and guests many times. I've used other fruits that are in season, but we like peaches best.

- 1 cup sugar
- 2 tablespoons all-purpose flour
- 1/4 teaspoon ground nutmeg
- 4 cups sliced peeled fresh peaches

TOPPING:
- 1 cup sugar
- 1 cup all-purpose flour
- 1 teaspoon baking powder
- 1 teaspoon salt
- 1/3 cup cold butter
- 1 egg, beaten

Ice cream, optional

1. In a bowl, combine sugar, flour and nutmeg. Add peaches; stir to coat. Pour into a greased 11-in. x 7-in. x 2-in. baking pan. For topping, combine sugar, flour, baking powder and salt; cut in the butter until the mixture resembles fine crumbs. Stir in egg. Spoon over the peaches.

2. Bake at 375° for 35-40 minutes or until filling is bubbly and topping is golden. Serve hot or cold with ice cream if desired. **Yield:** 8-10 servings.

🎀 🎀 🎀

Raspberry Trifle

Betty Howlett, Elmira, Ontario

The first time I served my trifle was for a family dinner. Every-one loved it! I've since found that it also goes over well at potlucks and at buffet dinners.

3 tablespoons cornstarch
1/4 cup sugar
3 cups milk
4 egg yolks, beaten
2 teaspoons vanilla extract
1 loaf (1 pound) frozen pound cake, thawed
3/4 cup raspberry jam
3 cups fresh or frozen unsweetened raspberries, thawed and drained
1 cup heavy whipping cream
2 tablespoons confectioners' sugar

2 tablespoons sliced almonds, toasted
Fresh raspberries, optional

1. In a saucepan, combine the cornstarch and sugar. Stir in milk until smooth. Cook and stir over medium heat until thickened and bubbly. Reduce heat; cook and stir 2 minutes longer. Remove from heat. Stir a small amount of hot filling into egg yolks; return all to pan, stirring constantly.

2. Bring to a gentle boil; cook and stir 2 minutes longer. Remove from heat. Stir in vanilla. Pour into a bowl and cover with waxed paper. Chill 20 minutes.

3. Meanwhile, cut cake into 3/4-in. slices; spread with jam. Cut each slice into thirds; place with jam side up in a 3-qt. trifle dish or a deep salad bowl. Cover with berries. Top with custard. Cover and chill overnight. Just before serving, whip cream and sugar until stiff; spread over custard. Garnish with almonds and berries if desired. **Yield:** 10-12 servings.

🎀🎀🎀
Vanilla Cream Fruit Tart

Susan Terzakis, Andover, Massachusetts

It's well worth the effort to prepare this spectacular tart, which is best made and served the same day.

- 3/4 cup butter, softened
- 1/2 cup confectioners' sugar
- 1-1/2 cups all-purpose flour
- 1 package (10 to 12 ounces) vanilla *or* white chips, melted and cooled
- 1/4 cup heavy whipping cream
- 1 package (8 ounces) cream cheese, softened
- 1 pint fresh strawberries, sliced
- 1 cup fresh blueberries
- 1 cup fresh raspberries
- 1/2 cup pineapple juice
- 1/4 cup sugar
- 1 tablespoon cornstarch
- 1/2 teaspoon lemon juice

1. In a mixing bowl, cream butter and confectioners' sugar. Beat in flour (mixture will be crumbly). Pat into the bottom of a greased 12-in. pizza pan. Bake at 300° for 25-28 minutes or until lightly browned. Cool.

2. In another mixing bowl, beat melted chips and cream. Add cream cheese; beat until smooth. Spread over crust. Chill for 30 minutes. Arrange berries over filling.

3. In a saucepan, combine pineapple juice, sugar, cornstarch and lemon juice; bring to a boil over medium heat. Boil for 2 minutes or until thickened, stirring constantly. Cool; brush over fruit. Chill 1 hour before serving. Store in the refrigerator. **Yield:** 12-16 servings.

🎀🎀🎀
Caramel Pear Crumble

Karen Ann Bland, Gove, Kansas

This is the first recipe I turn to after my mother shares juicy pears from her orchard. The down-home flavor of the not-too-sweet dessert is a welcomed alternative to apple crisp. Its crumbly topping and hint of caramel keep friends asking for more.

- 1-1/4 cups all-purpose flour
- 1 cup quick-cooking oats
- 1 cup packed brown sugar
- 1 teaspoon ground cinnamon
- 1/2 cup butter, melted
- 20 caramels
- 1 tablespoon milk
- 3 medium pears, peeled and sliced
- Whipped topping and additional cinnamon, optional

1. In a bowl, combine the flour, oats, brown sugar and cinnamon. Stir in butter (mixture will be crumbly); set aside 1 cup. Press the remaining mixture into an ungreased 8-in. square baking dish.

2. In a small saucepan over low heat, cook and stir caramels and milk until caramels are melted and mixture is smooth. Remove from the heat. Arrange pears over crust; spoon caramel mixture over pears. Sprinkle with the reserved crumb mixture.

3. Bake at 350° for 30-35 minutes or until the pears are tender and top is golden brown. Serve warm. Garnish with whipped topping and cinnamon if desired. **Yield:** 6 servings.

🎀🎀🎀
Banana Bread Pudding

(Pictured on page 209)

Mary Detweiler, West Farmington, Ohio

When I visited my grandmother in summer, I always looked forward to the comforting pudding she'd make. With its crusty golden top, custard-like inside and smooth vanilla sauce, this bread pudding is a real homespun dessert.

> 4 **cups cubed day-old French *or* sourdough bread (1-inch pieces)**
> 1/4 **cup butter, melted**
> 3 **eggs**
> 2 **cups milk**
> 1/2 **cup sugar**
> 2 **teaspoons vanilla extract**
> 1/2 **teaspoon ground cinnamon**
> 1/2 **teaspoon ground nutmeg**
> 1/2 **teaspoon salt**
> 1 **cup sliced firm bananas (1/4-inch pieces)**

SAUCE:
> 3 **tablespoons butter**
> 2 **tablespoons sugar**
> 1 **tablespoon cornstarch**
> 3/4 **cup milk**
> 1/4 **cup light corn syrup**
> 1 **teaspoon vanilla extract**

1. Place the bread cubes in a greased 2-qt. casserole; pour butter over and toss to coat. In a medium bowl, lightly beat eggs; add milk, sugar, vanilla, cinnamon, nutmeg and salt. Stir in bananas. Pour over bread cubes and stir to coat. Bake, uncovered, at 375° for 40 minutes or until a knife inserted near the center comes out clean.

2. Meanwhile, for sauce, melt butter in a small saucepan. Combine sugar and cornstarch; add to butter. Stir in milk and corn syrup. Cook and stir over medium heat until the mixture comes to a full boil. Boil for 1 minute. Remove from the heat; stir in the vanilla. Serve warm sauce over warm pudding. **Yield:** 6 servings.

🎀🎀🎀
Marbled Orange Fudge

Diane Wampler, Morristown, Tennessee

This decadent treat doesn't last long at our house. The soft fudge is guaranteed to get smiles because it has the familiar taste of frozen Creamsicles. Bright orange and marshmallow swirls make it the perfect take-along for autumn events and get-togethers.

> 1-1/2 **teaspoons plus 3/4 cup butter, *divided***
> 3 **cups sugar**
> 3/4 **cup heavy whipping cream**
> 1 **package (10 to 12 ounces) vanilla *or* white chips**
> 1 **jar (7 ounces) marshmallow creme**
> 3 **teaspoons orange extract**
> 12 **drops yellow food coloring**
> 5 **drops red food coloring**

1. Grease a 13-in. x 9-in. x 2-in. pan with 1-1/2 teaspoons butter. In a heavy saucepan, combine the sugar, cream and remaining butter. Cook and stir over low heat until sugar is dissolved. Bring to a boil; cook and stir for 4 minutes. Remove from the heat; stir in chips and marshmallow creme until smooth.

2. Remove 1 cup and set aside. Add orange extract and food colorings to remaining mixture; stir until blended. Pour into prepared pan. Drop the reserved marshmallow mixture by tablespoonfuls over top; cut through mixture with a knife to swirl. Cover and refrigerate until set. Cut into squares. **Yield:** about 2-1/2 pounds.

We vacation often in Vermont and always come home with some real maple syrup. This dessert is a terrific way to use the syrup, and it reminds us of the wonderful time we had while on vacation.

1 cup real maple syrup
2 cups milk, *divided*
2 tablespoons cornstarch
1/4 teaspoon salt
2 eggs, lightly beaten
1 cup finely chopped walnuts

1. In a large saucepan, heat syrup and 1-3/4 cups milk over medium heat until bubbles form around side of saucepan. Combine cornstarch, salt and remaining milk until smooth; gradually add to syrup.

2. Cook and stir over medium-high heat until thickened and bubbly. Reduce heat; cook and stir 2 minutes longer. Remove from the heat. Stir a small amount of hot filling into egg; return all to pan, stirring constantly. Bring to a gentle boil; cook and stir 2 minutes longer. Remove from the heat. Pour into serving dishes. Sprinkle with walnuts; cool. **Yield:** 6 servings.

🎀 🎀 🎀
Maple Walnut Cream
Ida Hartnett, Sparta, New Jersey

🎀 🎀 🎀
Chocolate Peanut Ice Cream Dessert
Jeanette Neufeld, Boissevain, Manitoba

If you're expecting company or simply want a convenient on-hand dessert, try this. It's easy, but people will think that you spent hours making it.

1 cup vanilla wafer crumbs
1/2 cup finely chopped peanuts
1/4 cup butter, melted
2 tablespoons confectioners' sugar
6 cups chocolate ice cream, softened, *divided*
FILLING:
1 package (3 ounces) cream cheese, softened
1/3 cup crunchy peanut butter
3/4 cup confectioners' sugar
1/4 cup milk
1/2 cup heavy whipping cream, whipped

1. Line the bottom and sides of a 9-in. x 5-in. x 3-in. loaf pan with heavy-duty aluminum foil. Combine the first four ingredients; press half onto the bottom of the pan. Freeze for 15 minutes. Spread half of the ice cream over crust; freeze for 1 hour or until firm.

2. Meanwhile, for filling, beat cream cheese and peanut butter in a mixing bowl. Add sugar and milk; mix well.

Fold in whipped cream. Spread over ice cream; freeze for 1 hour or until firm. Spread with remaining ice cream (pan will be very full). Press remaining crumb mixture on top.

3. Cover and freeze for several hours or overnight. Remove from the freezer 10 minutes before serving. Using foil, remove loaf from pan; discard foil. Cut into slices using a serrated knife. **Yield:** 10-12 servings.

General Recipe Index

This handy index lists every recipe by food category, major ingredient and/or cooking method, so you can easily locate recipes to suit your needs.

✓ Recipe includes Nutritional Analysis and Diabetic Exchanges

Alphabetical Index

This handy index lists every recipe in alphabetical order,
so you can easily find your favorite recipes.

✓ Recipe includes Nutritional Analysis and Diabetic Exchanges